IMAGES of Rail

CHICAGO & WESTERN INDIANA RAILROAD

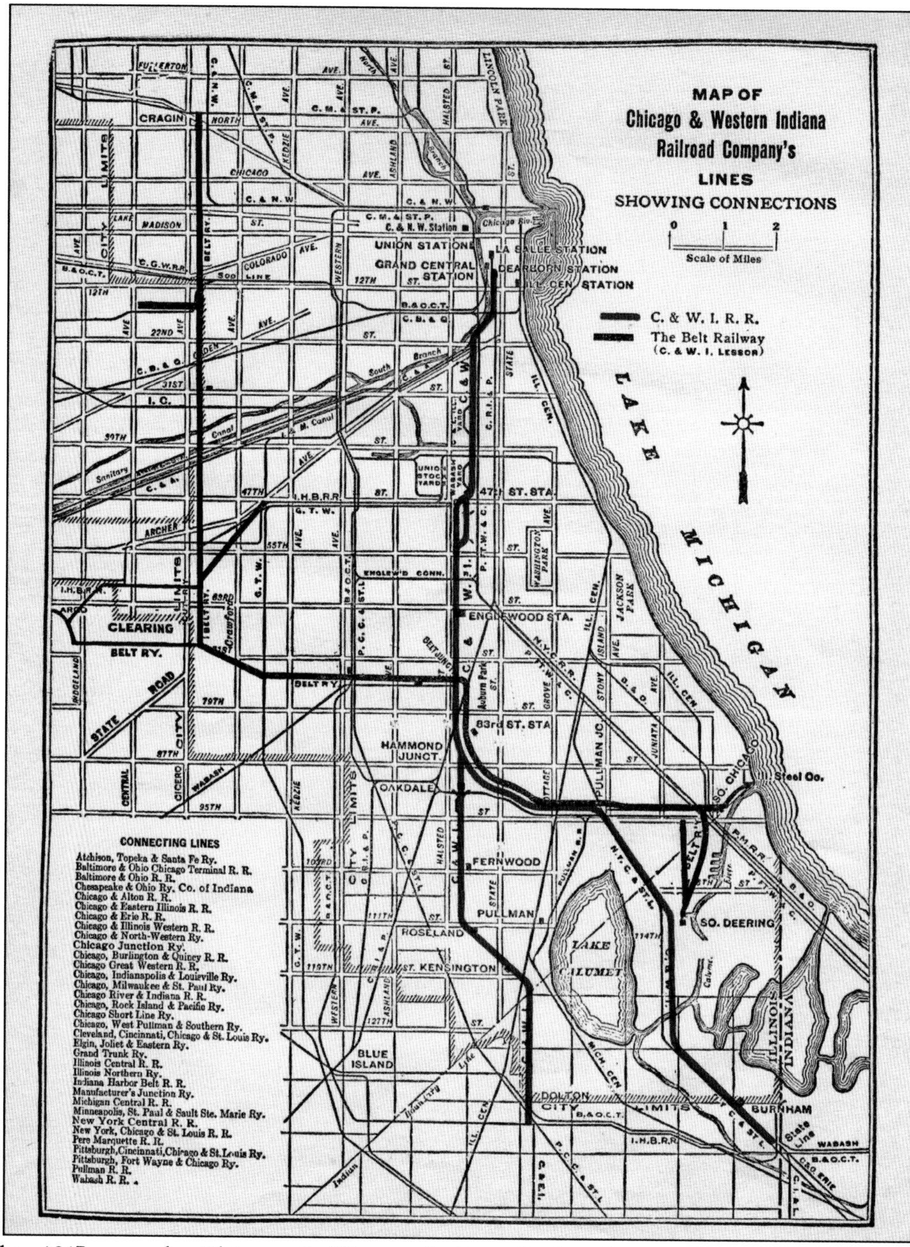

On this 1917 map, the Chicago & Western Indiana Railroad's main line is shown connecting Dearborn Station at Polk and Dearborn Streets in downtown Chicago with Yard Center in Dolton, Illinois, 18 miles to the south, and with the Indiana state line at Hammond, 20 miles to the south and east. The rail line crossing it and running east–west and then north is the Belt Railway of Chicago. (Courtesy of Bill Molony.)

On the Cover: The Chicago & Western Indiana (C&WI) Railroad's class J-1 2-6-0 Moguls, such as No. 209, shown here, were purchased from the Baldwin Locomotive Works in 1913, and its class J-2 2-6-0 Moguls were purchased from the Lima Locomotive Works in 1914. These simple but reliable steam locomotives remained in revenue service on the C&WI until the late 1940s, when they were replaced with ALCO RS-1 diesels. (Courtesy of Bill Molony.)

IMAGES
of Rail

CHICAGO & WESTERN INDIANA RAILROAD

Cynthia L. Ogorek and Bill Molony

ARCADIA
PUBLISHING

ISBN 978-1-4671-1668-8

Published by Arcadia Publishing
Charleston, South Carolina

Printed in the United States of America

Library of Congress Control Number: 2015956732

For all general information, please contact Arcadia Publishing:
Telephone 843-853-2070
Fax 843-853-0044
E-mail sales@arcadiapublishing.com
For customer service and orders:
Toll-Free 1-888-313-2665

Visit us on the Internet at www.arcadiapublishing.com

Contents

Acknowledgments

The authors wish to thank the following people for all their assistance, suggestions, and contributions of photographs and historical information.

Robin Scheldberg and Ed Smith of the South Holland Historical Society were always accommodating with the use of their society's collection. Paul Petraitis provided insights on the Roseland area. Marlene Cook was ever eager and happy to help with matters of local history, especially information about Dolton and the "Seeny-I." Richard Lytle went above and beyond to help with photographs from the Hammond Public Library's collection of Hammond railroadiana. Thanks to Marge Loitz at the Village of Thornton Historical Society for the use of its collection and pointing out what would be useful among the museum's exhibits. Rod Sellers of the Southeast Chicago Historical Society was very accommodating and allowed us "free range" in the collection. He was there to answer all sorts of questions, too.

Finally, thank you to Mark Lluanza and Bob Lalich for coming through at the last minute with photographs and insights.

Unless otherwise noted, all the photographs came from the collection of Bill Molony.

INTRODUCTION

The primary purposes of the Chicago & Western Indiana Railroad (C&WI) were to provide access to Chicago and to provide switching service for the passenger and freight cars of its owner railroad companies. Therefore, it was known as a "terminal company."

Following the Panic of 1873, the US economy began improving, and by the late 1870s more and more eastern trunk-line railroads clamored for access to the Chicago market. However, the high cost of real estate in downtown Chicago, along with opposition from the Chicago City Council due to complaints about congestion, smoke, and noise, deterred them from doing so individually. Leasing track rights, too, was often very expensive and not always the best way to get into the city.

A promoter by the name of John B. Brown came up with a solution: a one-rail right-of-way with a terminal that would serve as the gateway to Chicago. Earliest support for the plan came from the Chicago & Eastern Illinois Railroad (C&EI), which had been using an inconvenient and inefficient route via the Pennsylvania Railroad's tracks to go from its terminal at Dolton, Illinois, to the city. Brown's proposed route would be much more direct and would not depend on leasing agreements with other lines.

In order to spread the costs, C&EI approached four other railroads to become investors in the new line. They were the Grand Trunk Western; the Chicago, Indianapolis & Louisville (later Monon); the Chicago & Atlantic (known commonly as the Erie); and the Wabash, St. Louis & Pacific (Wabash). Each bought a 20-percent share of the company, which gave them seats on the board of directors and access to the terminal that would be built at the far south end of Chicago's Loop where Dearborn Street ended at Polk Street. The new company, now known as the Chicago & Western Indiana Railroad Company (C&WI), was incorporated in the state of Illinois on June 5, 1879.

Construction of the right-of-way began the following month at Dolton, working its way north to the city limits, which at that time were around Thirty-Fifth Street, along a line that would meet the existing Dearborn Street in downtown Chicago. This route was approximately 17 miles long and would serve the C&EI well, but the other railroads needed to connect to it. Another consideration was getting a business toehold in the developing region called the Calumet, which lay south of the city on the eastern side of Hyde Park Township along Lake Michigan and the Indiana border. Heavy industry was already staking claim to various sections of it, especially along the Calumet River. It would probably become a prime market for the eastern rail lines.

To route the C&WI through this area, two new companies were incorporated. They were the South Chicago & Western Indiana Railroad Company (SC&WI) and the Chicago and Western Indiana Belt Railway Company (C&WIBRC). The first was incorporated on April 20, 1880, and the latter on April 22, 1881. With them, the organizers created a complete belt line that connected with every railroad entering the city from the Indiana border to areas far northwest of the city. Then, on January 26, 1882, all three were consolidated into the Chicago & Western Indiana Railroad Company. After further discussion and experience, another corporation, the Belt Railway Company of Chicago (BRC) was organized in November. Under a lease from the C&WI, it took over the operation of what was known as the "Belt Division," which handled the freight interchange and industrial operations. In 1912, the BRC signed another lease with the C&WI which gave it rights to 53 miles of the main track and 327 miles of yards and sidings around Chicago. The portion of the C&WI which was not leased to the BRC became known as the "Terminal Division."

The C&EI determined the route between Dolton and the city that became known as the Dolton Line. It was already serving the communities of Momence, Crete, Chicago Heights, Glenwood, Thornton, and South Holland on its way north from Danville, Illinois. By the time the C&WI was organized, it had gained a right-of-way north from Dolton to a village called Roseland, where a local landowner, Jan Ton, had offered land to the railroad if the C&EI would build a station at 103rd Street and guarantee a fare of 1¢ per mile. Just south of Roseland, at 112th Street, it had negotiated the right to cross the existing tracks of the Illinois Central. At that point, the Dolton Line curved northwest then north to Twenty-First Street or Alton Junction, where it crossed the Pittsburgh, Fort Wayne & Chicago Railroad, the St. Charles Air Line, and the Chicago, Rock Island & Pacific Railroad on an angle, after which it swung north to the Dearborn Station about three blocks south of Chicago's Loop.

Probably due to the influence of Joseph T. Torrence, also one of the incorporators of the C&WI, a significant section of the Dolton Line from Oakdale to Dearborn Station was elevated. The Main Line from Eighty-First Street east as far as Pullman Junction was also elevated.

The Main Line was also known as the Hammond Line for its endpoint at the Indiana border. From Pullman Junction, the Main Line headed in a southeasterly direction between the west shore of the Calumet River and Torrence Avenue through South Deering (now a neighborhood of Chicago). It crossed the Calumet River near 126th Street and continued southeast through Hegewisch (also a Chicago neighborhood) and then through the Burnham Yard at Burnham, Illinois, ending at the Indiana border, where an interlocking tower was built.

From a starting point in South Deering, the BRC also followed the Calumet River's west bank but veered northeast to serve the mills closest to Lake Michigan. It had an east-west leg that intersected with the New York Central and Pennsylvania Railroads in South Chicago before traversing Pullman Junction and Burnside and then turning north to parallel the C&WI. At Seventy-Fourth Street it went west to hand off or pick up cars at the Clearing Yard. From Clearing, it went north as far as the Cragin Yard, with spur lines running to the east and west at various points.

The symbol of the Terminal Division of the C&WI was its Dearborn Station, located prominently at the foot of Dearborn Street in downtown Chicago. The company already owned land about three blocks north of its location, on Van Buren Street, when it applied to the City of Chicago for permission to build. The mayor, Carter Harrison, did not favor putting yet another railroad station and its attendant yards and warehouses so close to downtown. He and the city council argued for a location at Seventeenth Street. In the end, a compromise was made, and the C&WI was able to bring its owners' trains into the city as far as the area between Taylor and Polk Streets. While the legal wrangling went on, the C&WI installed a terminal at Archer Avenue and State Street that was later moved to State and Twelfth Street.

Construction of the final terminal got underway in the middle of 1883. Dearborn Station, also known as Polk Street Station, opened for business on May 8, 1885. By 1890, seven rail lines used it as their Chicago terminal. One-hundred-twenty-two trains and approximately 17,000 people passed through the building daily either as suburban commuters or cross-country travelers. Business continued to increase with the addition of the Atchison, Topeka & Santa Fe as a tenant in 1887 and the Chesapeake & Ohio Railroad as a tenant in 1910. By 1912, 144 trains came and went daily, even though the C&EI, now owed by the Frisco and the Rock Island lines, had moved most of its passenger and commuter service to the Rock Island's LaSalle Street station.

Due to bankruptcy actions and the reorganizations of its controlling railroads, the C&EI moved back to Dearborn Station in 1913. To handle the crush of trains, people and freight, a one-story annex was built east of the station in 1914 for the suburban service of the C&WI, Wabash, and Grand Trunk along with some intercity trains and mail handling.

All was well until 1922, when fire damaged the clock tower and the third floor of Dearborn Station. The C&WI engineers, however, handled the situation well, with almost no inconvenience to their owner lines and their passengers. Service was practically uninterrupted. In fact, all scheduled trains during the day of the fire, December 21, were delayed by only two hours and thereafter ran on time.

While the C&EI was the driving force behind the C&WI, the terminal company needed the other owners—the Monon, Erie, Grand Trunk Western, and Wabash—to keep it profitable.

The predecessor name of the Monon was the Louisville, New Albany & Chicago, and it was under that name that the line became one-fifth owner of the C&WI. It was incorporated in 1847 as the New Albany & Salem Railroad Company for the purpose of connecting a port on the Ohio River with a port on Lake Michigan. Cargo was transferred to watercraft at either end. It was not until 1873 that the railroad had an owner interested in moving freight and people to Chicago over land instead of by steamship from Michigan City. In 1881, a branch line was built northwest from Indianapolis to Dyer, Indiana, and north from there to Hammond, where it connected with the C&WI's Main Line at the Illinois state line.

The Grand Trunk Western's history prior to 1880 was full of buyouts and mergers with smaller lines from the Canadian border through Michigan and across northern Indiana. As a Canadian railroad (its parent was the Grand Trunk Railway of Canada) seeking an entry into Chicago, it formed the Chicago & State Line Railroad in order to purchase the Chicago & Southern line from the C&EI. When its tracks reached Valparaiso, Indiana, it continued west to Griffith, crossed into Illinois, then crossed the C&EI at a point between South Holland and Thornton. Making another purchase, it now owned the C&EI's former western approach to Chicago, which carried it through Harvey and Blue Island and finally to Forty-Ninth Street, where it connected to the C&WI as an owner in 1883. C&WI provided GTW with switching service between its Elsdon Yard at Fifty-Fifth and Central Park and Dearborn Station.

Until 1884, the Erie Railroad used the Monon's tracks through Hammond to make its connection with the C&WI at the state line. Before that, it had made its way into Chicago via the lakeshore routes of other railroads. It was always a secondary passenger carrier between New York City and Chicago due to its terminal being on the New Jersey side of the Hudson River and its meandering route through the middle of Ohio and northern Indiana. It entered the Calumet region through Crown Point, Indiana, southeast of Hammond. But it was a viable freight competitor, especially after it acquired the Chicago & Atlantic, which connected Hammond directly to the eastern coal mining districts of Ohio and Pennsylvania and gave the Erie its own track bed through Hammond to the state line.

The Wabash entered and left the C&WI at two junctions, from the east via the Main Line at the Illinois-Indiana state line and from the west on the Dolton Line at Seventy-Fourth Street. Its traffic between Chicago and St Louis and Kansas City used the latter route. The Toledo-to-Chicago route across northern Ohio and Indiana was never very busy, and it used the Chicago & Atlantic/Erie Railroad tracks through Hammond until it moved north about a mile to use those of the Baltimore & Ohio and the Indiana Harbor Belt.

The Terminal Division of the C&WI grew to include a freight yard at Eighty-Third Street with 14 tracks and a 647-car capacity. A coach yard at Fifty-First Street comprised 36 acres of track, car repair shops, a power plant, and storehouses. At Twenty-Sixth and Canal Streets, by the 1950s, there was a team track development and perishable terminal that had concrete driveways connecting to 26 unloading tracks. A gantry crane was on hand, and the facility provided an unloading capacity of 400 cars per day. The C&EI maintained its yard between Thirty-First and Thirty-Eighth Streets with a capacity of 352 cars. The Wabash freight yard was located between Forty-Third and Forty-Seventh Streets and had a capacity of 753 cars. The Erie had its freight yard between Forty-Ninth and Fifty-Fifth Streets with 46 tracks and a capacity of 1,262 cars.

There were seven freight houses located in the vicinity of Dearborn Station. One was leased to the Railway Express Agency, and the other six were operated by the owner railroads for the handling of their respective inbound and outbound less-than-carload freight.

The Atchison, Topeka & Santa Fe Railroad held a 99-year lease with the C&WI. As the premier long-term tenant, it used Dearborn Station and track rights between the station and Twenty-First Street for all its west-coast passenger trains.

Over the years, the BRC also leased trackage rights from the C&WI over another 18 miles of the Terminal Division, which gave it access to the Ford Assembly Plant on Torrence Avenue and 130th Street as well as a connection with the Chicago, South Shore & South Bend Railroad, which incidentally also used the C&WI's interlocking tower at the Indiana state line.

At the peak of its existence in the 1950s, the C&WI furnished its owner railroads with switching of their passenger cars, plus cleaning, repairing, servicing, and other jobs for them at the coach yard and in their car shops. It operated an industrial switching service and a suburban passenger service between Dearborn Station and Dolton. It had changed from steam locomotives to diesels in the late 1940s and on an average day was handling approximately 135 freight trains and 61 passenger trains over its tracks. In an average year, that came to approximately 71,500 trains and 1,470,000 cars.

That was in the 1950s. By then, passenger revenues had already decreased significantly from their wartime highs, and the Dearborn Station annex was closed. Then all remaining passenger and commuter service was returned to the main station. Mail handling, too, was experiencing a shift to other places in the city and other means of transportation.

In the 1960s, passenger service declined further as air travel and private automobiles beckoned to travelers with limited vacation time and commuters who preferred the autonomy of their own automobiles. More and more freight was moving by air and truck. What remained to be handled by railroads was being relocated to terminal facilities on the outskirts of the city or even to the suburbs. At the end of the decade, one by one, the owner railroads were merged into bigger concerns; their passenger services cut back drastically or discontinued all together. The mail and package express business took to the airlines and over-the-road trucking. On July 26, 1963, C&WI discontinued its own suburban service between Dearborn and Milepost 16 at Dolton. It continued, however, to switch cars for its owners at Dearborn.

In 1971, when Amtrak took over most of the intercity passenger train service in the United States, it moved all the remaining passenger trains in Chicago to Union Station on the west side of the downtown area. Dearborn Station was closed. With no further need for them, the C&WI began removing the station tracks and demolishing the train shed. At the end of May 1976, only the head-house, or main station building, was standing.

The land previously occupied by the train shed became Dearborn Park, surrounded by a quiet development of townhouses and apartment buildings. Soon after, Dearborn Station itself underwent a conversion and rehabilitation program turning it into commercial office space. The C&WI, however, continued to switch freight cars for its owners until the closing of the mills in the Calumet delivered the death blow. By 1985, the C&WI was reduced to merely maintaining the remaining tracks and yards. It did so for another nine years, until in 1994, after 115 years of service, the Chicago & Western Indiana went out of existence.

One

The Early Years of the Chicago & Western Indiana

In the late 1870s, the Calumet Region, that part of Lake Michigan's southern shore that straddles the Indiana-Illinois border, was beginning to be developed. For decades, there had been tiny settlements and farms here and there, with two or three railroads coming in from the east hugging the lakeshore after 1852. The coming of heavy industry to the southern tier of the region brought with it the second phase of railroad building across the region. The C&WI played a key role in this development by providing four eastern trunk lines with a right-of-way from the Indiana border into downtown Chicago. Along the way, the owners were also provided with spurs and sidings with which to serve the steel mills, rolling stock manufacturers, and food processing plants that were springing up along the Calumet River in South Chicago, Hegewisch, East Side, and South Deering—none of which were part of the city of Chicago until 1889. Once the lawsuits in Chicago were cleared up and junctions with other railroads were agreed upon, all five owners had access to the Dearborn Station. C&WI, meanwhile, established a suburban commuter service of its own and created a subsidiary called Belt Railway Company of Chicago, which provided switching and access to the industries in the Calumet on the Illinois side and those west of the C&WI right-of-way. C&WI developed into a terminal operation with 52.24 miles of main track. Its total mileage, though, was 596.

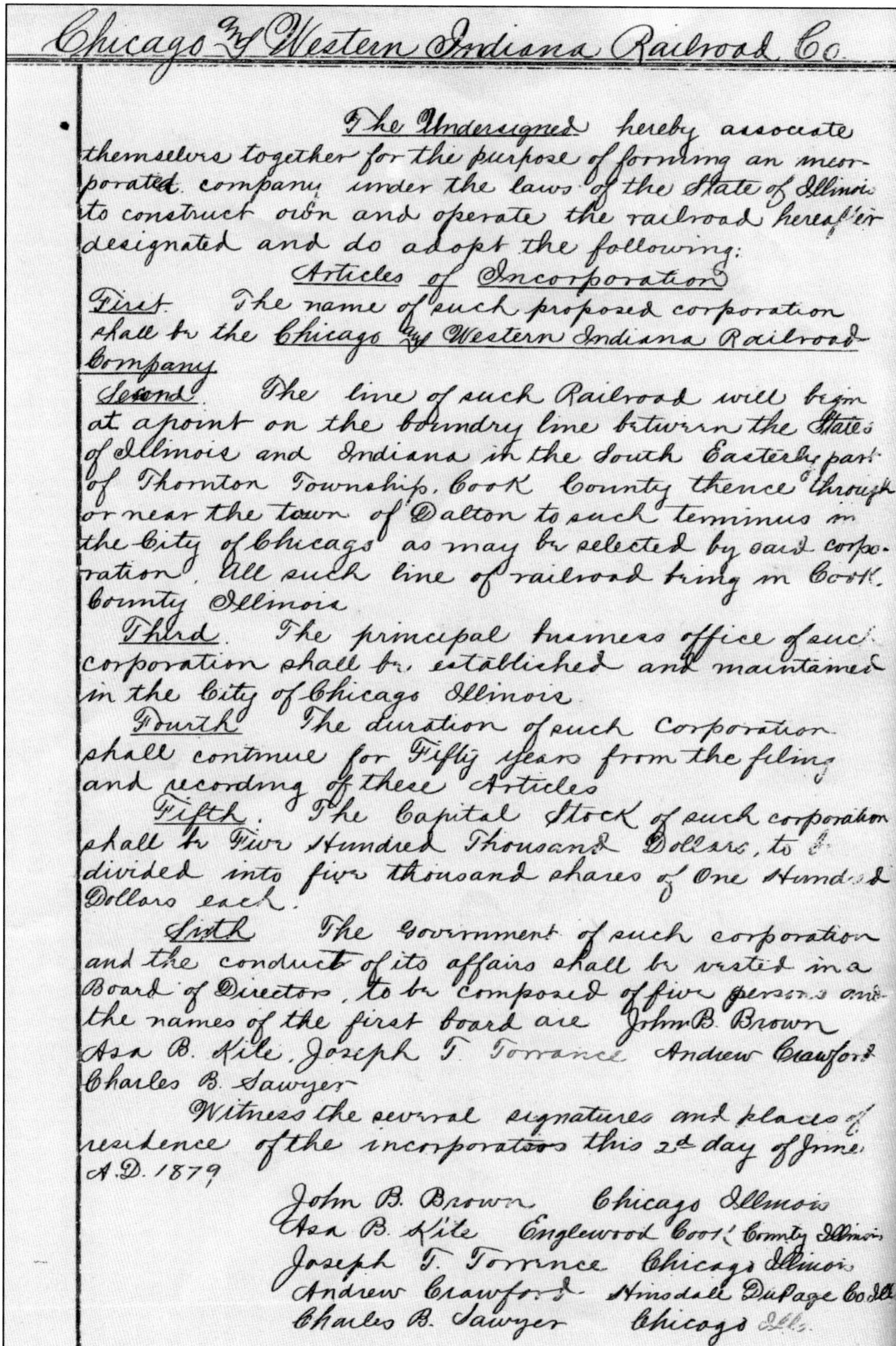
Chicago & Western Indiana Railroad Co.

The Undersigned hereby associate themselves together for the purpose of forming an incorporated company under the laws of the State of Illinois to construct own and operate the railroad hereafter designated and do adopt the following:

Articles of Incorporation

First. The name of such proposed corporation shall be the Chicago & Western Indiana Railroad Company

Second. The line of such Railroad will begin at a point on the boundry line between the States of Illinois and Indiana in the South Easterly part of Thornton Township, Cook County thence through or near the town of Dalton to such terminus in the City of Chicago as may be selected by said corporation. All such line of railroad being in Cook County Illinois

Third. The principal business office of such corporation shall be established and maintained in the City of Chicago Illinois

Fourth The duration of such Corporation shall continue for Fifty years from the filing and recording of these Articles

Fifth. The Capital Stock of such corporation shall be Five Hundred Thousand Dollars, to be divided into five thousand shares of One Hundred Dollars each.

Sixth The Government of such corporation and the conduct of its affairs shall be vested in a Board of Directors, to be composed of five persons and the names of the first board are John B. Brown Asa B. Kile, Joseph T. Torrance Andrew Crawford Charles B. Sawyer

Witness the several signatures and places of residence of the incorporators this 2d day of June A.D. 1879

John B. Brown Chicago Illinois
Asa B. Kile Englewood Cook County Illinois
Joseph T. Torrance Chicago Illinois
Andrew Crawford Hinsdale DuPage Co Ill
Charles B. Sawyer Chicago Ills

OPPOSITE: The incorporation document of the Chicago & Western Indiana Railroad, above, was written by hand in June 1879. By that time, a legislative act was no longer necessary for the chartering of a railroad in Illinois. Witnesses to the incorporation were John B. Brown, Joseph Thatcher Torrence, and Charles B. Sawyer of Chicago. Asa B. Kite lived in Englewood, Illinois, and Andrew Crawford, was from Hinsdale. These men also made up the company's first board of directors. Torrence was perhaps the most famous of the group of incorporators. He was a partner in the Joseph H. Brown iron mill, constructed in 1875 between the Calumet River and the future C&WI right-of-way in the South Deering neighborhood, and he took a term as president of the C&WI in the 1880s. Torrence was also instrumental in the development of the town of East Chicago, Indiana, and some of the belt lines that connected the trunk lines with industries from Gary, Indiana, to the stockyards of Chicago and beyond.

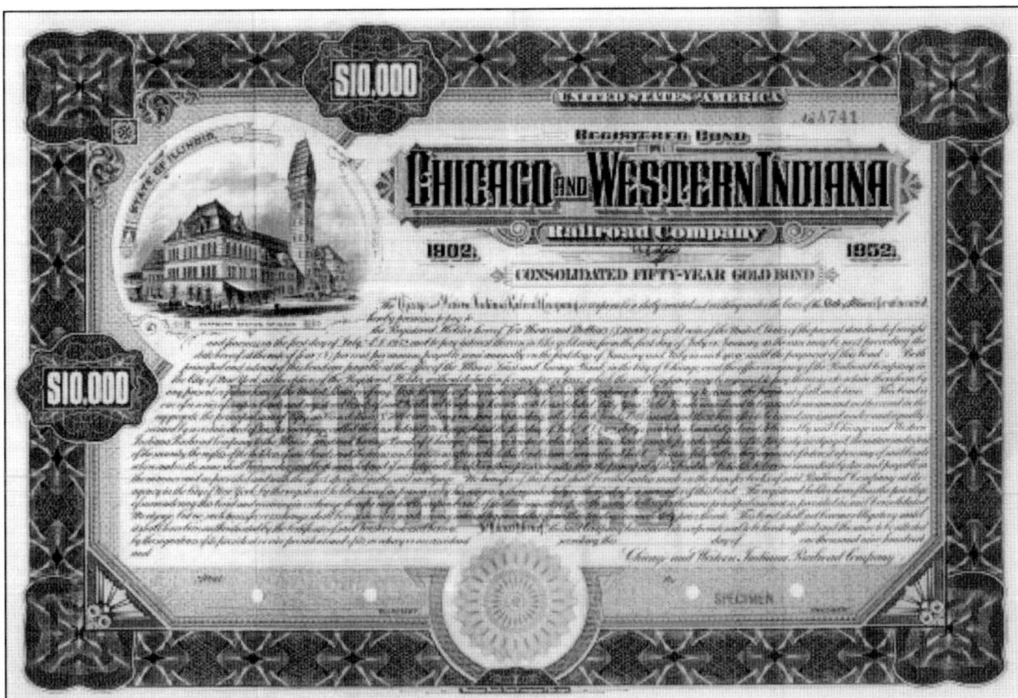

The offices of the Chicago & Western Indiana Railroad Company were located in Chicago, eventually on the second and third floors of the Dearborn Station. The company's initial stock offering was for $500,000, and each certificate sold for $100. The above bond was issued in 1902, scheduled to mature in 1952. Although the railroad did indeed stay within the boundaries of Cook County as mentioned in the articles of incorporation, its route when built deviated from that which was planned. The point on the Indiana-Illinois border was not specified. "Thornton Township" was really Thornton Fractional Township, and the route of the C&WI that touched the Indiana border, known as the Main Line or sometimes the Hammond Line, ran northwest through Burnham, Illinois, and the territory that later became known as Chicago's Southeast Side before it joined the Dolton Line at Eighty-Seventh Street.

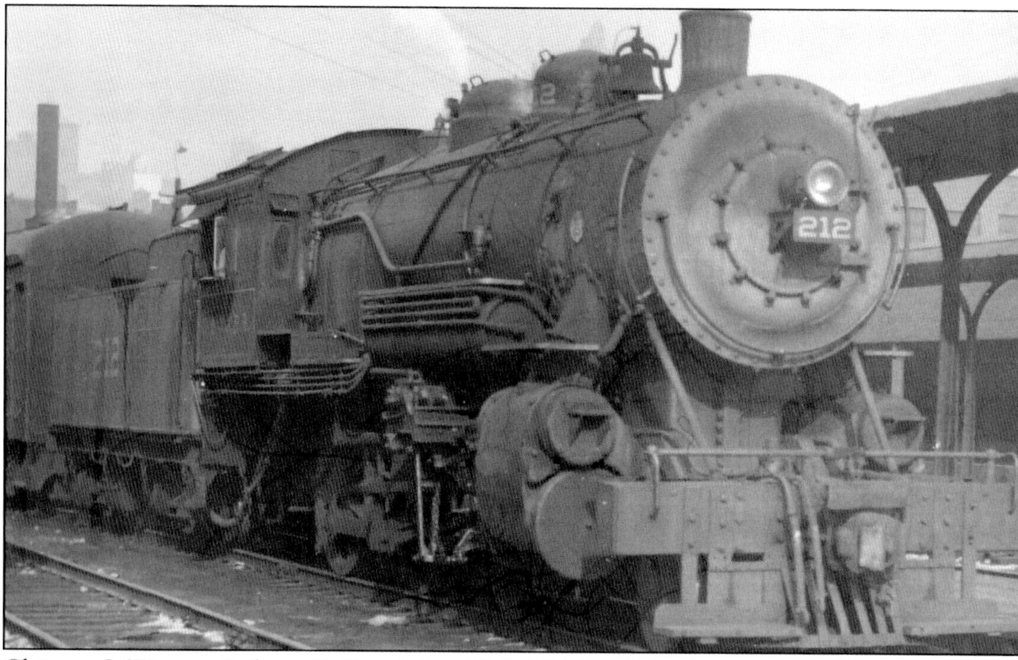

Chicago & Western Indiana Railroad class J-1 2-6-0 Mogul-type No. 212 switches passenger cars at Dearborn Station in Chicago in January 1948. Most other railroads retired their 2-6-0 steam locomotives in the 1920s or 1930s or converted them to 0-6-0 switch engines. The C&WI was one of the very few railroads that still operated their Moguls in the late 1940s.

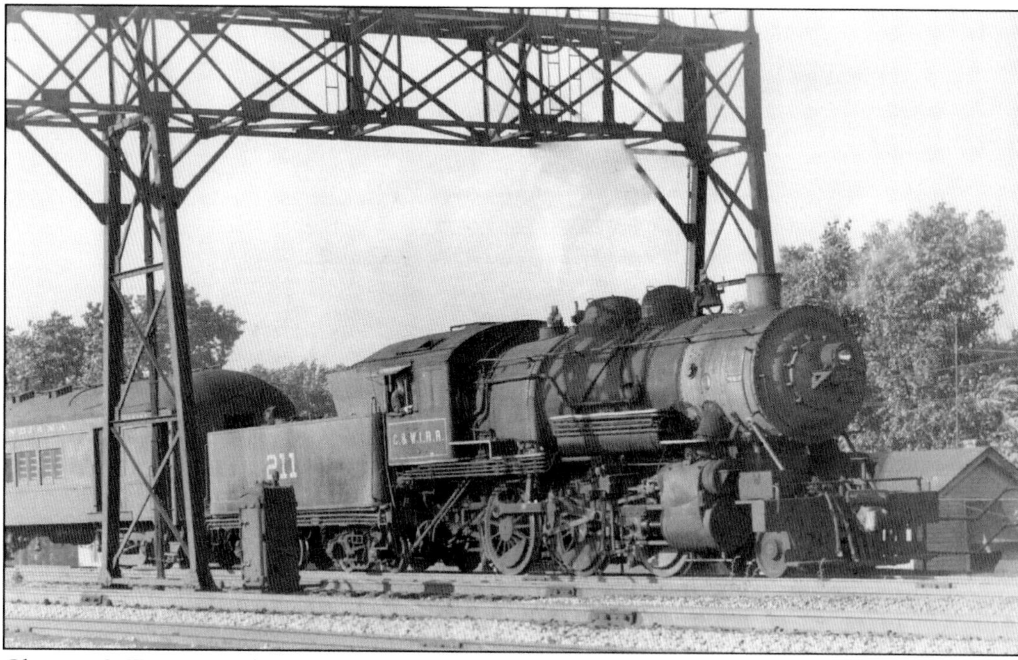

Chicago & Western Indiana Railroad class J-1 2-6-0 Mogul-type No. 211, hustles down the tracks near the Eightieth Street junction with a midday train that includes combination car No. 40. The train is passing under the signal bridge, which supported the signals used to control the interlocking of the C&WI tracks with those of the Belt Railway Company of Chicago.

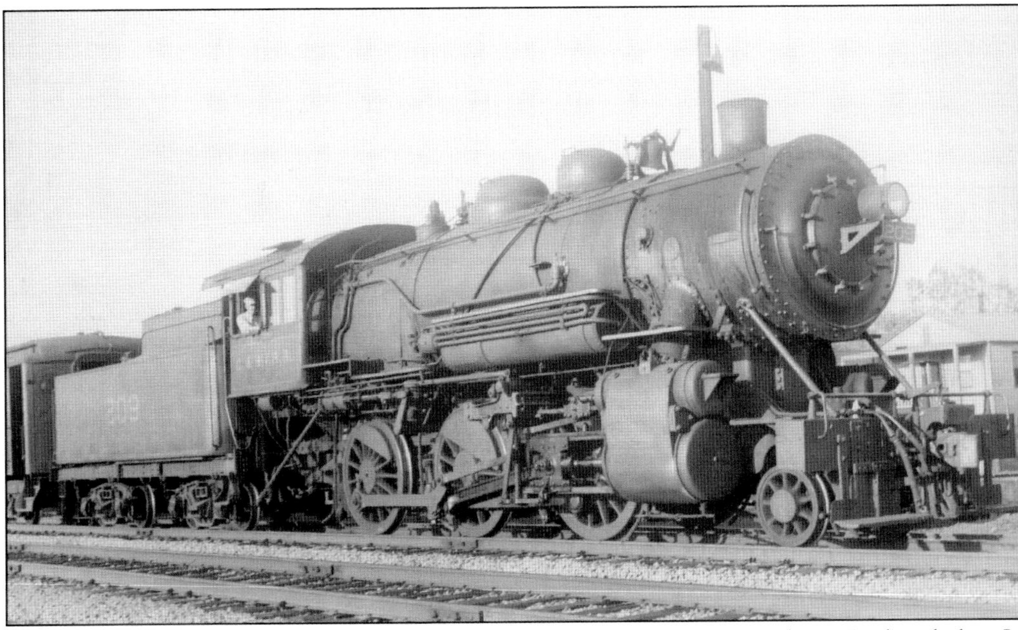

The engineer can be seen in the cab window of Chicago & Western Indiana Railroad class J-1 2-6-0 Mogul-type steam locomotive No. 209, waiting to open the throttle and proceed with its commuter train. The 209 remained in revenue service until 1950, when C&WI replaced all of its remaining steam locomotives with new diesel locomotives.

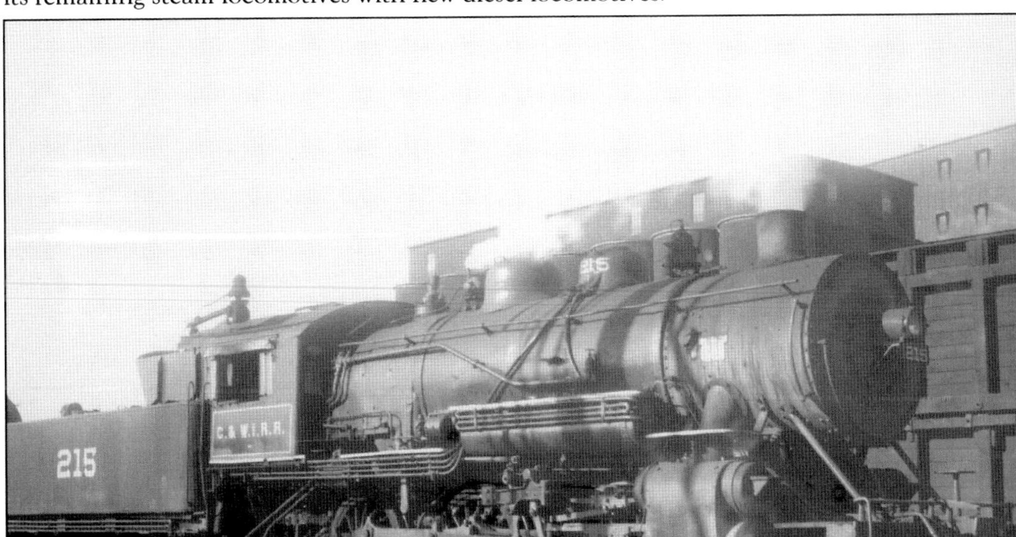

Chicago & Western Indiana Railroad's class J-2 2-6-0 Mogul-type steam locomotive No. 215 was equipped with 63-inch drive wheels and 23-inch-by-28-inch cylinders and operated with a maximum of 180 pounds of boiler pressure. Most railroads replaced their 2-6-0 Mogul locomotives with more powerful 4-6-2 Pacific-type locomotives early in the 20th century.

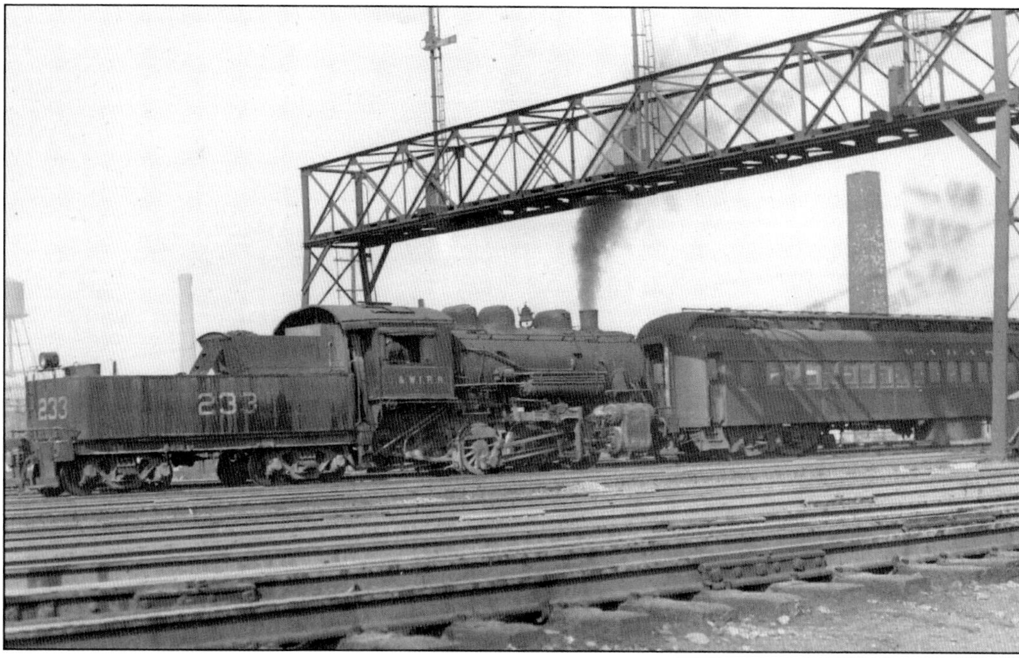

The Lima Locomotive Corporation of Lima, Ohio, built the Chicago & Western Indiana Railroad's class L-1 0-6-0 switch engine No. 233 in 1914. It is shown here switching some Wabash Railroad passenger cars at Dearborn Station in February 1949. The C&WI provided switching service for all of the railroads using Dearborn Station except for the Atchison, Topeka & Santa Fe.

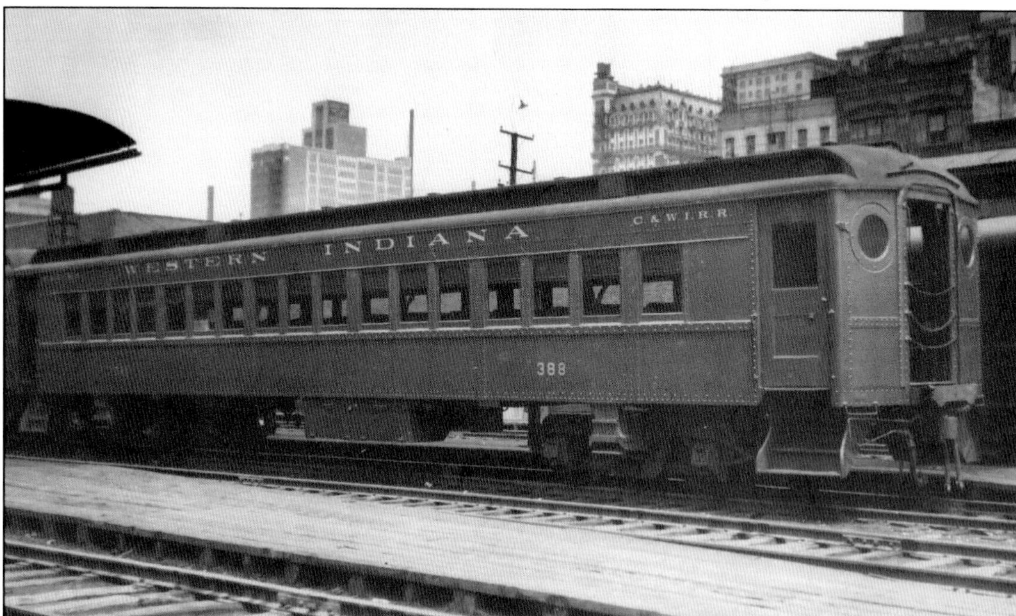

Chicago & Western Indiana Railroad coach No. 388 was typical of the passenger cars used by the C&WI for suburban service between Dearborn Station and Dolton. This particular car was a Pennsylvania Railroad P54 coach that the C&WI acquired third-hand from the Norfolk & Western Railroad. These cars were only 64 feet long, but they seated 68 passengers.

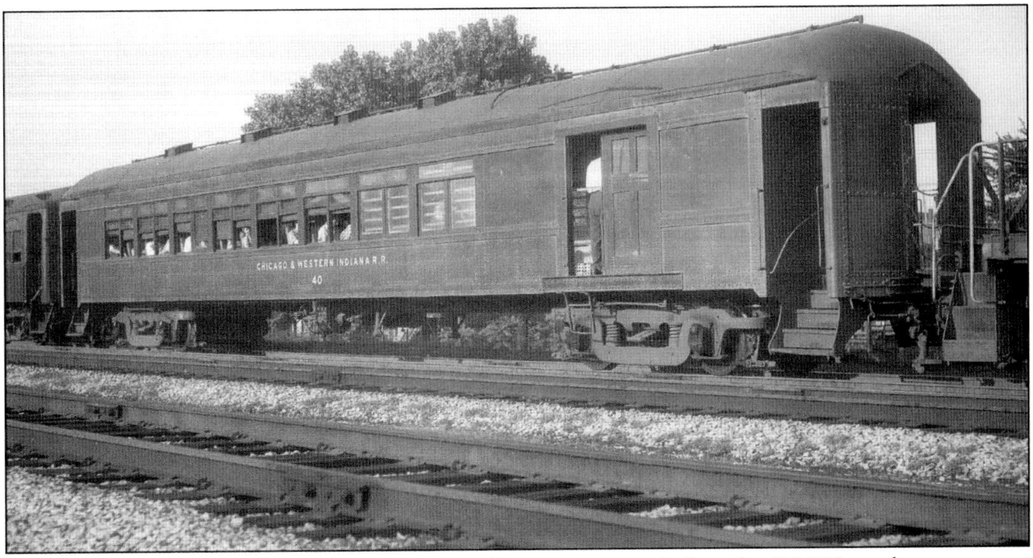

Car No. 40 was a combination baggage car and passenger coach that the C&WI used to transport daily newspapers and Railway Express Agency packages to the various stations along the line. It was normally used only on the midday trains. It is shown here in August 1955 coupled behind American Locomotive Company (ALCO) RS-1 diesel engine No. 253.

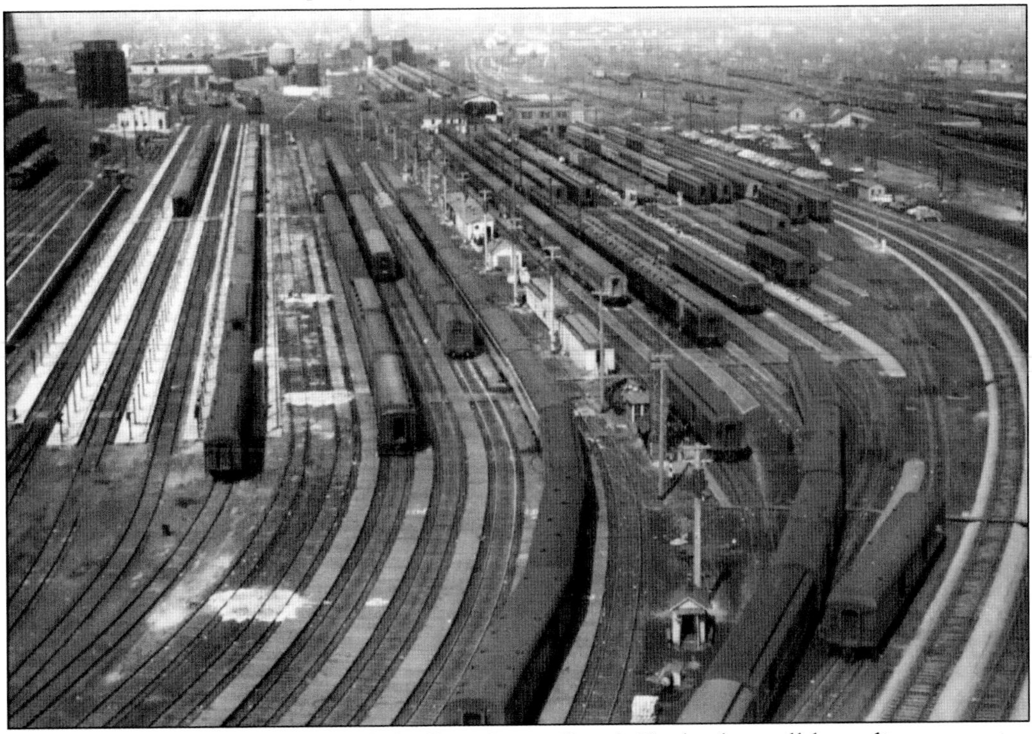

The aerial above shows C&WI's Fifty-First Street Coach Yard, where all long-distance trains out of Dearborn except the Santa Fe's were serviced. Fresh bed linens were brought in, food was restocked, washroom water tanks were refilled, and the trains were cleaned. After air brakes and other mechanicals were checked out, the cars were returned to Dearborn in time for the next departure.

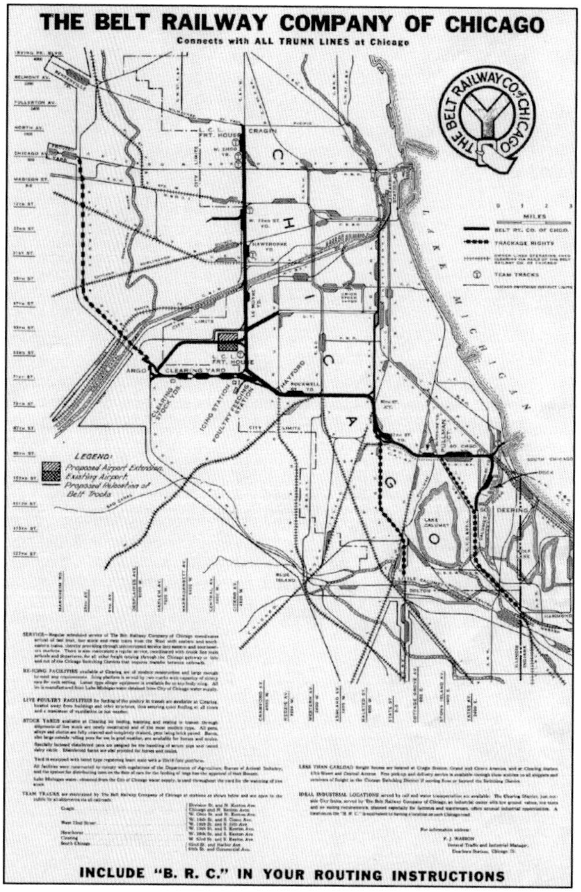

The Chicago & Western Indiana was instrumental in the development of the Belt Railway Company of Chicago (BRC) in 1882. Called the Belt Division, its purpose was to connect all the trunk lines in Chicago in order to facilitate the interchange of freight cars among the five owner railroads and various tenants. By 1900, the BRC was handling nearly 675,000 cars a year, providing access to 29 railroads and 450 industrial sites.

The Chicago & Western Indiana Railroad interlocking tower in Chicago's South Deering neighborhood, near 112th Street and Torrence Avenue, controlled the junction of the Belt Railway Company of Chicago's South Deering District branch and the C&WI's Main Line to Hammond. The single track next to the tower belongs to the BRC, and the C&WI double-track Main Line can be seen in the distance.

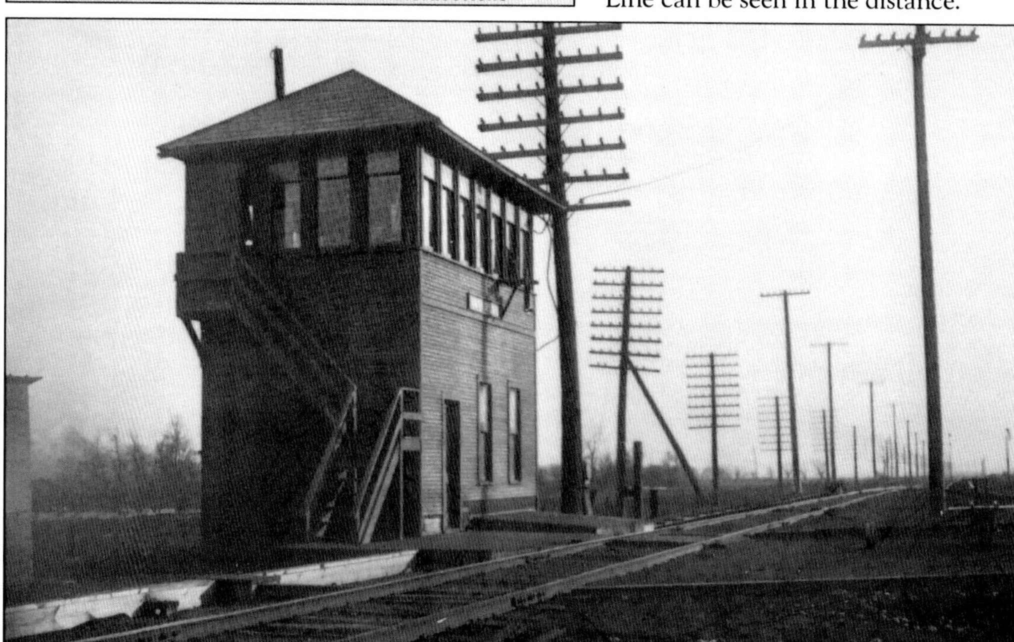

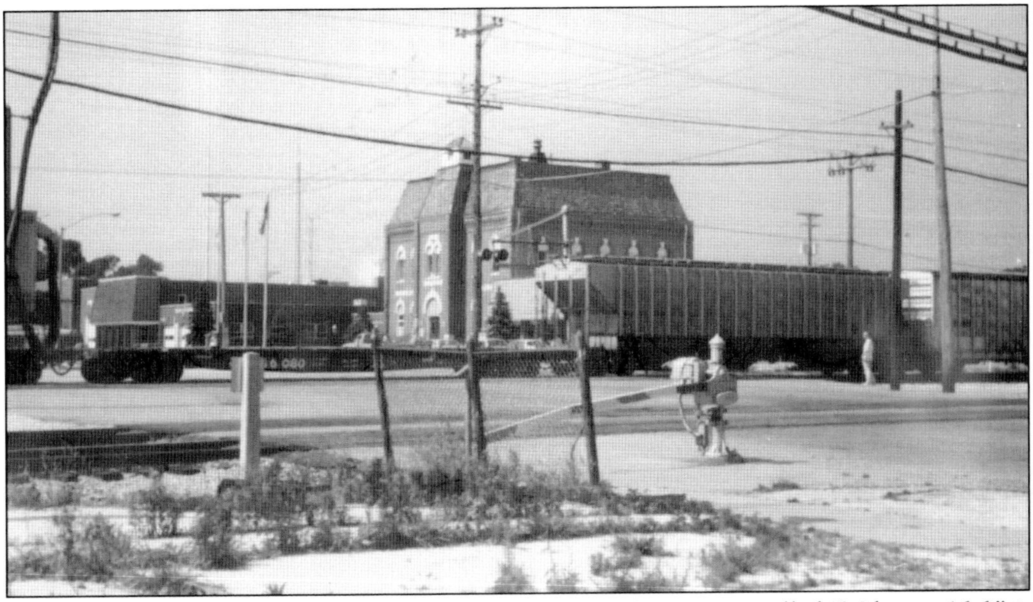

Dolton Junction was 16.6 miles from Dearborn Station. Sometimes called "Milepost 16.6," it was located near the crossing of Lincoln and South Park Avenue in Dolton. It was the southern terminal of the C&WI. Freight trains of the Baltimore & Ohio, Pennsylvania, and Indiana Harbor Belt (IHB) Railroads crossed here. (Courtesy of the South Holland Historical Society.)

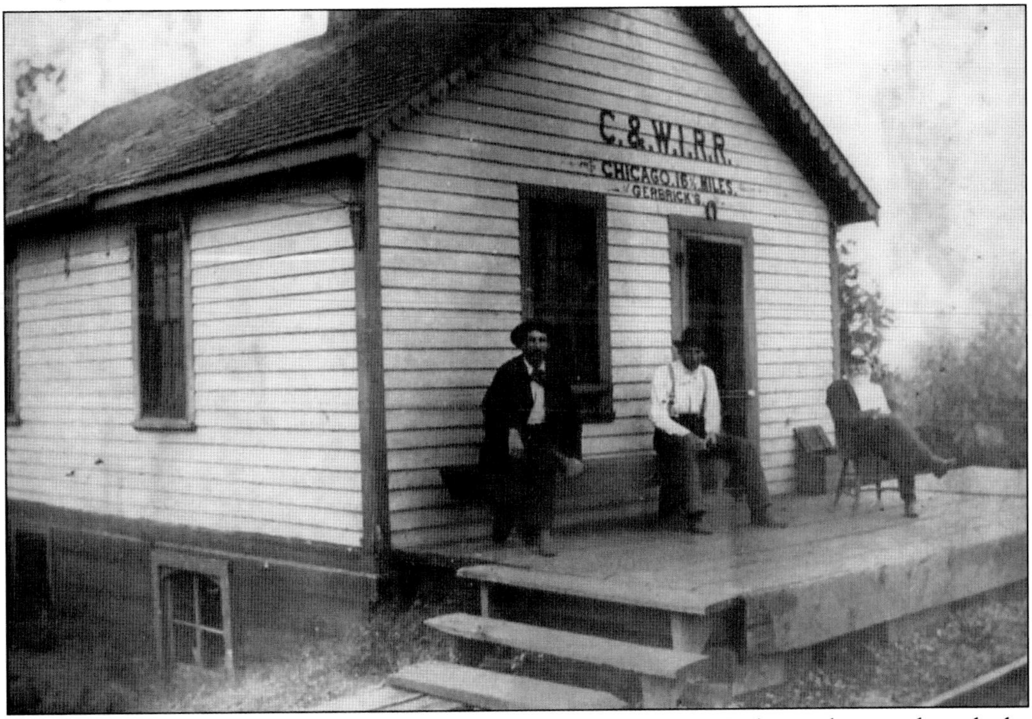

Proudly announcing its connection with the Chicago & Western Indiana along with its lucky horseshoe above the door, Gerbrick's depot or maintenance building was located just north of Dolton Junction. The names of the gentlemen presumably waiting for the train are unknown. (Courtesy of the Southeast Chicago Historical Society.)

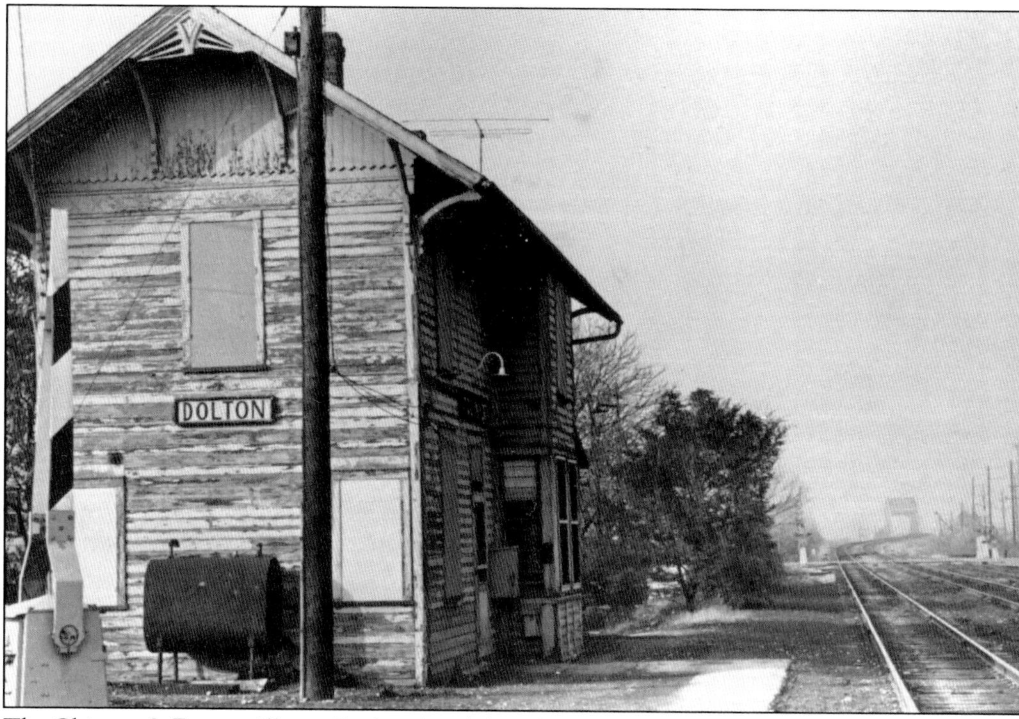

The Chicago & Eastern Illinois Railroad and the Chicago & Western Indiana Railroad shared this two-story station at Dolton, 16.6 miles south of Dearborn Station, in the early years of the 20th century. This was the southern terminal for the C&WI's suburban trains. The C&EI's through passenger trains from Evansville, Indiana, and St. Louis, Missouri, passed through Dolton without stopping. (Courtesy of Marlene Cook.)

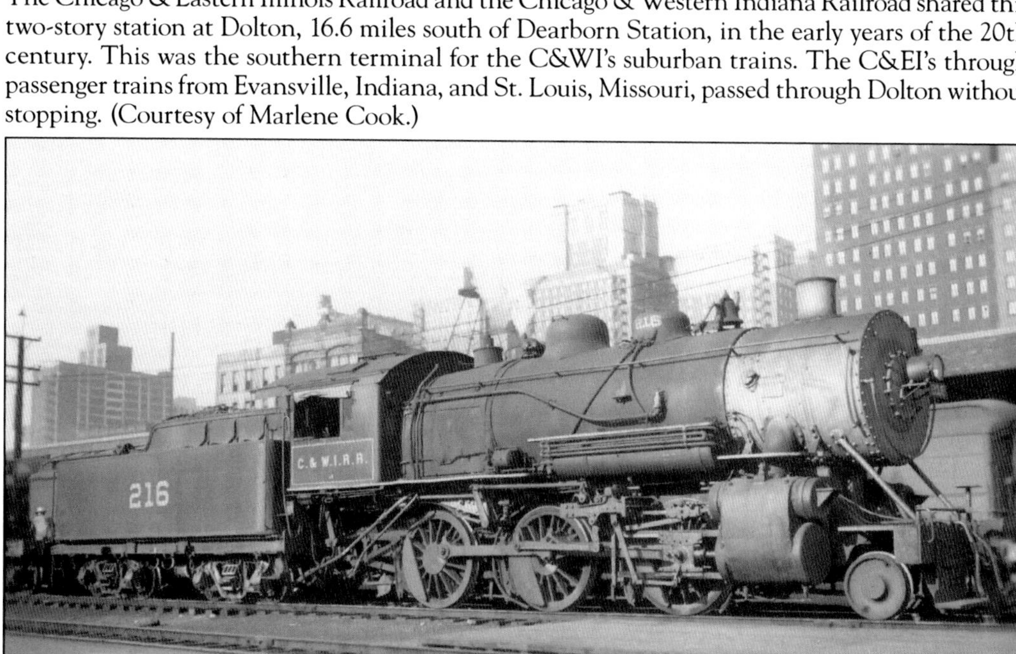

The C&WI's No. 216 is another class J-2 2-6-0 Mogul-type that was built by the Lima Locomotive Works of Lima, Ohio, in 1914. The C&WI regularly used its 2-6-0 locomotives for pulling suburban trains between Dolton and Dearborn Station in Chicago. They were also used for a variety of switching assignments in town. It is shown here on a sunny afternoon in downtown Chicago, steamed up and ready for its next assignment.

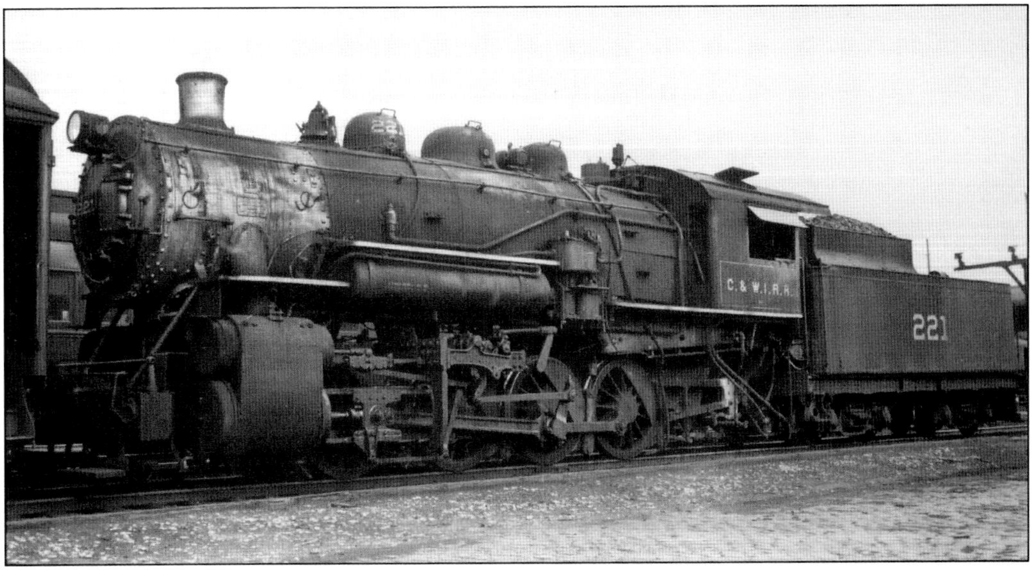

The American Locomotive Company in Schenectady, New York, built C&WI's class K-1 0-8-0 switch engine No. 221 in 1913. It was equipped with 57-inch-diameter drivers and 24-inch-by-30-inch cylinders and operated with a maximum boiler pressure of 190 pounds per square inch. It is shown here on June 23, 1939, working at the C&WI's coach yard, coupled to a heavyweight passenger car. It was retired from service in the late 1940s.

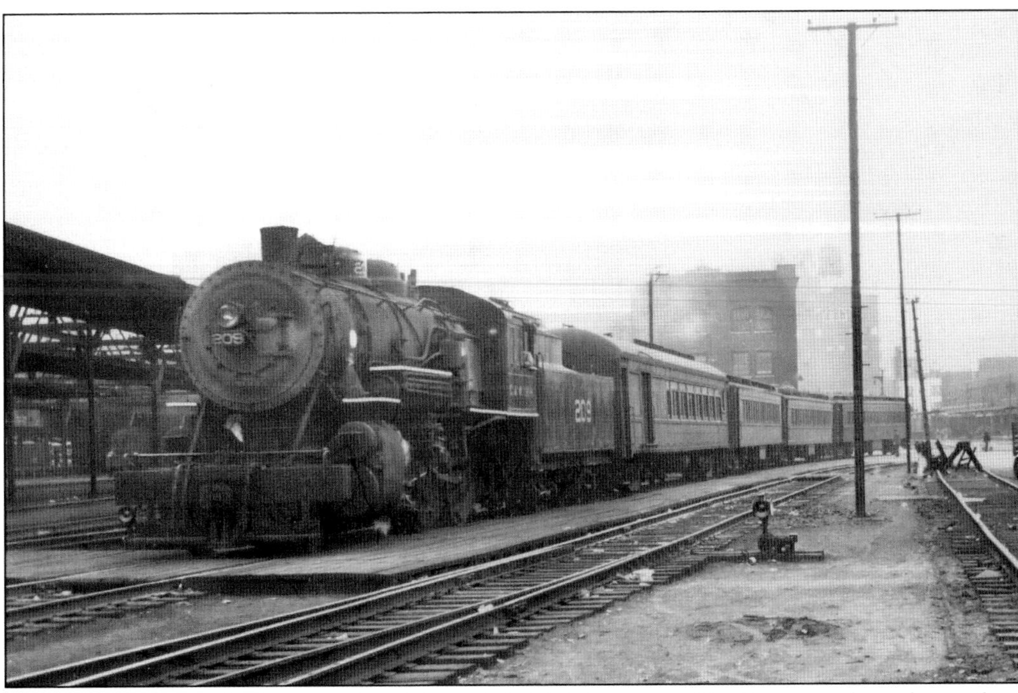

Chicago & Western Indiana Railroad class J-1 2-6-0 Mogul-type No. 209 is ready to depart from Dearborn Station in Chicago with a four-car suburban train bound for Dolton in 1946. The train was heated in cold weather by steam from the locomotive, but ventilation in warm weather was provided by just opening the windows.

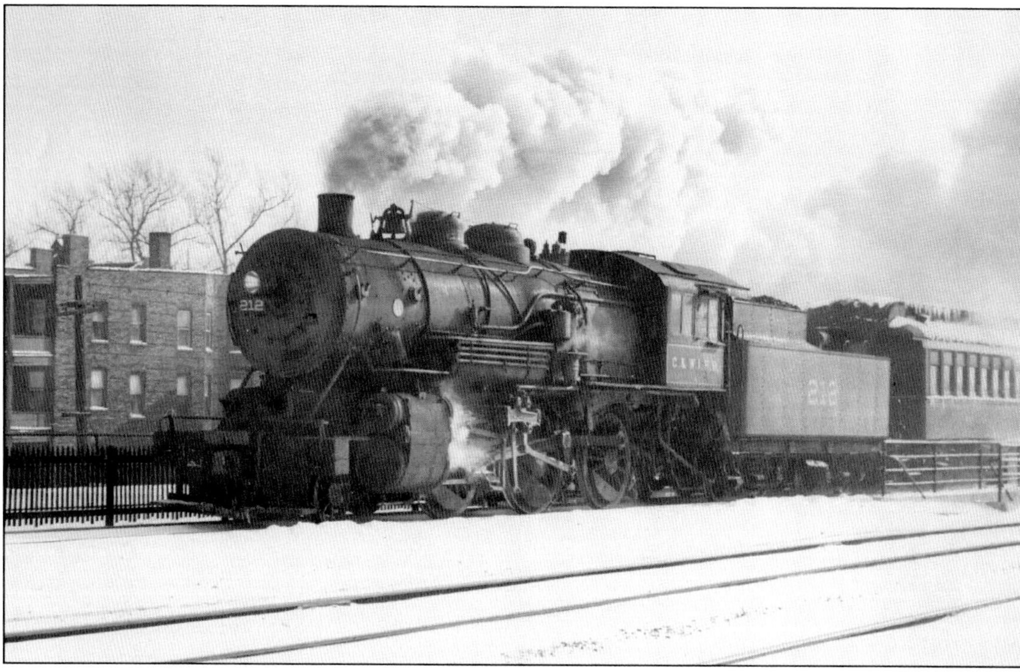

Chicago & Western Indiana Railroad class J-2 2-6-0 Mogul-type No. 212 was built by the Baldwin Locomotive Works of Eddystone, Pennsylvania, in 1913. It is shown here at Englewood Station (Sixty-Third and Wallace Streets) on a very cold day in January 1940. This locomotive provided reliable service to the C&WI for 37 years, both in suburban train service and in switching service. (Courtesy of Sid Davies.)

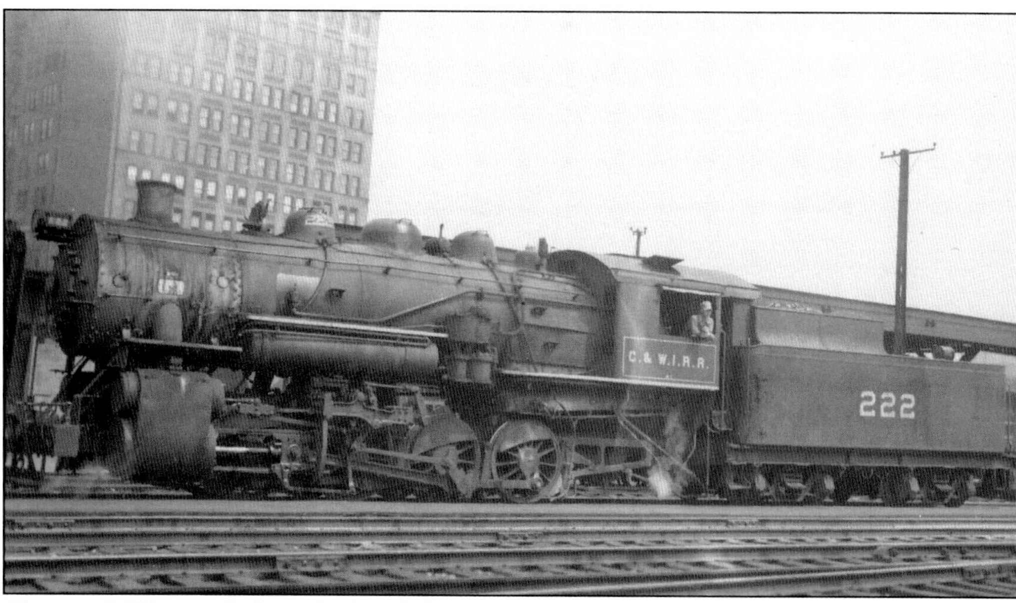

Chicago & Western Indiana Railroad class K-1 0-8-0 switch engine No. 222 was built by ALCO in 1913. This was one of the C&WI's heaviest locomotives, and it was used to move passenger trains between Dearborn Station and the C&WI's coach yard at Fifty-First Street.

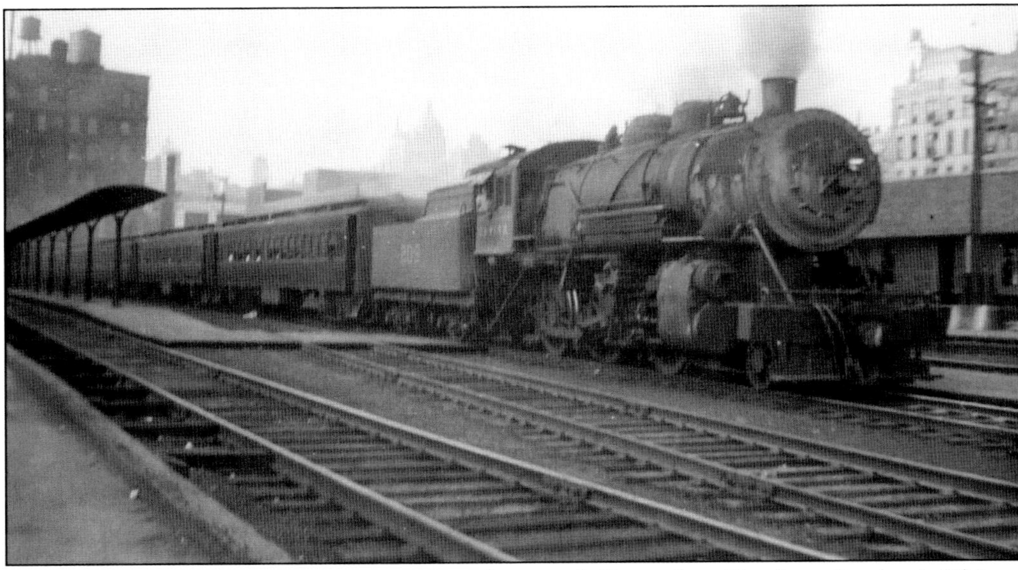

Class J-1 2-6-0 Mogul-type No. 209 is ready to depart at 5:48 p.m. from Dearborn Station in Chicago with Chicago & Western Indiana train No. 75 in July 1939. This train would make stops at Forty-Seventh Street, Fifty-Fifth Street, Fifty-Ninth Street, Englewood, Normal Park, Hamilton Park, Auburn Park, Eighty-First Street, Oakdale, Euclid Park, Fernwood, North Roseland, Roseland, Sheldon Park, Kensington, and Dolton.

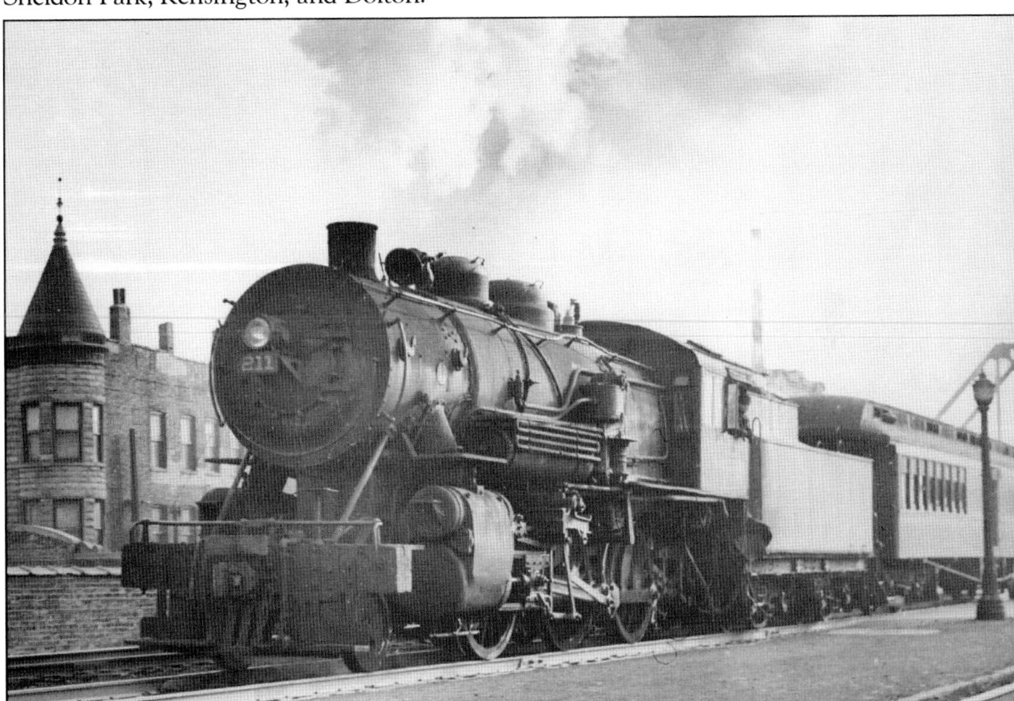

The Chicago & Western Indiana Railroad's class J-1 2-6-0 Mogul-type steam locomotive No. 211 was built by the Baldwin Locomotive Works of Eddystone, Pennsylvania, in 1913. It is shown here with a suburban passenger train stopped at the C&WI's Englewood Station at Sixty-Third and Wallace Streets on the South Side of Chicago in 1940. (Courtesy of Sid Davies.)

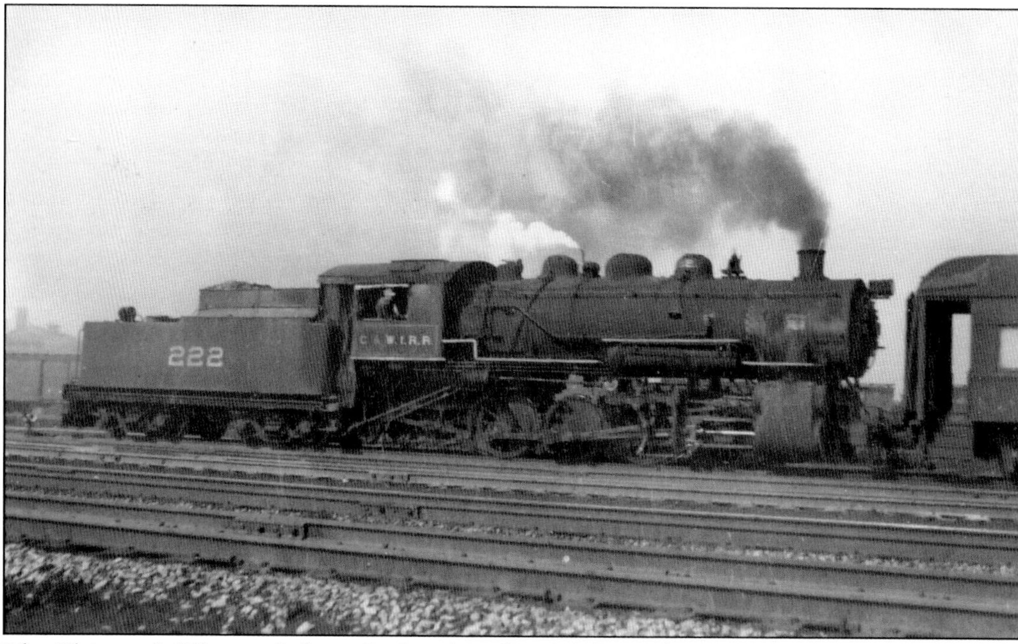

The Chicago & Western Indiana Railroad used its 0-8-0 switch engines, such as No. 222, shown here pushing an unidentified heavyweight passenger car, to move passenger trains between Dearborn Station and the Fifty-First Street coach yard. These low-speed but powerful locomotives were well suited for this duty and remained in service on the C&WI for over 35 years.

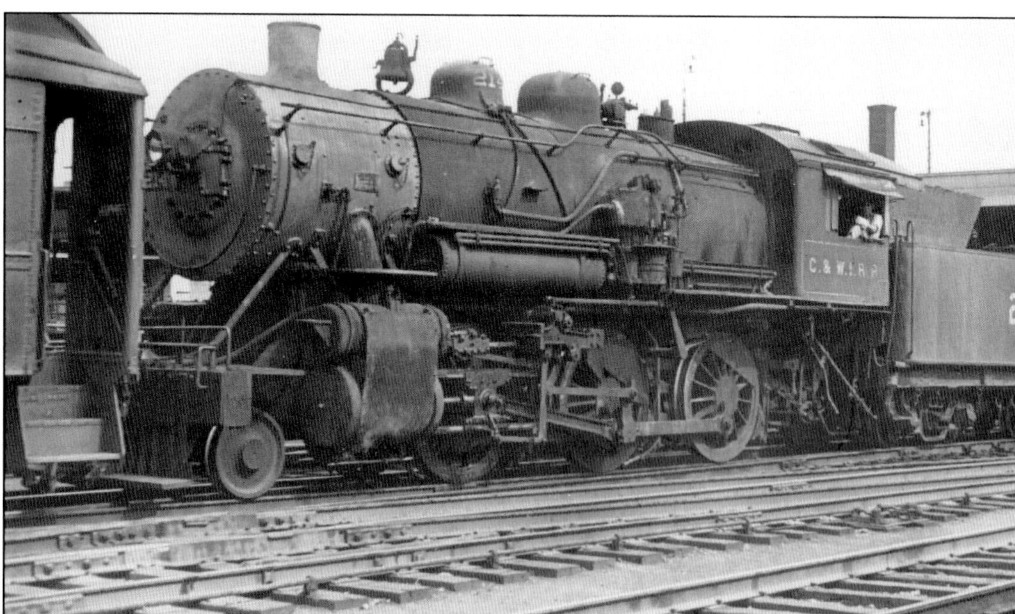

Class J-2 2-6-0 Mogul-type No. 214 is shown here switching passenger cars at Dearborn Station in Chicago in July 1948. The 214 was built by the Lima Locomotive Corporation for the Chicago & Western Indiana in 1914 and was retired from revenue service in 1950, when the C&WI acquired new diesel locomotives from the American Locomotive Company.

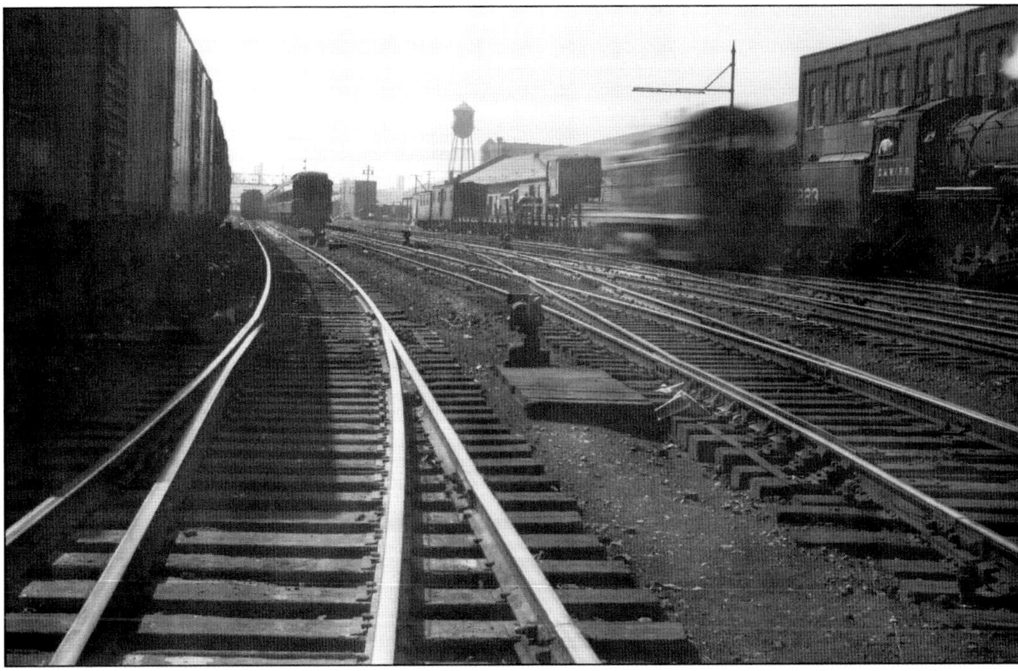

C&WI locomotive No. 223 is on the far right of the photograph pulling a work train with a crane and a crew car. The latter was used as quarters for maintenance employees. This photograph was taken at the Fifty-First Street switchyard. Coaches can be seen in the background, with freight cars on the left. It was a busy day in the switchyard, as indicated by the unattached and blurry engine moving parallel to the work train.

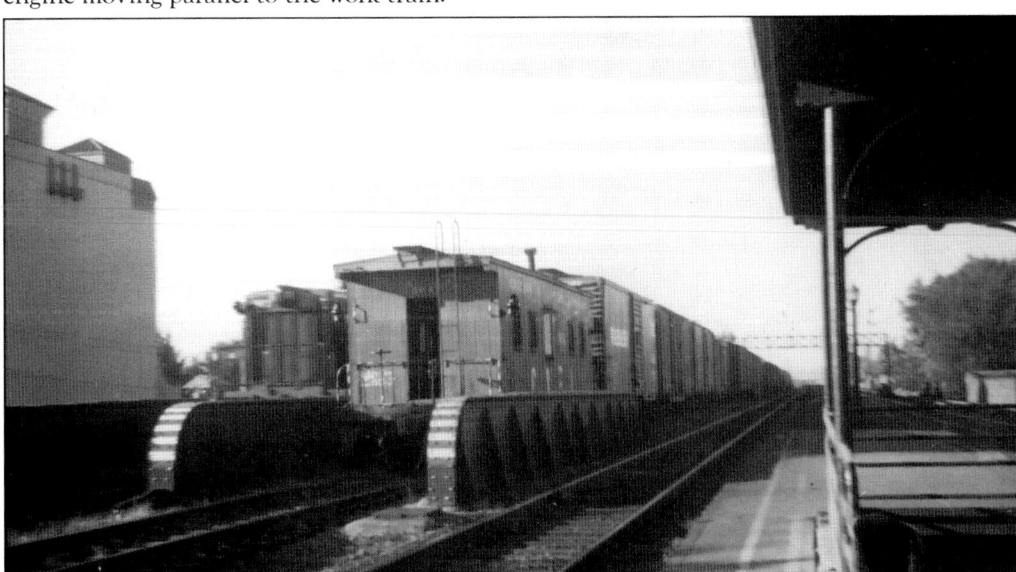

A northbound C&EI freight passing through Englewood was captured on film by the young Bill Molony in August 1956. On the left is the front end of an Erie switch engine, EMD-NW-2, which took him by surprise. The fact that the caboose has no cupola or bay window indicates that it was a transfer caboose headed for a western connection with the Santa Fe, the Chicago Northwestern, or the Burlington line.

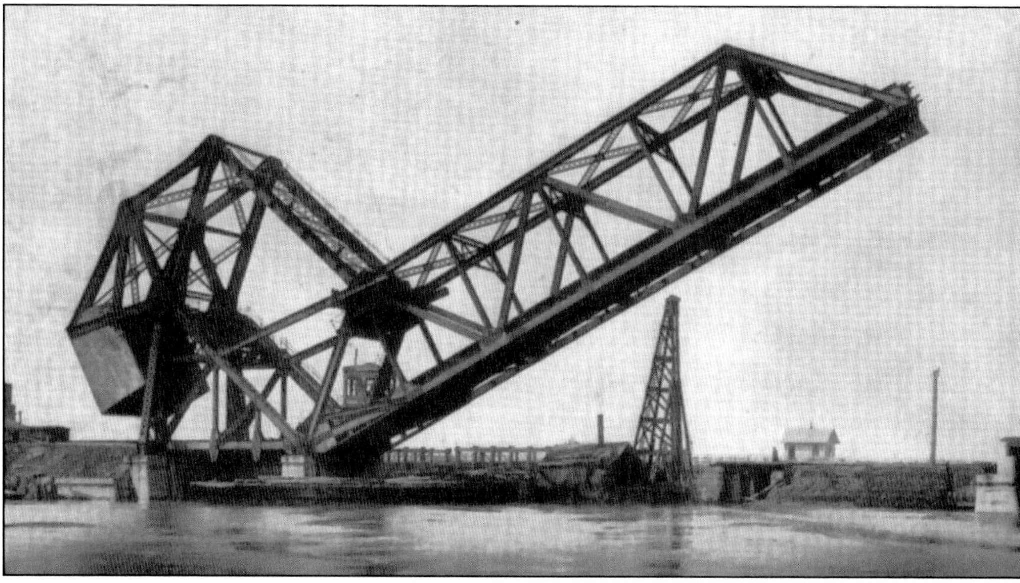

This bascule bridge, the second Main Line Bridge of the Chicago & Western Indiana, went into service in 1912. The previous version was a swing bridge mounted in the center of the Calumet River channel. Both were located just east of Torrence Avenue, connecting South Deering industrial sites along the line with those in Hegewisch. (Courtesy of the Southeast Chicago Historical Society.)

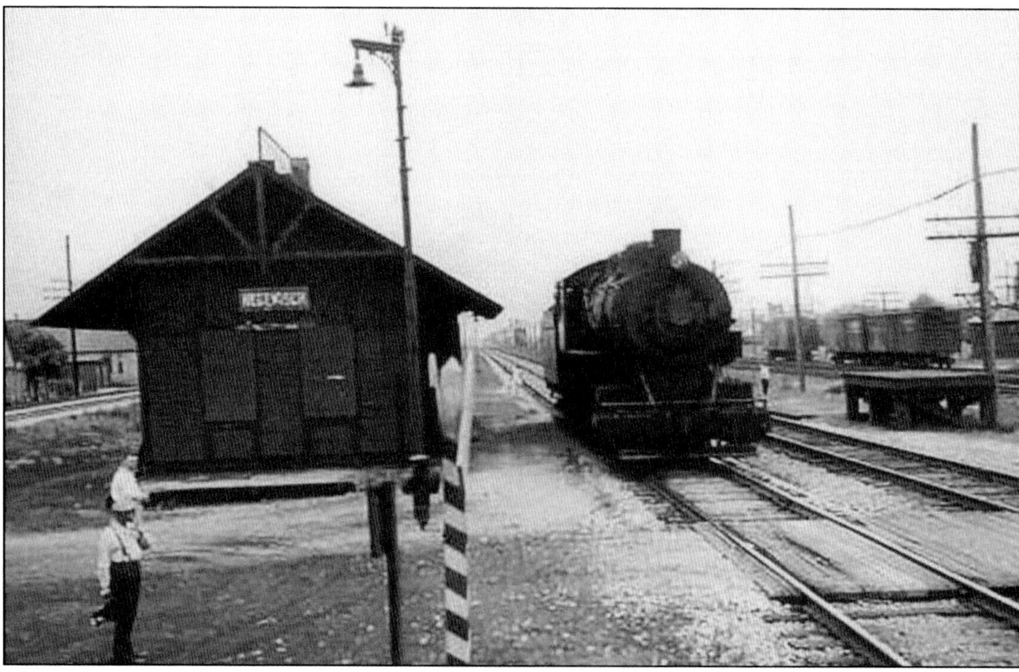

The C&WI station at Hegewisch, 18.2 miles from Dearborn Station, was mainly used by the Cincinnati, Indianapolis & Louisville line or Monon. The equipment on the tracks appears to be a switch engine with tender, probably working in the late 1920s. The right-of-way for the Chicago South Shore & South Bend interurban is to the left; the employee entrance to Western Steel Car Company is to the right. (Courtesy of the Southeast Chicago Historical Society.)

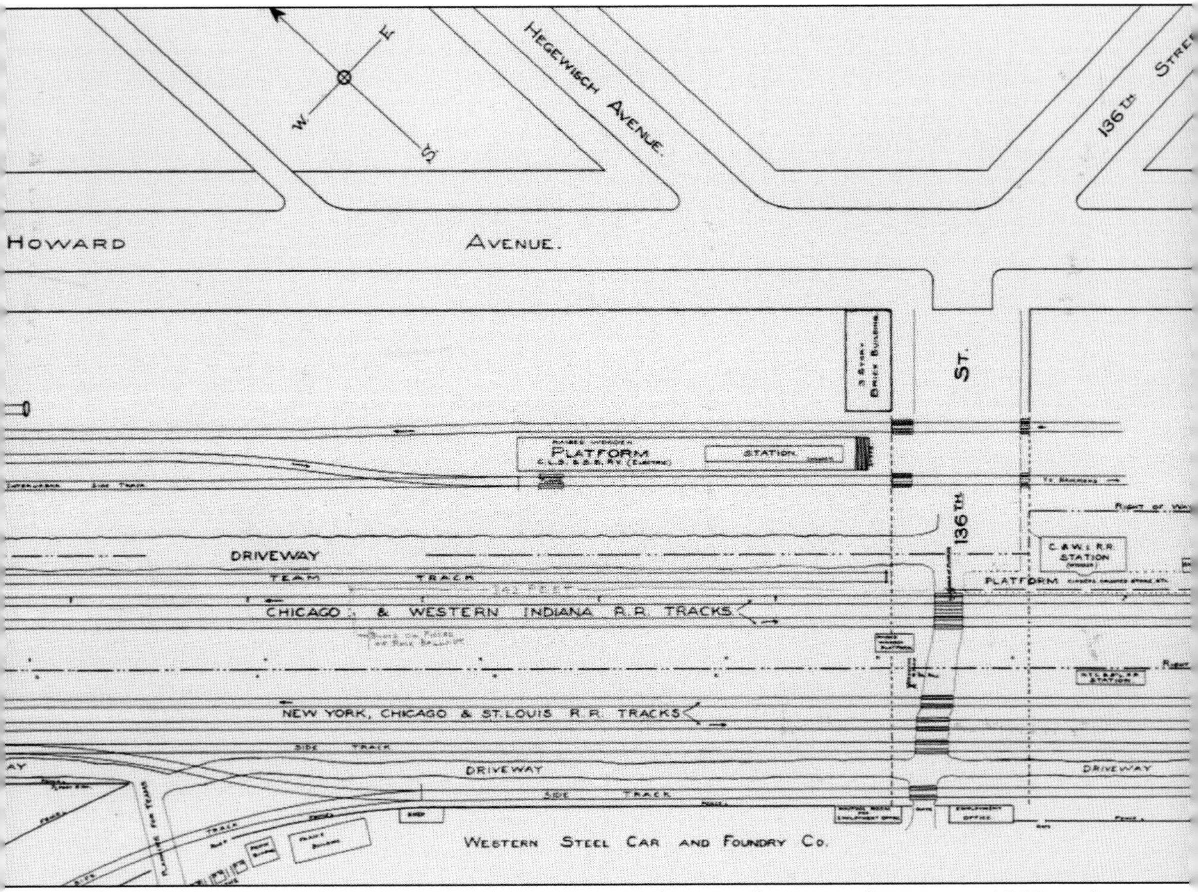

The Hegewisch station of the Chicago & Western Indiana is shown on this map at 136th and Howard Streets (later Brainard Avenue) approximately two miles from the Indiana state line. This placed it in the Burnham Yard (Burnham, Illinois), although the station sign reads "Hegewisch," which after 1889 was a part of Chicago. Restaurants, taverns, hotels, and small service businesses lined the nearby streets to serve workers from Western Steel Car and Foundry and commuters who rode the Chicago South Shore & South Bend (CSS&SB) electric. In 1880, the C&WI junction at the Indiana state line was a complicated affair involving the Monon, Erie, Wabash, and several non-C&WI railroads. A small, wooden tower originally controlled traffic manually. In 1907, it was replaced with a brick and concrete building 100 feet long and 15 feet wide. Inside, a mechanical locking bed and signal equipment were built and installed by National Switch and Signal Company. The locking bed, at over 95 feet long, had 196 levers and was the largest of its kind in North America at the time. (Courtesy of the Southeast Chicago Historical Society.)

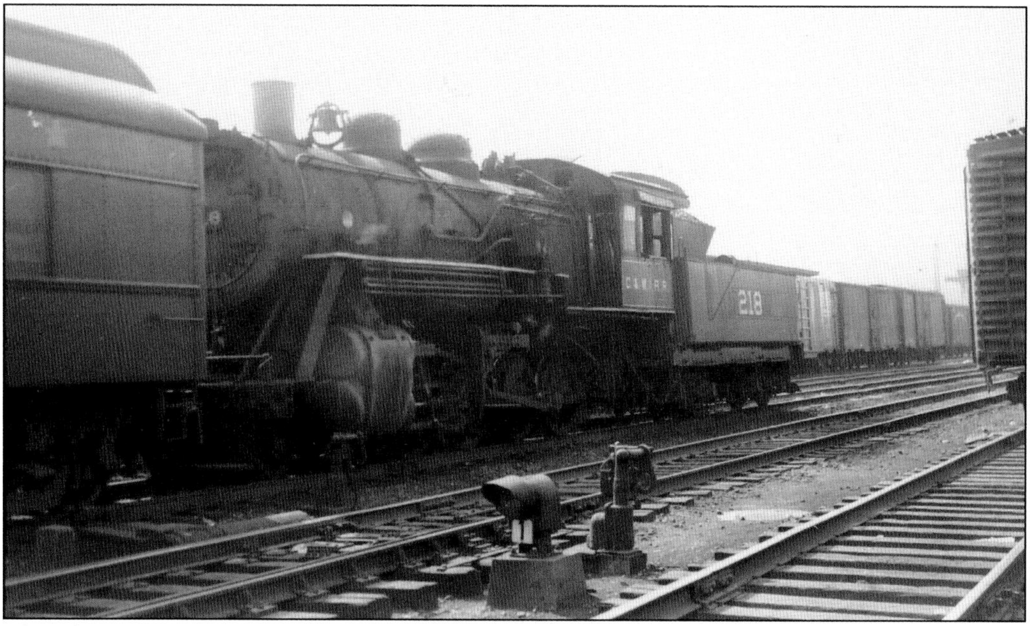

The Chicago & Western Indiana Railroad used its Class K-1 0-8-0 switch engines to move inbound and outbound trains between Dearborn Station and the C&WI coach yard about five miles south. C&WI 0-8-0 No. 218, shown here at the coach yard, is coupled to a heavyweight passenger car. These engines were built by the American Locomotive Company in 1913 and remained in service until 1950, when they were replaced with diesel switch engines.

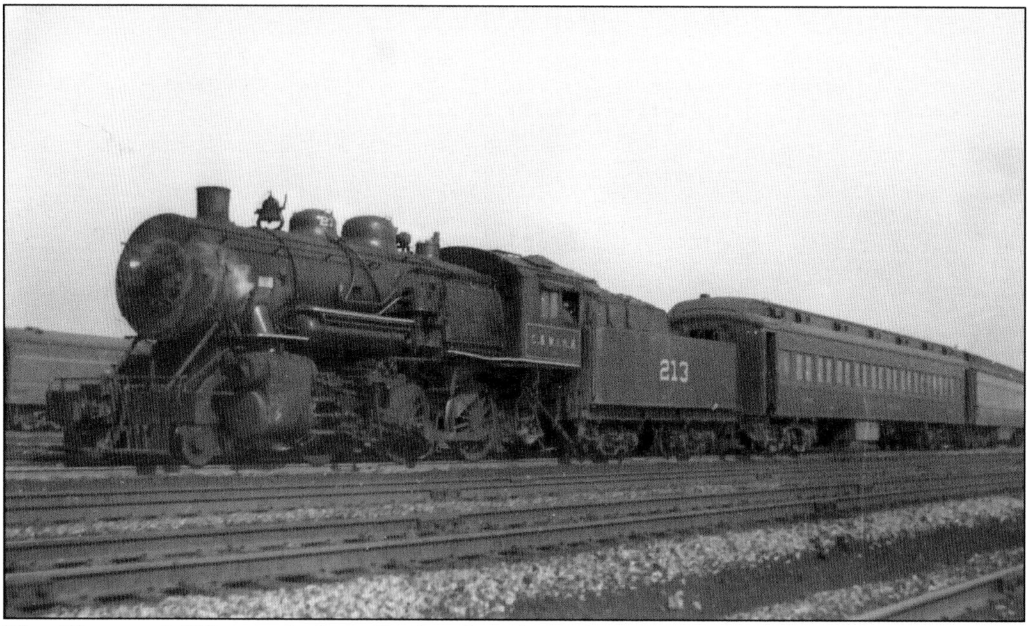

The Chicago & Western Indiana Railroad performed switching duties for all of the railroads using Dearborn Station except for the Atchison, Topeka & Santa Fe. C&WI 2-6-0 Mogul-type No. 213 is shown in this undated photograph coupled to two Wabash Railroad heavyweight chair cars at the Fifty-First Street coach yard. These cars were assigned to the Wabash passenger trains operating between Chicago; Decatur, Illinois; and St. Louis, Missouri.

Two

Dearborn Station 1885–1922

Immediately after the opening of C&WI, all its owner rail lines needed a terminal in downtown Chicago. This would be one of their selling points in order to get freight and passenger customers. The City of Chicago, however, was reluctant to buy into this project because it would cost the city a lot of money to put in a new street, and at the same time, business owners and residents already on the right-of-way would have to be moved. Lawsuits ensued. For the first years of the C&WI, there was a head-house at Twenty-Second Street and Archer Avenue; later it was at Twelfth and State Streets. Finally, the grand Dearborn Station was unveiled in 1885. But it had its problems. The track yard behind it was too long and crossed busy Taylor Street, so trains with passengers disembarking could not spend too much time on the platforms before the trains had to be broken or moved south of Taylor Street. The owner rail lines also built warehouses south of Dearborn along the right-of-way, and in 1914, a station annex was added. Although Dearborn Station was a grand building in the best elaborate style of the late Victorian period, it was not the "front door" of Chicago, as many a small-town station was often considered to be, nor was it a "railroad cathedral" like many other big-city terminals of the time. It was a utilitarian but handsome backdoor entrance for visitors to the Columbian Exposition, European immigrants, and commuters from the south and southwest neighborhoods of the city and beyond. In fact, it was situated in what had been and for some time thereafter continued to be an area of saloons, drug dens, and brothels, also known as Conley's Patch or the Levee. By the early 20th century, though, more respectable businesses had taken hold, and the neighborhood was referred to as Printers Row.

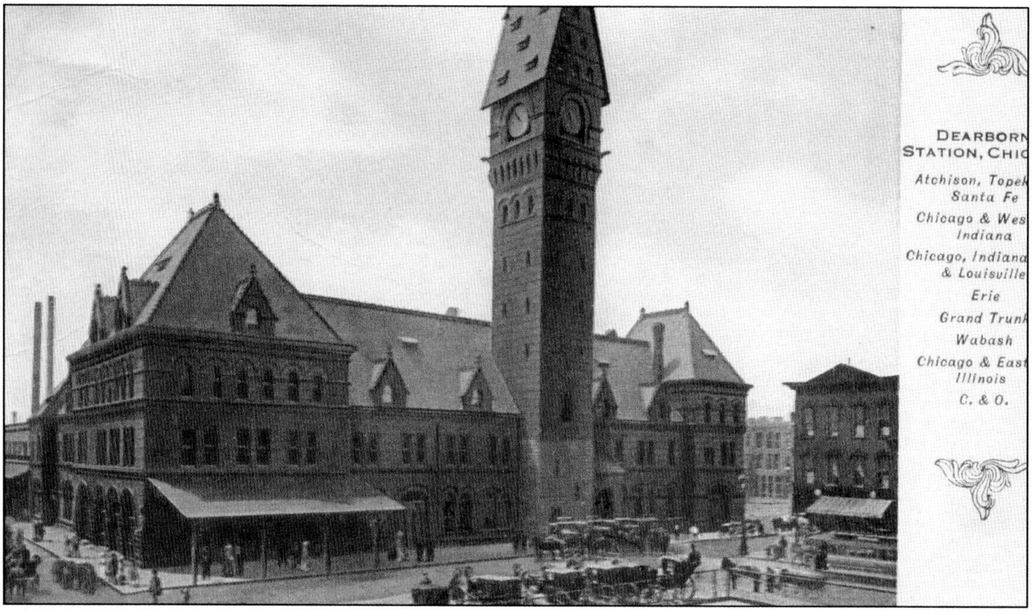

The C&WI built Dearborn Station as the downtown terminal for its five owner railroads in 1885. The architect was Cyrus L. Eidletz, whose firm was located in New York City. Of the user lines listed on the postcard, the Santa Fe and the Chesapeake & Ohio were tenants, not owners. The Chicago, Indianapolis & Louisville was commonly called the Monon. (Courtesy of the V.O. Hammon Publishing Co.)

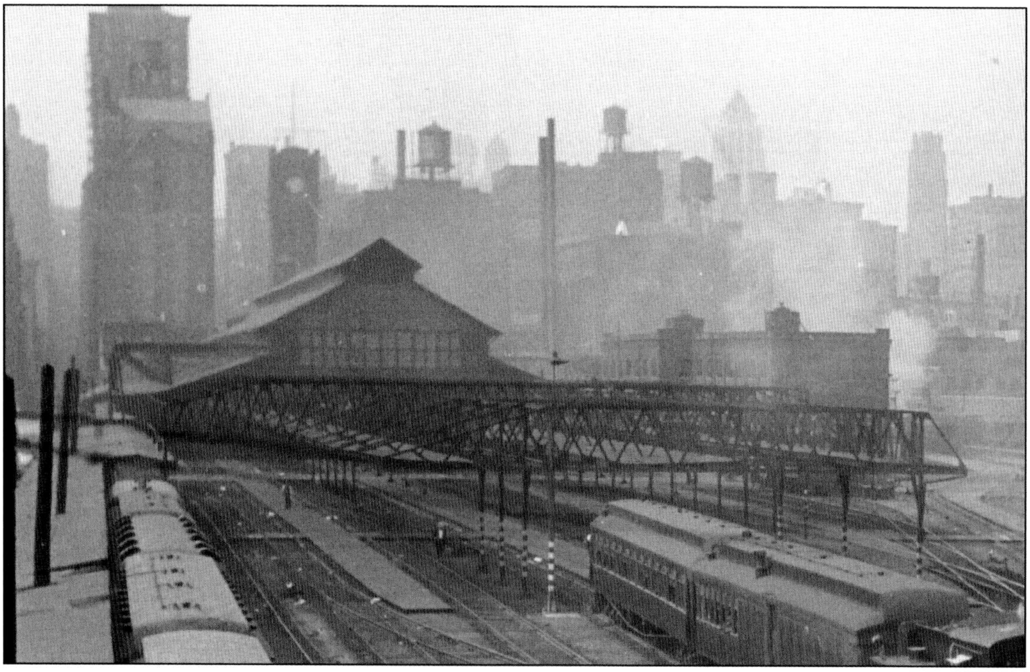

In 1912, the C&WI, Wabash, C&EI, and Grand Trunk Western were running up to 104 daily through trains and 42 suburban trains out of Dearborn Station. Due to the heavy traffic, an annex was built east of the main station to handle the suburban trains and any intercity trains that had extensive "head-end" business.

In the golden era of Chicago railroading, the 1920s and 1930s, the city boasted six main-line stations. Only two blocks to the west was Grand Central Station. Similar in appearance to Dearborn, it was owned and operated by the Baltimore & Ohio, with the Wisconsin Central (Soo Line), Chicago & Great Western Railway, and the Pere Marquette Railway as tenants. Grand Central closed in 1969 and was demolished in 1971. (Courtesy of Cynthia Ogorek.)

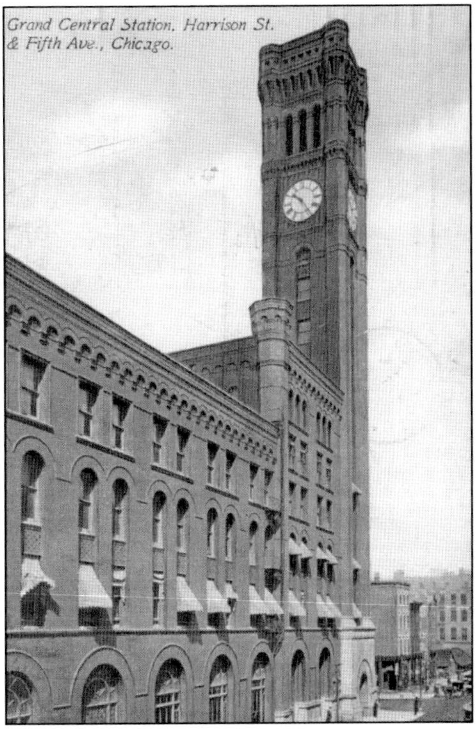

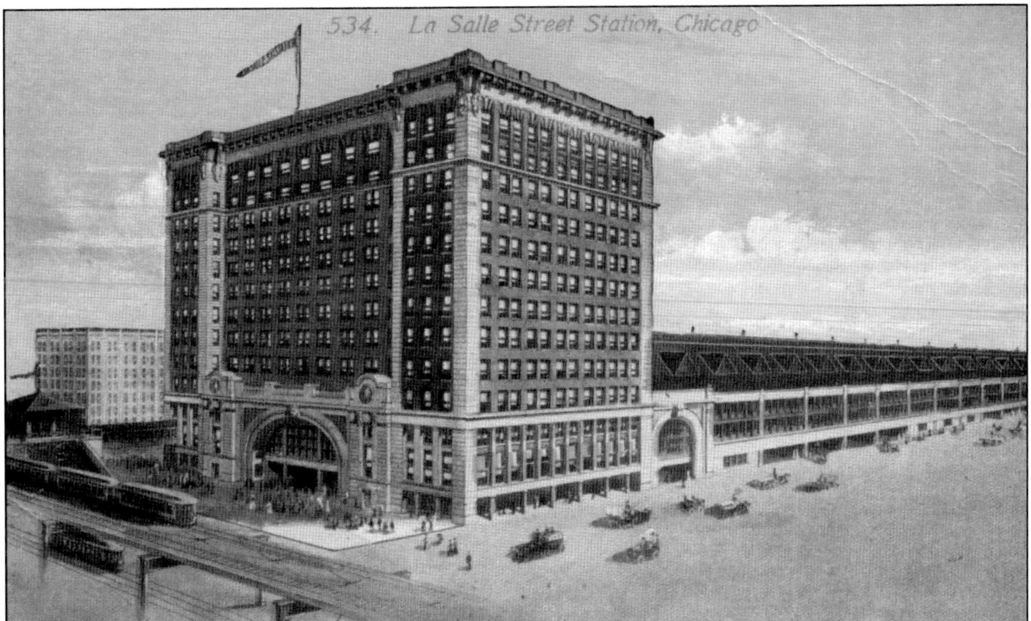

LaSalle Street Station in Chicago was located on Van Buren Street between LaSalle Street and Sherman Street. It was the terminal for the Chicago, Rock Island & Pacific, the New York Central, and the New York, Chicago & St. Louis (Nickel Plate) Railroads. Most of the passenger trains of the Chicago & Eastern Illinois Railroad moved from Dearborn Station over to La Salle Street Station on July 31, 1904. Nine years later, on August 1, 1913, the C&EI trains moved back to Dearborn Station.

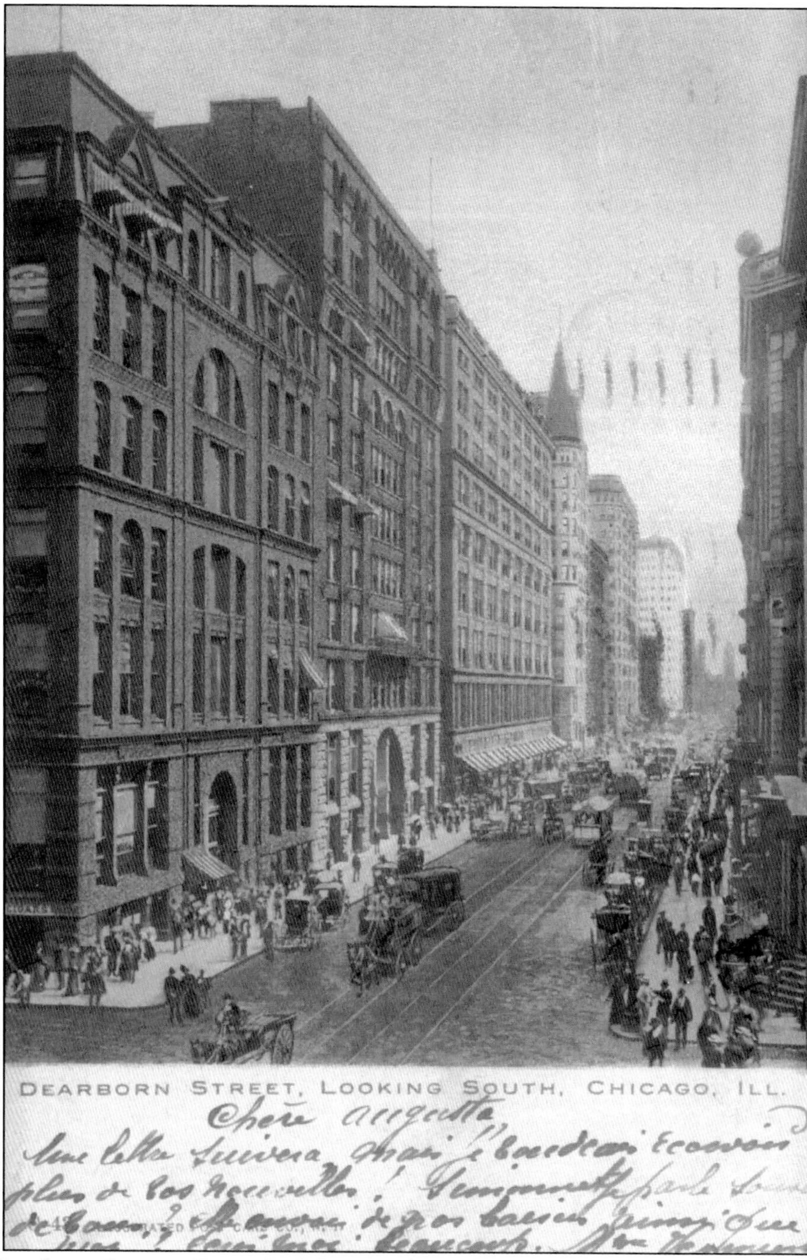

In 1885, Dearborn Station (far end of the street) was located in the middle of one of Chicago's most notorious vice districts. By the late 1890s, however, the neighborhood was attracting respectable printing and publishing businesses, which were housed in the earliest of Chicago's skyscrapers. The street soon became known as Printers Row. Many of the railroad companies that used Dearborn Station also had their general offices in the neighborhood. In the days before telephones, travelers arriving at their destinations would purchase a penny postcard such as this one and send it by adding a penny stamp. Getting their "two cents worth," the folks back home were informed that they had arrived safely. This one, however, required a 2¢ stamp because it went to Belgium. The writer told the recipient, "dear Augusta," that a letter would soon follow. (Courtesy of Cynthia Ogorek.)

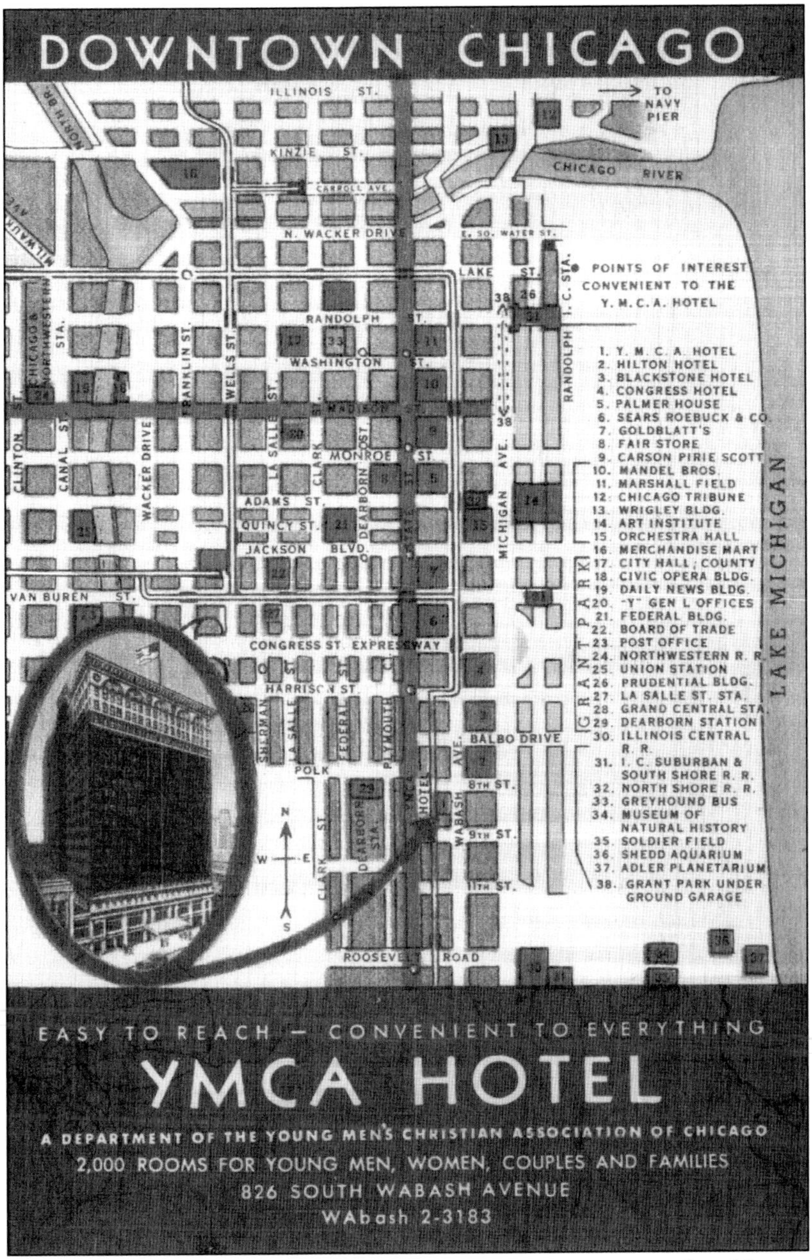

While some critics said that Dearborn was not a very convenient or comfortable station, it was located within walking distance of many downtown Chicago sites and hotels, as well as business offices. Taxi service was also available, and connections were easily made via public transportation with other train stations for cross-country travelers. This map was published by the YMCA Hotel, which was located east of the station. Further east was Grant Park. From Roosevelt Road, visitors would find three of Chicago's nationally known museums: Adler Planetarium, the Shedd Aquarium, and the Field Museum of Natural History. The theater and shopping districts were just a few blocks north on Dearborn or State Street. The fact that trains came right into the heart of a city like Chicago made getting in and out of town much simpler than a drive to some far-flung airport would prove in the not-so-distant future. (Courtesy of Cynthia Ogorek.)

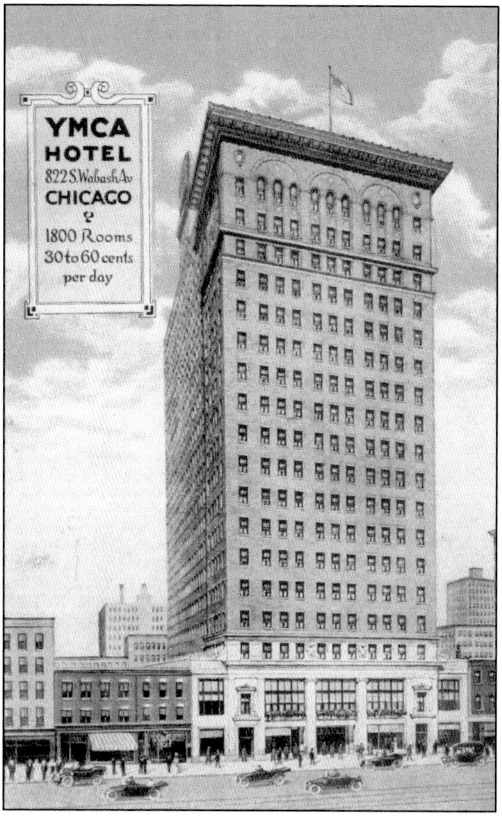

The YMCA on Wabash was only three blocks east of Dearborn Station and yards. Since its mission was to provide inexpensive lodgings for transient men, it is easy to assume that railroad crewmembers stayed at the hotel. In fact, for decades, the YMCAs in New York City, Cleveland, and elsewhere across the nation had been setting aside rooms for railroad workers who wanted decent room and board. (Courtesy of Cynthia Ogorek.)

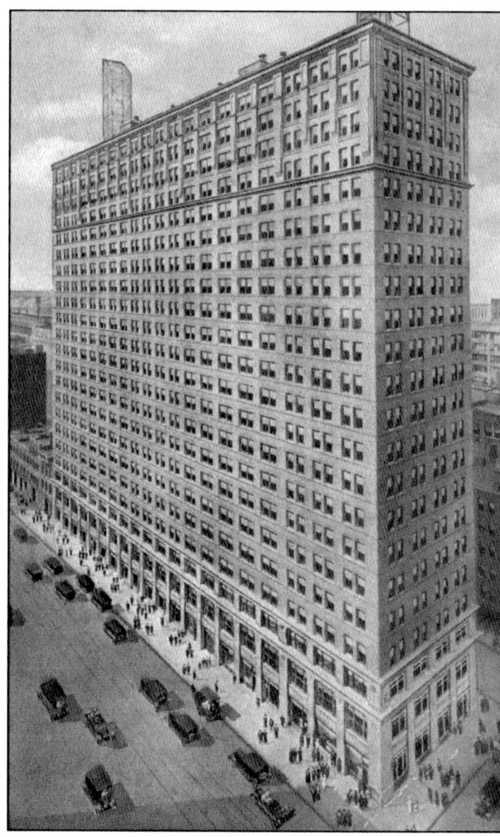

The Transportation Building was the tallest structure on Printers Row. It was designed by John Van Osdel and built by Fred V. Prather in 1911 to house railway, shipping, and other commercial businesses. The famous Elliott Ness had an office on the third floor. It is now in use at 600 South Dearborn Street for residential living. (Courtesy of Cynthia Ogorek.)

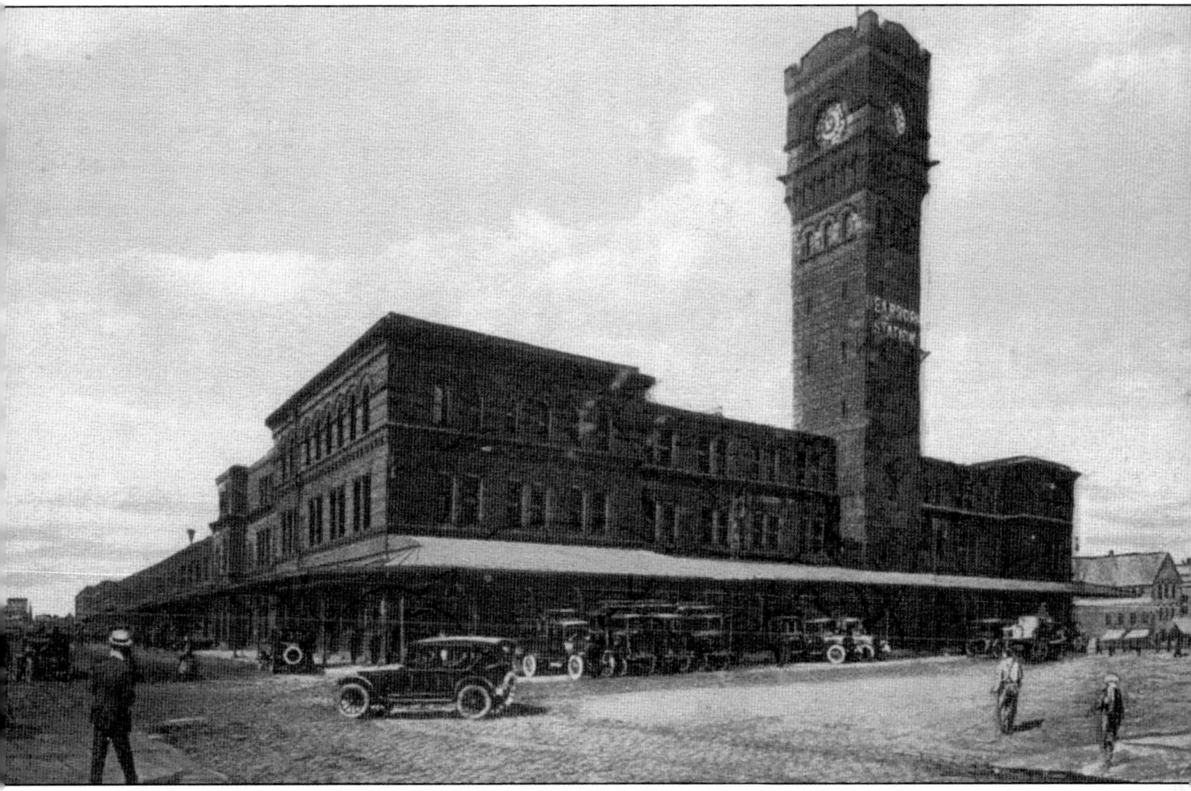

On December 21, 1922, fire nearly destroyed the Dearborn Station, which at 37 years of age was considered a Chicago landmark. While firefighters worked to put out the blaze, office workers and holiday travelers stood in Dearborn and Polk Streets watching as flames turned the tower into a blazing torch. They watched as one by one the clock hands dropped to the ground, and when the flagpole from the very top of the tower crashed to the ground, the crowd cheered. Meanwhile, C&WI officials moved arrivals and departures to the sheds behind the building and the annex while railroad and postal employees secured tons of holiday mail from the flames. Workers were on the job early the next morning to clean up and assess the damage. It was estimated that repairs to the roof and third floor would take about three months. In the meantime, C&WI's offices were relocated across the street to the Transportation Building, and the train floor was reopened on December 23. The photograph above shows the building in 1923.

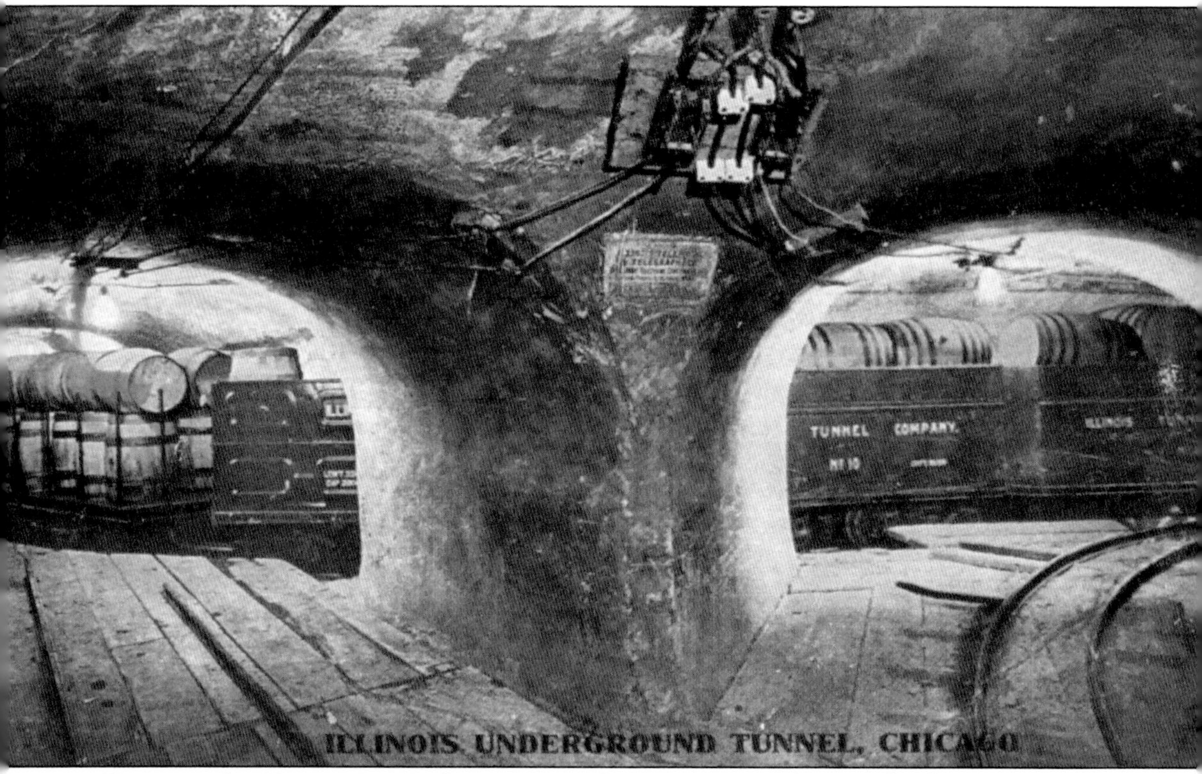

Known as the Chicago City Railway, among other names, an underground railroad with some 50 miles of track served Dearborn Station from Plymouth Court starting in October 1898. Originally, the tunnels were constructed just to handle telephone cables, but then a battery-operated railroad was added to run merchandise, mail, express packages, and checked passenger luggage among the freight houses south of Dearborn and rail stations elsewhere in the city. The motorman drove the train, loaded and unloaded its cars, and when necessary, re-railed cars that had fallen off the track. The short-lived service was particularly handy for delivering bales of paper to the local printing houses and ran regularly until 1901. General Electric extended the line west under Polk Street to Federal Street, then north to Harrison Street. From Polk Street it went south to Fourteenth Street, west to Dearborn Street, and south on Dearborn Street to Archer Avenue. In 1905, it was complete. The decline in use began in the 1920s. By 1940, street trucks had replaced the rail line. (Courtesy of Cynthia Ogorek.)

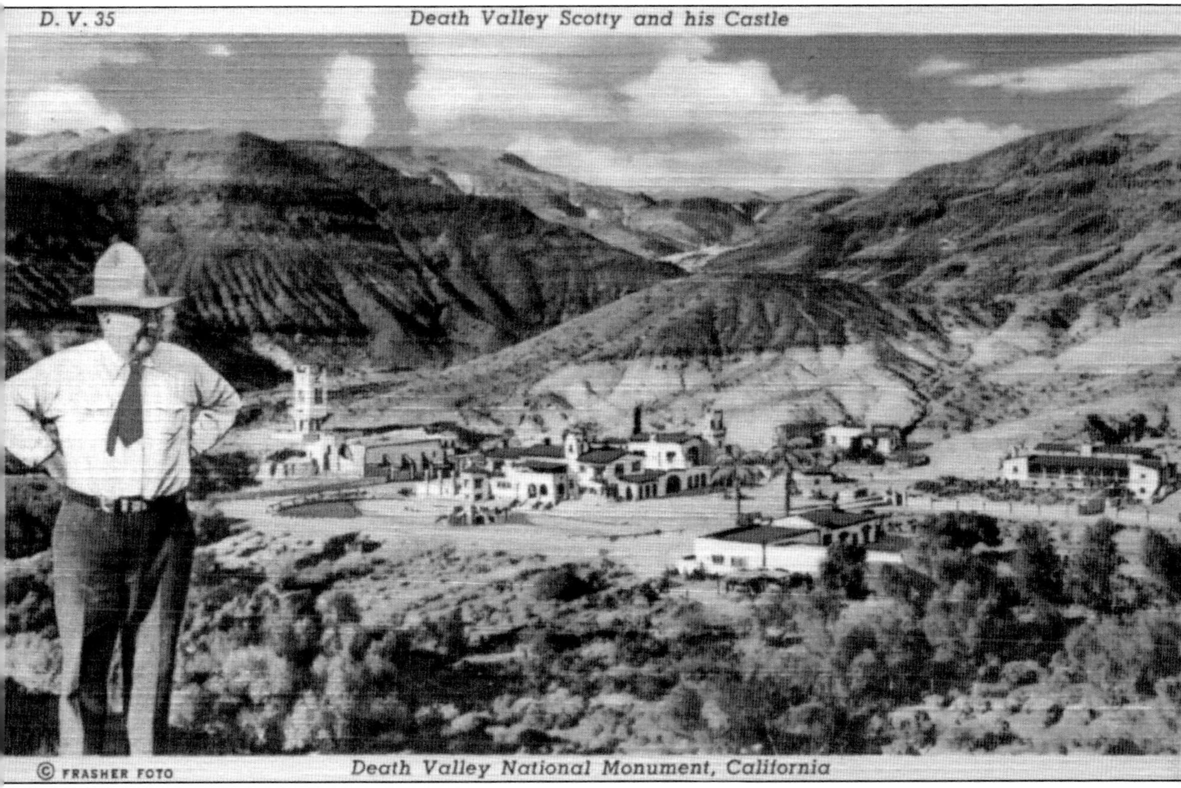

The story goes that on July 8, 1905, Walter "Death Valley Scotty" Scott walked into the Los Angeles office of the Santa Fe Railroad and challenged the line to break its own speed record between L.A. and Chicago. The railroad agreed. Twenty-four hours later, 15 crew members, Scotty, his wife Ella, a Santa Fe PR man, and a Los Angeles *Examiner* reporter boarded the *Scott Special.* Forty-four hours and 54 minutes later, it arrived at Dearborn Station approximately seven hours ahead of the normal trip time. Leaving Los Angeles, it was pulled by Ten-Wheeler No. 442. From La Junta, Colorado, to Chicago, it was powered with balanced compound 4-4-2 Atlantics built by Baldwin in 1904. Every two hours, engines were changed in 80-second to four-minute "pit stops," and the train averaged 50.4 miles per hour for the 2,265-mile journey. The consist included baggage car No. 210, dining car No. 1407 and Pullman sleeper *Muskegon*, also built in 1904. "Scotty's Castle," shown in the image above, was owned by Chicago insurance executive Albert Johnson and is today a part of Death Valley National Park. (Courtesy of Cynthia Ogorek.)

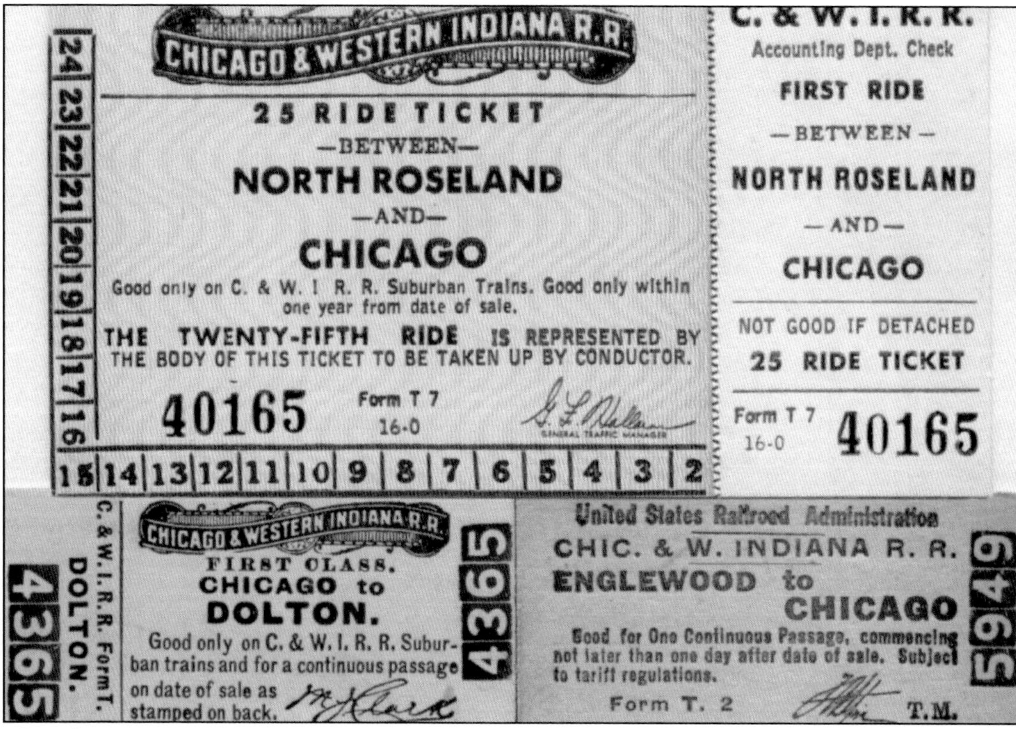

The Chicago & Western Indiana Railroad's suburban trains operated between downtown Chicago and Dolton, with intermediate station stops at Forty-Seventh Street, Fifty-Fifth Street, Fifty-Ninth Street, Englewood, Normal Park, Hamilton Park, Auburn Park, Oakdale, Euclid Park, Fernwood, North Roseland, Roseland, Sheldon Park, and Kensington. The Wabash used the same route but left it at Seventy-Second Street. The Erie and the Chicago, Indianapolis & Louisville (Monon) left it for the Main Line at Eighty-First Street, about seven and a half miles from Dolton. From there, passenger trains went southeast to their passenger stations in Hammond, a little over 20 miles away. Their freight yards were located in South Hammond. The Grand Trunk left this route at Forty-Ninth Street, while the Santa Fe used it for only 1.3 miles before heading west to California. Only the Chicago & Eastern Illinois went beyond Dolton.

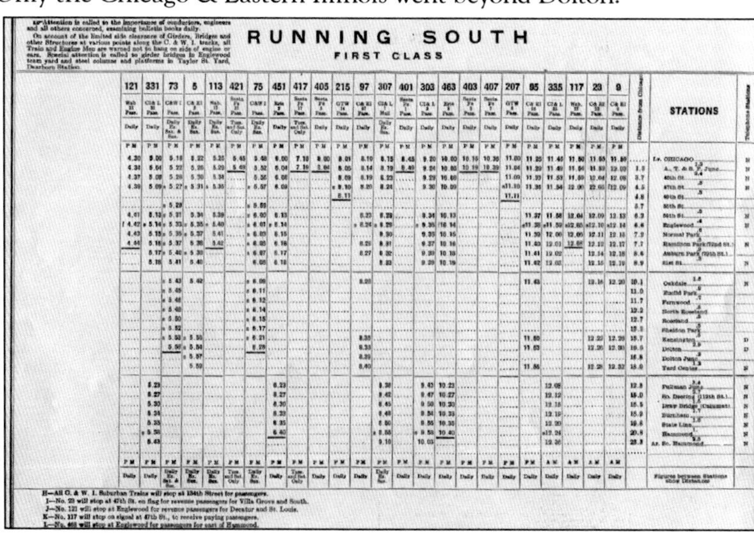

Three

Chicago & Eastern Illinois and the Dolton Line

Although the Chicago & Eastern Illinois was an equal partner in the C&WI venture with the other shareholding railroads, it must always be considered as the instigator of the railroad. The C&EI came about in 1877, after a merger of the Chicago, Danville & Vincennes Railroad with two other railroads, the result of which was named the Chicago & Eastern Illinois. Eventually, six subsequent corporations were called C&EI. The new railroad served many towns on both sides of the Indiana-Illinois border between Evansville, Indiana, and Chicago. The problem, however, was getting into downtown Chicago in the cheapest way possible. The solution was to form the C&WI, which would be some 17 miles long and give the C&EI a nearly straight and much less expensive route from Dolton to the Loop. In 1879, it incorporated the C&WI for this purpose. Once this Dolton Line was built and the Dearborn Street station was in service, the C&EI was able to run its passenger, commuter, and freight trains without any interference from lessor lines. Once the four other trunk lines joined it as full partners in the venture, its financial bottom line took a turn for the better. The C&EI became a local as well as long-distance transportation provider, which generated many stories about its stations and yards and the people and businesses that used it.

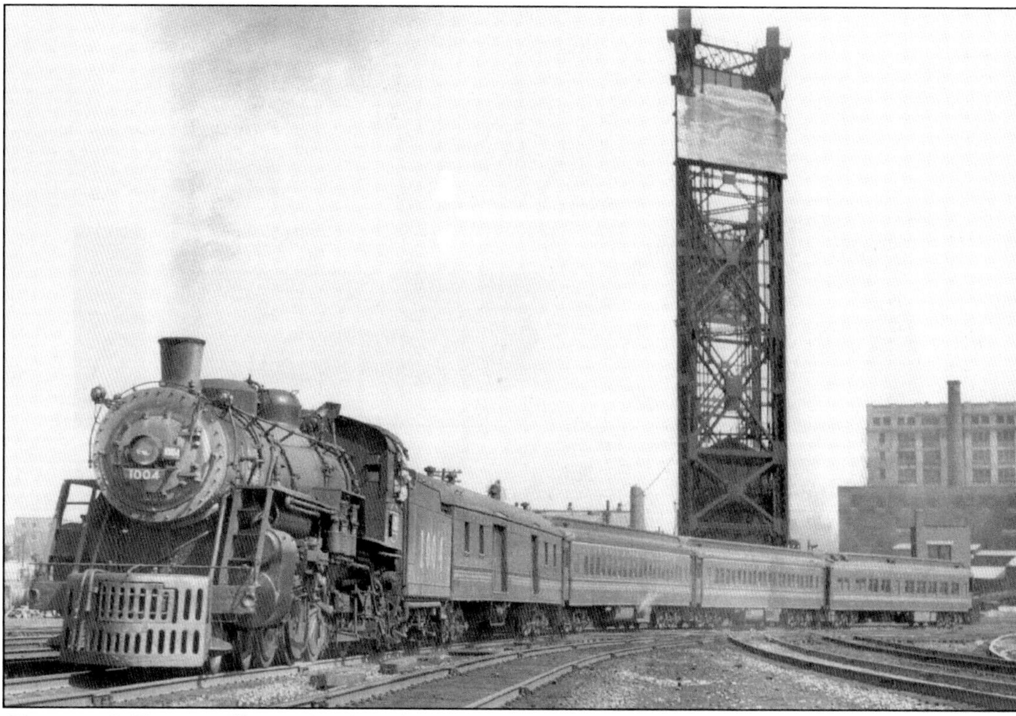

Chicago & Eastern Illinois Railroad class P34 4-6-2 Pacific-type No. 1004, with C&EI train No. 23, the *Cardinal*, heads out of Chicago in the fall of 1947. The *Cardinal* was the C&EI's day train that operated between Chicago and St. Louis. It was a conventional heavyweight train that was overhauled and repainted blue with orange stripes to match the company's newer streamlined trains.

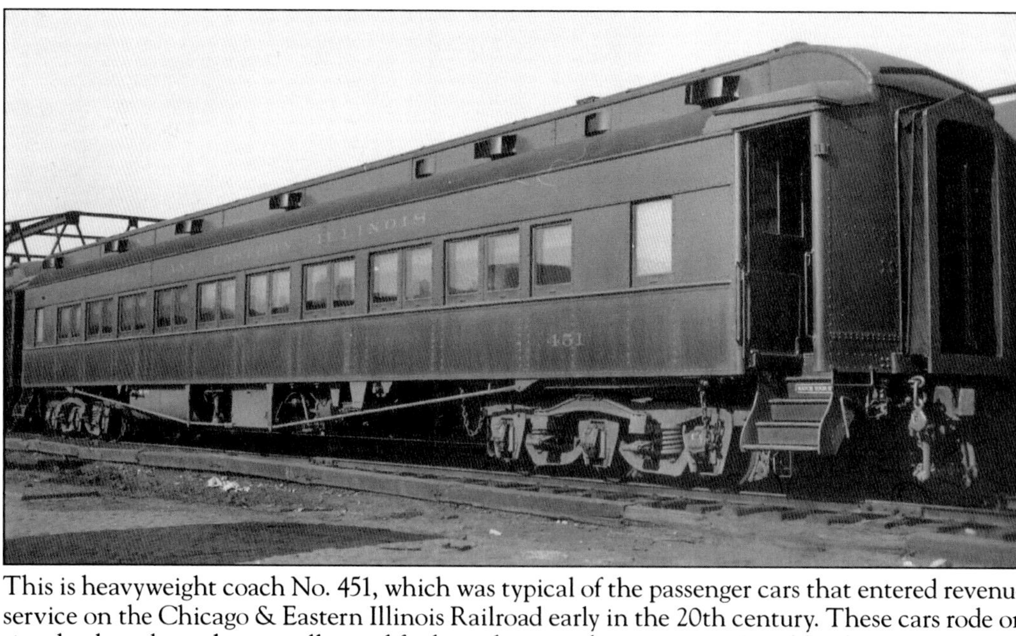

This is heavyweight coach No. 451, which was typical of the passenger cars that entered revenue service on the Chicago & Eastern Illinois Railroad early in the 20th century. These cars rode on six-wheel trucks and were well suited for long-distance daytime trips. Cars like this one remained in service well into the 1950s and 1960s.

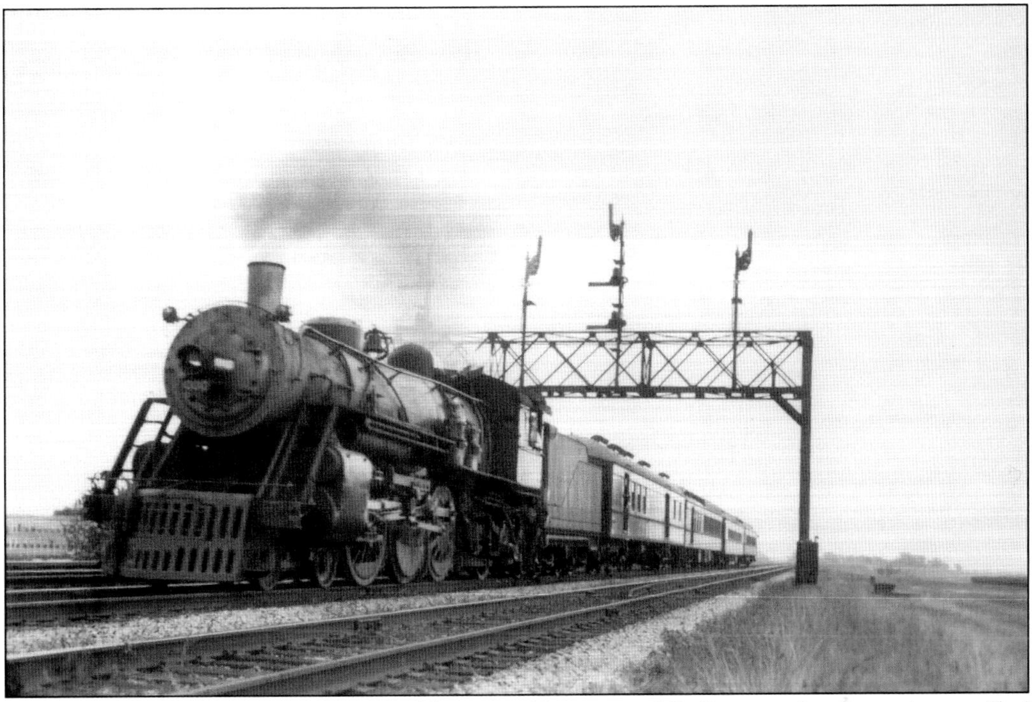

C&EI train No. 21, the *Zipper,* operated between Chicago and St. Louis and is shown here pulled by a Chicago & Eastern Illinois Railroad 4-6-2 Pacific-type on its way past Eighty-Third Street on the South Side of Chicago in August 1946. The *Zipper* at that time was equipped with just a mail car, a baggage car, and two coaches. It had no dining car, parlor car, or sleeping car.

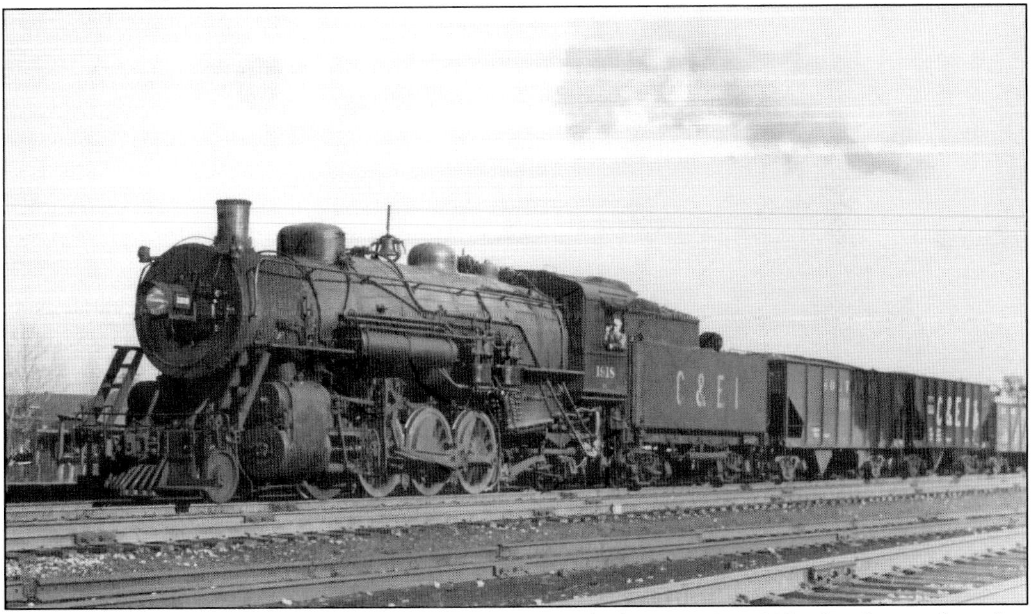

Chicago & Eastern Illinois Railroad class K55 2-8-2 Mikado-type No. 1919 is hard at work with a freight train on the Chicago & Western Indiana Railroad tracks on the South Side of Chicago. The C&EI used the C&WI tracks to get freight from its own yard in South Holland to the Belt Railway Company of Chicago's yard in Clearing.

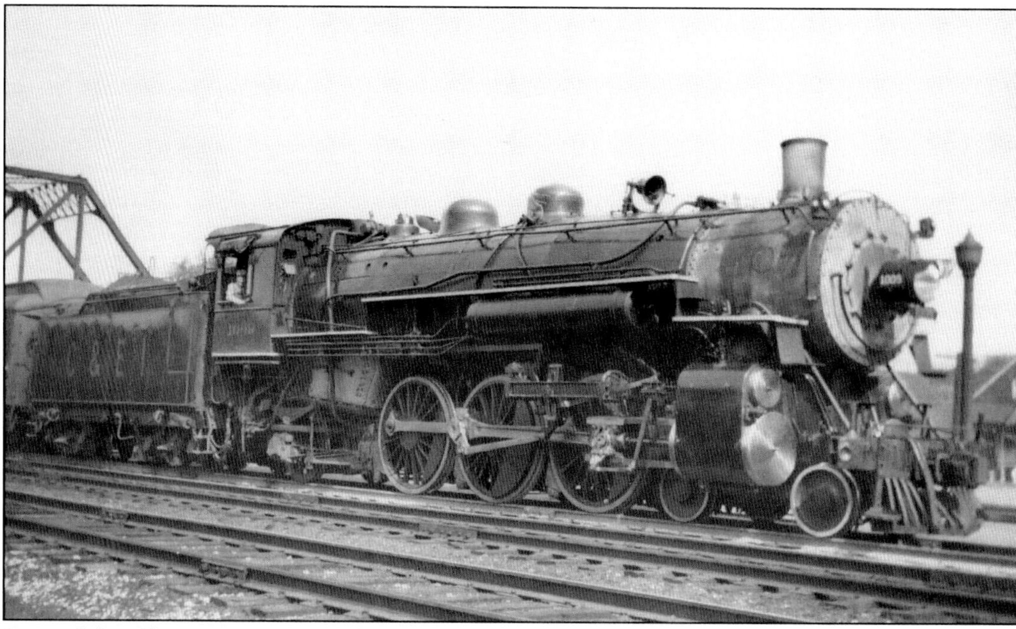

One of the Chicago & Eastern Illinois Railroad's class P34 4-6-2 Pacific-types is paused at the Chicago & Western Indiana Railroad's Englewood Station on the South Side of Chicago in the early 1930s. This magnificent locomotive would soon be departing northbound for the remaining 6.6 miles to Dearborn Station in downtown Chicago.

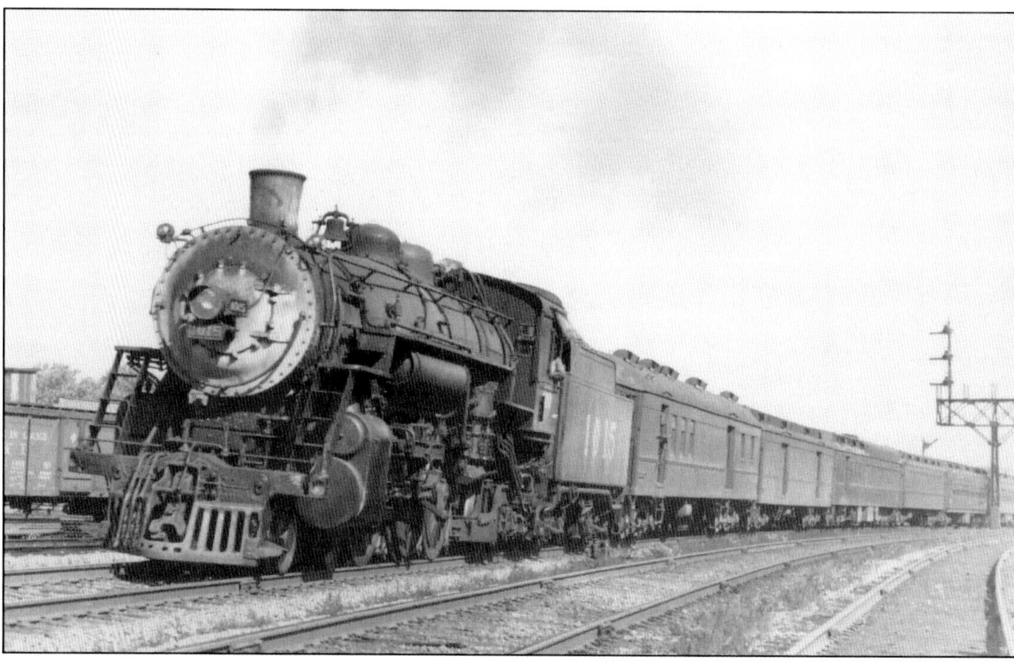

Another one of the Chicago & Eastern Illinois Railroad's class P34 4-6-2 Pacific-type steam locomotives heads out of Chicago on the Chicago & Western Indiana Railroad's tracks with a heavyweight passenger train. The C&EI continued to use its Pacifics for passenger train service until the late 1940s, when they were replaced with new diesel locomotives.

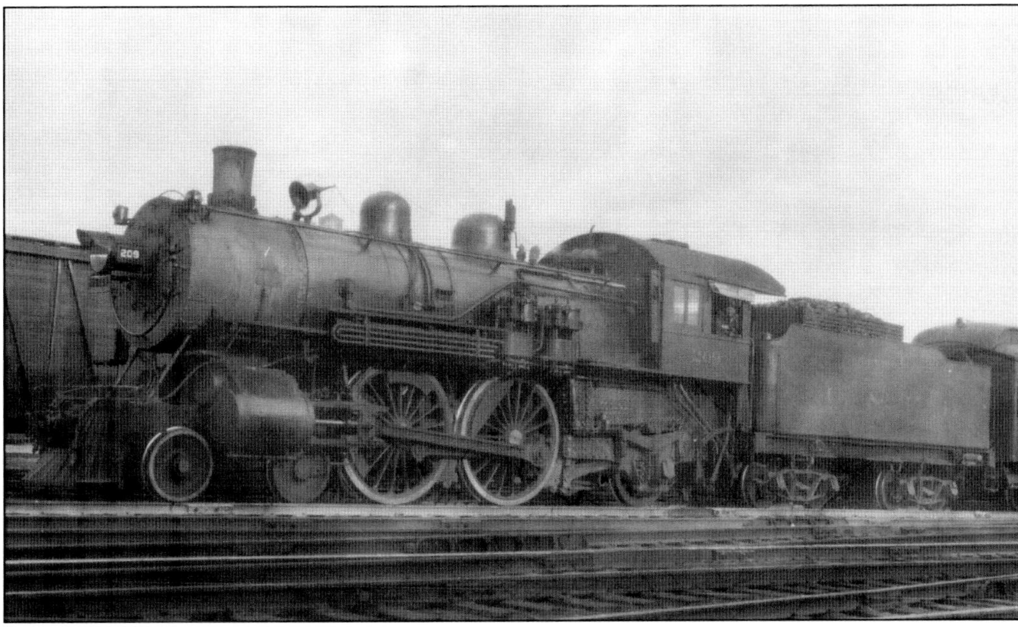

The American Locomotive Company of Schenectady, New York, built Chicago & Eastern Illinois Railroad class E-2 4-4-2 Atlantic-type No. 209 in March 1904. This was a beautifully proportioned locomotive that was bought by the C&EI for high-speed passenger service. Equipped with 78-inch drive wheels and 21-inch-by-26-inch cylinders, these little 4-4-2s were well suited to pull the two-, three-, or four-car passenger trains of the early 20th century. It was retired in 1934.

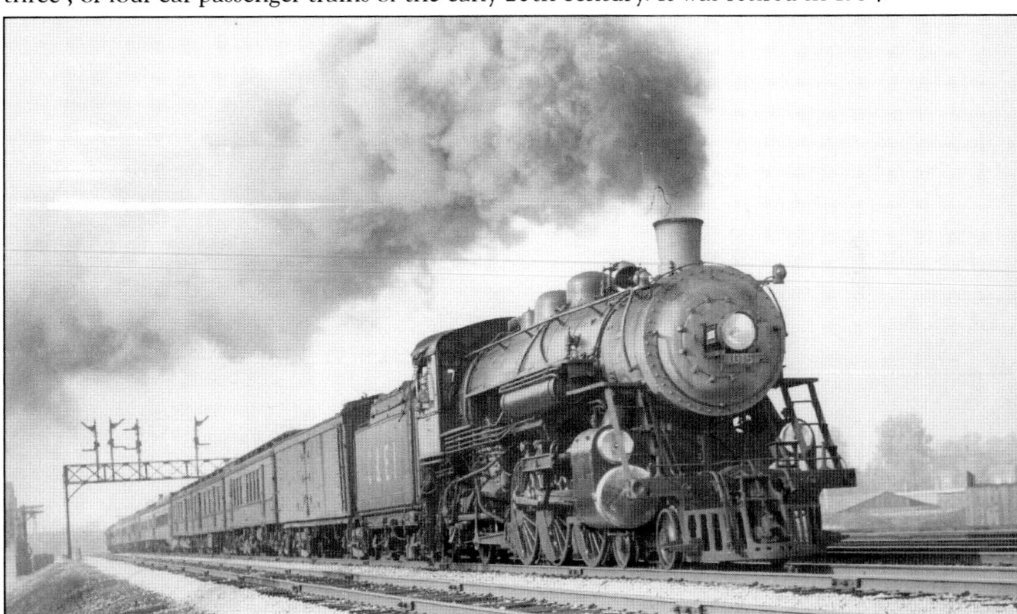

A Chicago & Eastern Illinois Railroad class P34 4-6-2 Pacific-type is pictured here pulling C&EI train No. 24, the *Silent Knight*, at about Seventy-Sixth Street on the Chicago & Western Indiana Railroad's tracks. The *Silent Knight* was the C&EI's overnight train between St. Louis and Chicago in the 1940s. It carried an express car, a Railroad Post Office car, a baggage car, a Pullman sleeping car, and coaches.

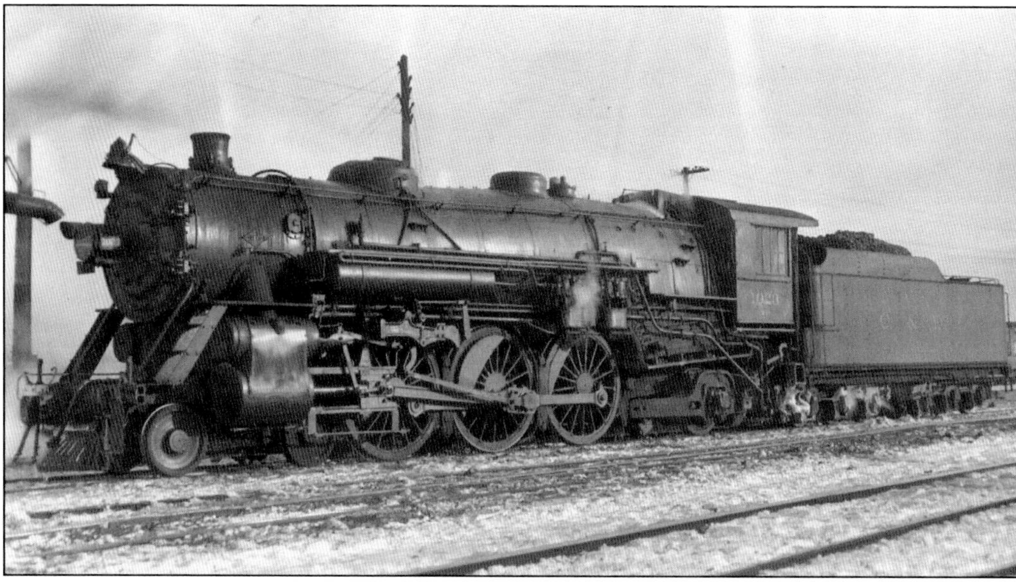

The Lima Locomotive Corporation of Lima, Ohio, built Chicago & Eastern Illinois Railroad class K3s 4-6-2 Pacific-type No. 1023 in January 1923. This was the very last 4-6-2 purchased by the C&EI. It was equipped with 79-inch drive wheels and 27-inch-by-28-inch cylinders, making it very well suited for powering the company's fast passenger trains. It remained in service until 1949.

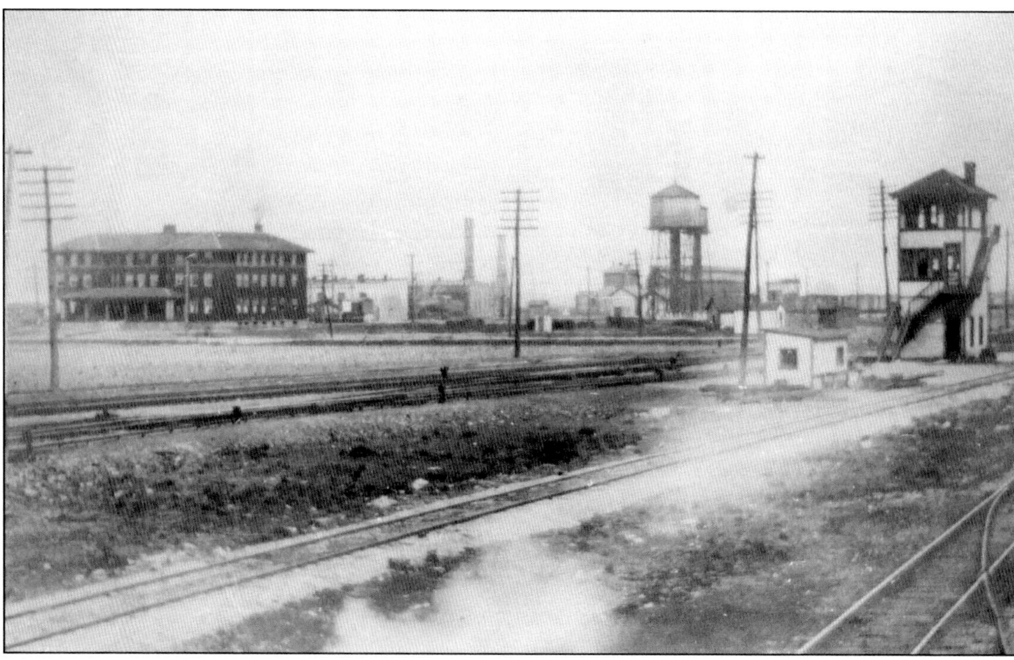

The C&EI's Yard Center was located on both sides of 147th Street between Chicago Road and State Street in Dolton. The YMCA building in the background provided rooms for crewmen on layovers. With over 20 tracks running through the yard, a viaduct was built on 147th Street to eliminate vehicular traffic mixing with rail traffic. Today, the yard does a brisk intermodal business. (Courtesy of the South Holland Historical Society.)

The control tower for the Dolton yard is shown here in 1912. The electric switches were operated by Charlie Berger. Emery Kauffman was the maintenance man. From the tower, the yardmaster kept an eye on yard activity and issued orders for transferring cars and making up new trains. (Courtesy of the South Holland Historical Society.)

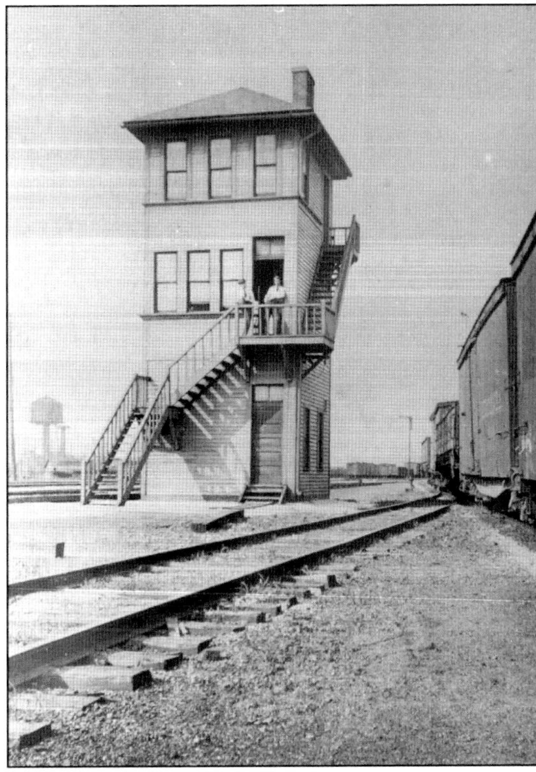

The Dolton Station on the C&EI is shown here with the bridge over the Little Calumet River down the tracks in the background. In some cases, a second story on a station house was used as quarters for the agent. But as towns grew bigger, most agents preferred to live elsewhere within walking distance. (Courtesy of Marlene Cook.)

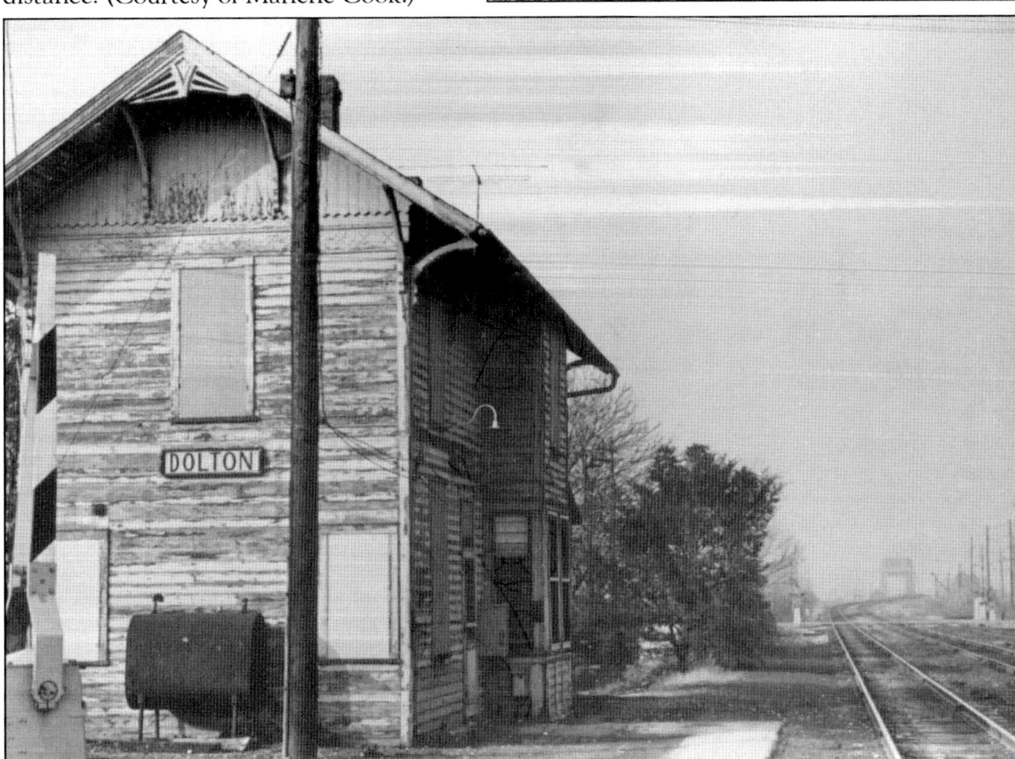

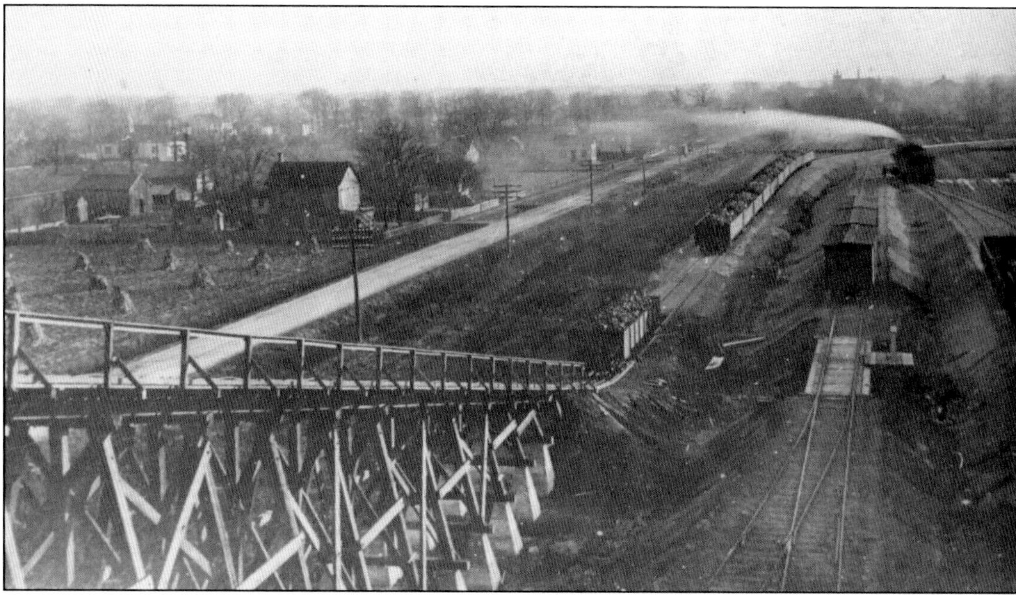

Located between the South Holland depot and Yard Center was the Deering coal grading plant at 154th Street and Chicago Road. It was operated by the Chicago & Eastern Illinois line in the early years of the 20th century. The view from the top of the elevator offers a panorama of the yard and the village of South Holland to the south. (Courtesy of South Holland Historical Society.)

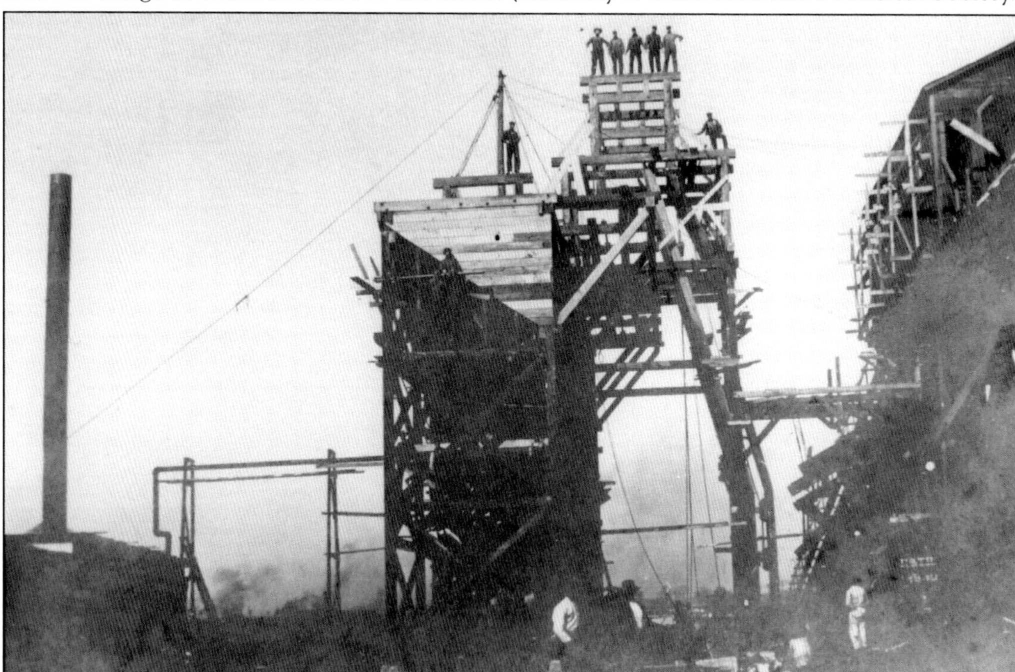

This is the coal elevator and ramp under construction over a C&EI siding. The entire structure burned in 1906. The Erie Railroad, which made a part of its freight revenue by hauling Pennsylvania coal, had a coal yard in Hammond, Indiana. There were others in Harvey, Illinois, just west of South Holland, and many more scattered across the South Side of Chicago. (Courtesy of the South Holland Historical Society.)

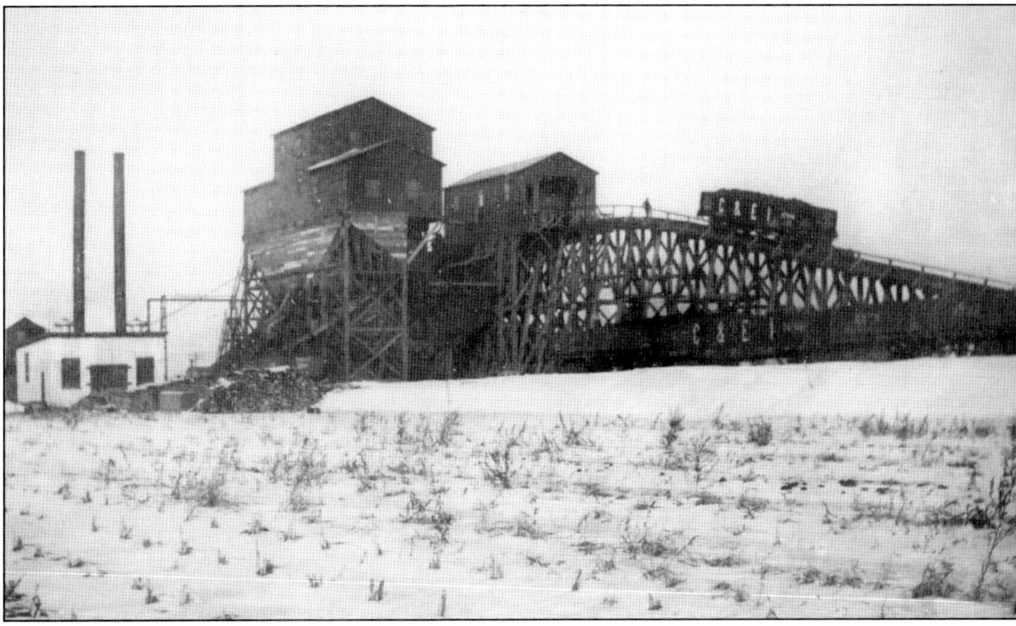

C&EI hopper cars trundled up the ramp, and after discharging a load of coal at the top, the empty cars came down by gravity. At the bottom, they were coupled to other empties before leaving to pick up more coal or some other commodity. Empty cars below the elevator waited for their payloads, which went to service other steam railroads and office buildings in Chicago. (Courtesy of South Holland Historical Society.)

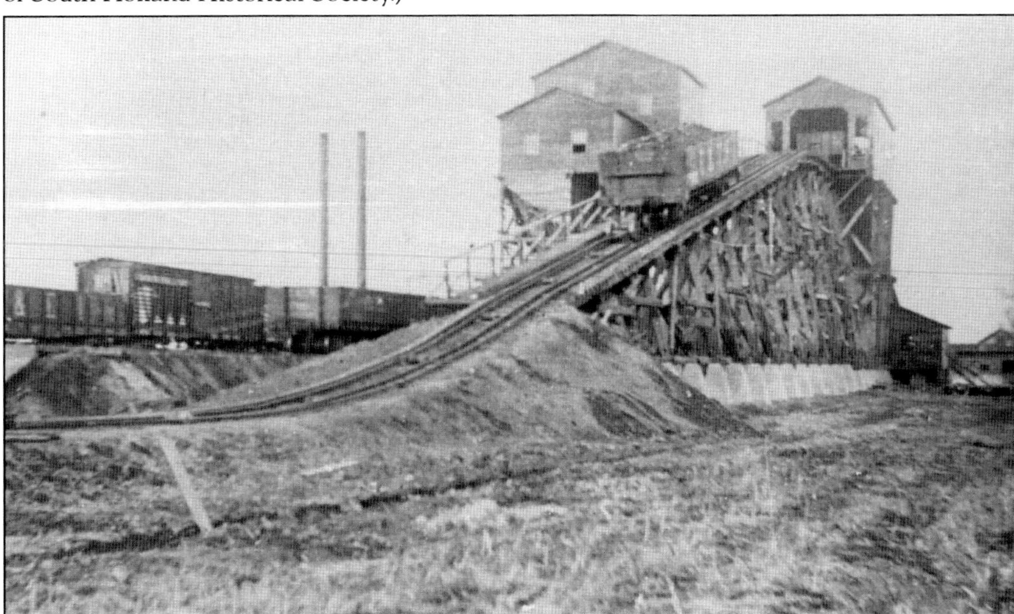

Coal from yards like this throughout the Chicago area was shipped to stores and office buildings in Chicago's Loop. The amount of coal needed daily to run the furnaces of skyscrapers of the day, like Marshall Field's or the Transportation Building, was enormous. The C&EI transferred coal to the Illinois Tunnel Railroad at the Dearborn yard. From there, it was delivered directly to boiler rooms across the city. (Courtesy of the South Holland Historical Society.)

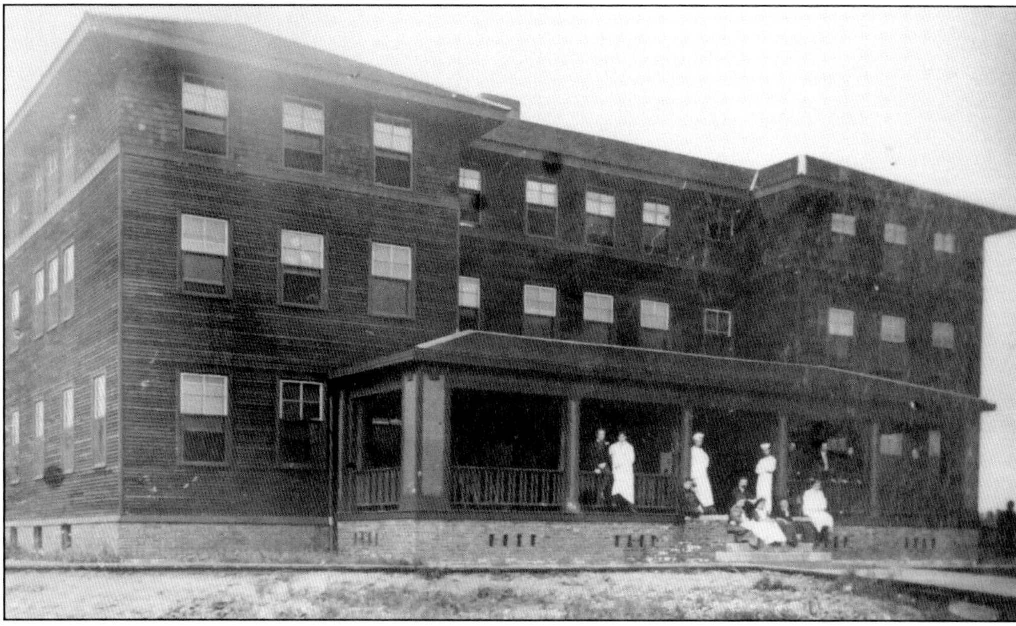

The YMCA Hotel at Yard Center was available to crew members on layover. In 1872, a Y near the Lake Shore Railroad in Cleveland offered railroad men clean rooms and some Bible reading. Railroad magnate Cornelius Vanderbilt supported the idea, because sober and well-rested employees did a better job. By 1910, there were about 240 railroad Ys located near yards and junctions across the country. (Courtesy of the South Holland Historical Society.)

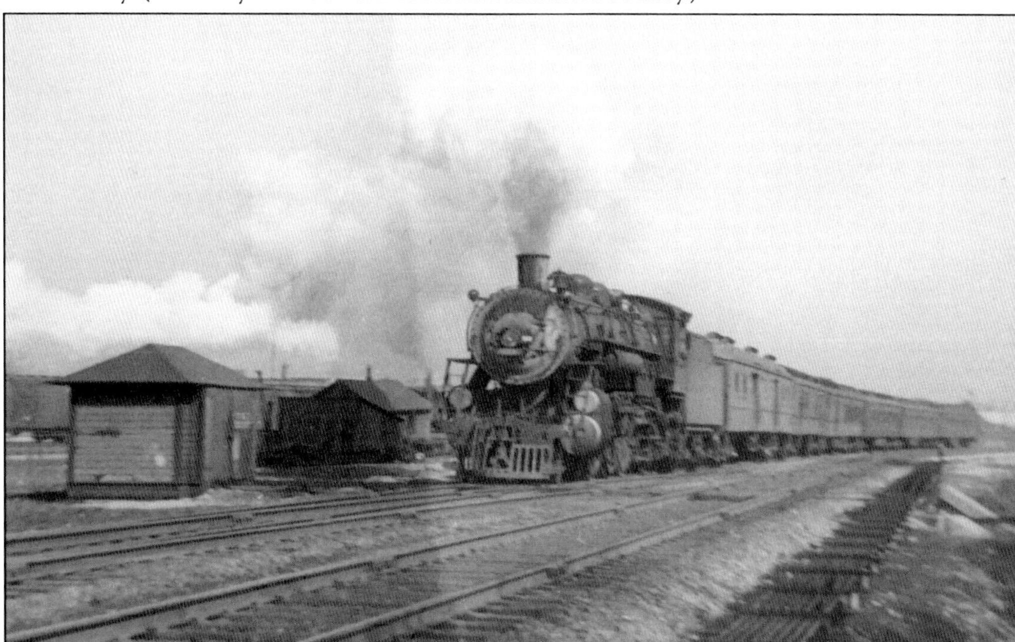

Another Chicago & Eastern Illinois Railroad 4-6-2 Pacific-type running at speed with a six-car passenger train is southbound on the Chicago & Western Indiana Railroad's tracks at Eighty-First Street on a bright morning in April 1944. This train is most likely C&EI No. 87, the *Dixieland*, which operated every third day between Chicago and Miami.

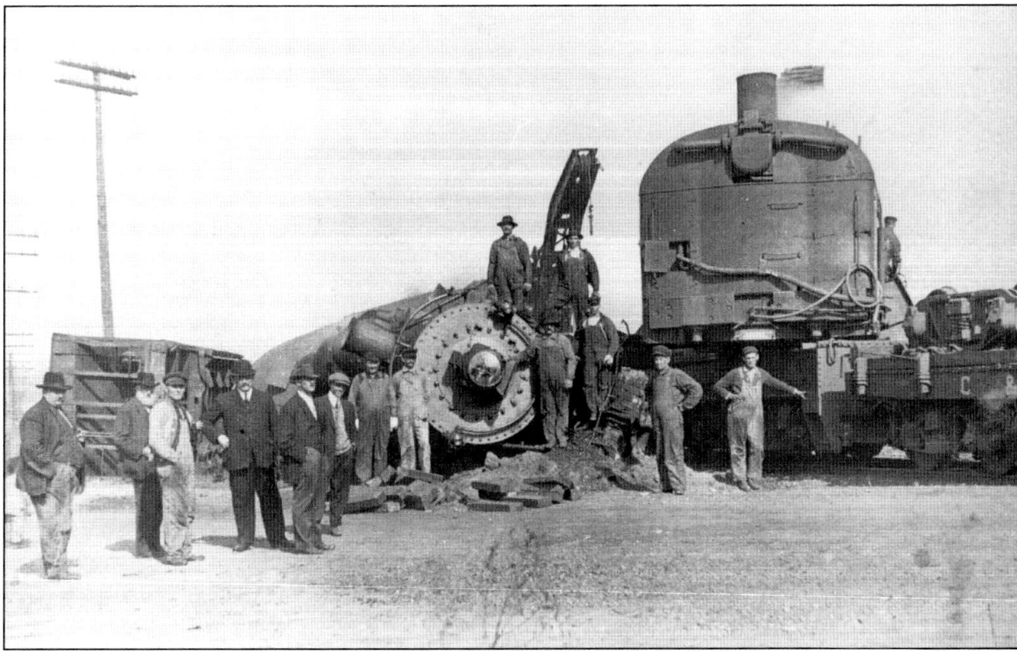

Working on the railroad was fraught with dangers both to crewmen and civilians. George Bales was the engineer on this C&EI train at the time of the accident. Cleanup was done by the crew at Yard Center in Harvey, where the accident occurred. (Courtesy of the South Holland Historical Society.)

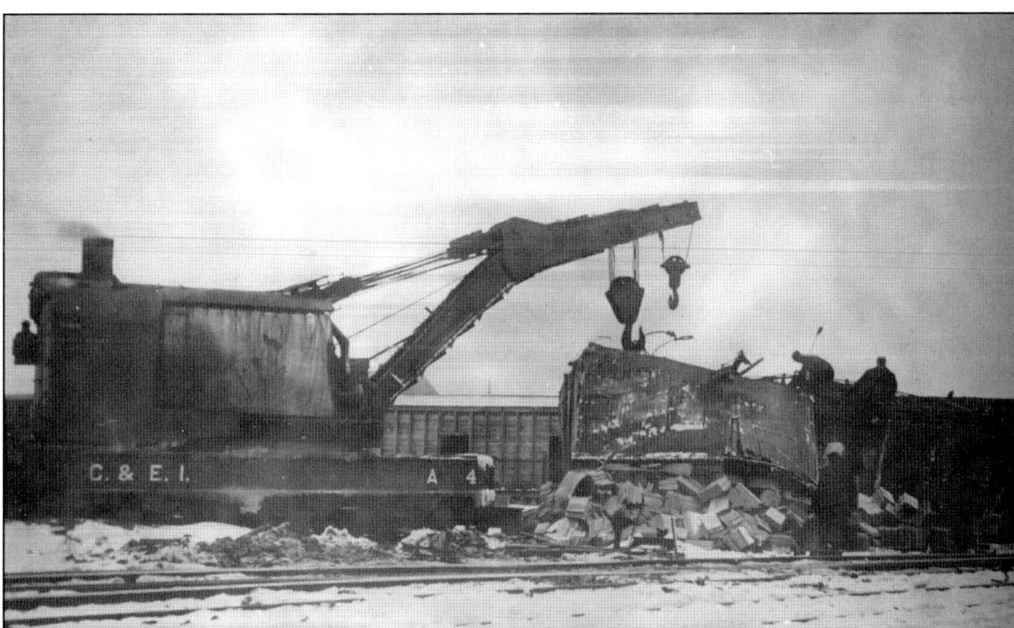

Cranes on rails were handy equipment to have at the ready for accidents. They were operated by steam, just like the locomotives, and took care of the heavy lifting. Manpower and elbow grease cleaned up the rest of the wreckage after the crane removed the bent car roof and sides. (Courtesy of the South Holland Historical Society.)

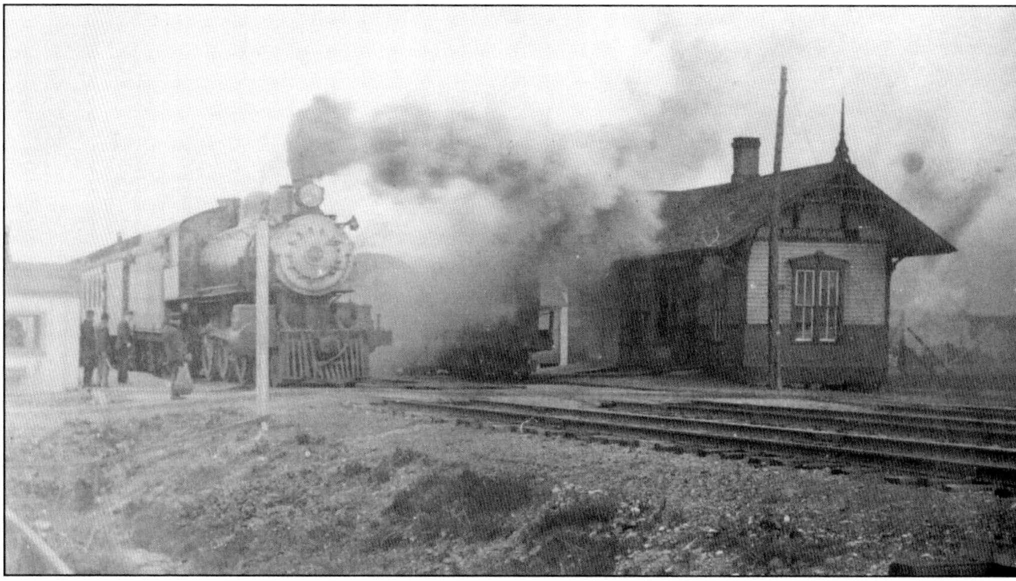

Farther south on the C&EI—sometimes referred to as the "Seeny-I" by locals—stations and depots were small wooden-frame buildings where people bought tickets and waited for trains. The agent was also a telegraph operator. Here the mail train stops at the depot on the west side of South Holland around 1900. (Courtesy of the South Holland Historical Society.)

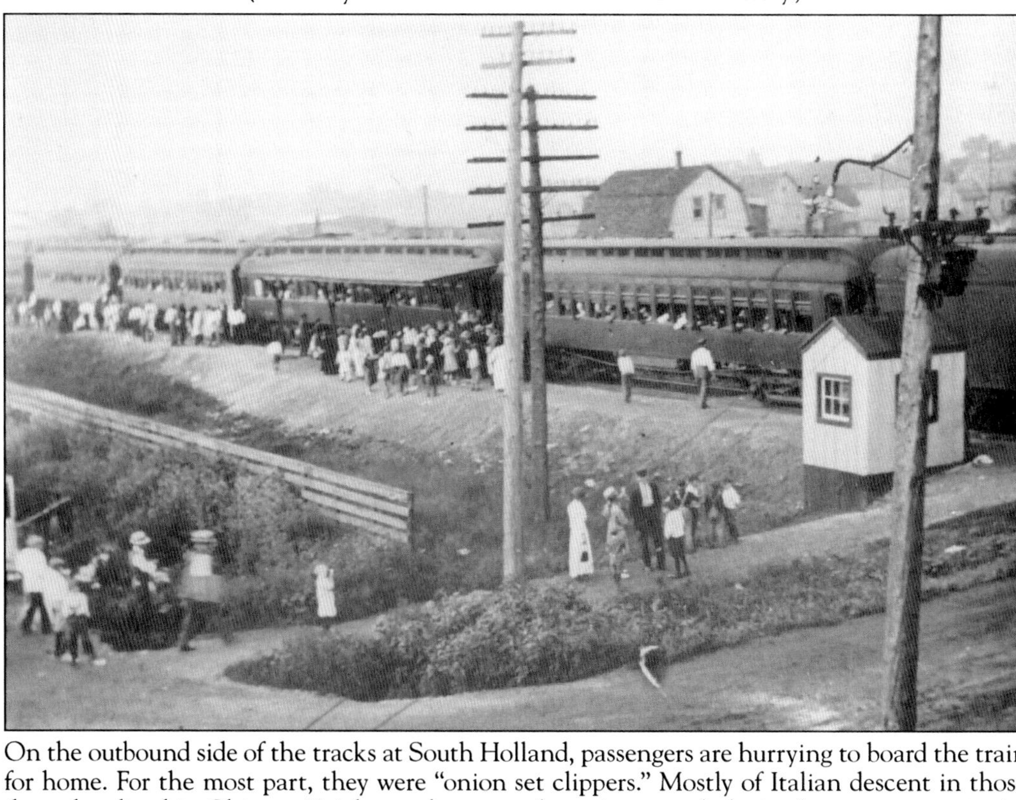

On the outbound side of the tracks at South Holland, passengers are hurrying to board the train for home. For the most part, they were "onion set clippers." Mostly of Italian descent in those days, they lived in Chicago Heights and came up by train to work during harvest season in the "Onion Set Capital of the World." (Courtesy of the South Holland Historical Society.)

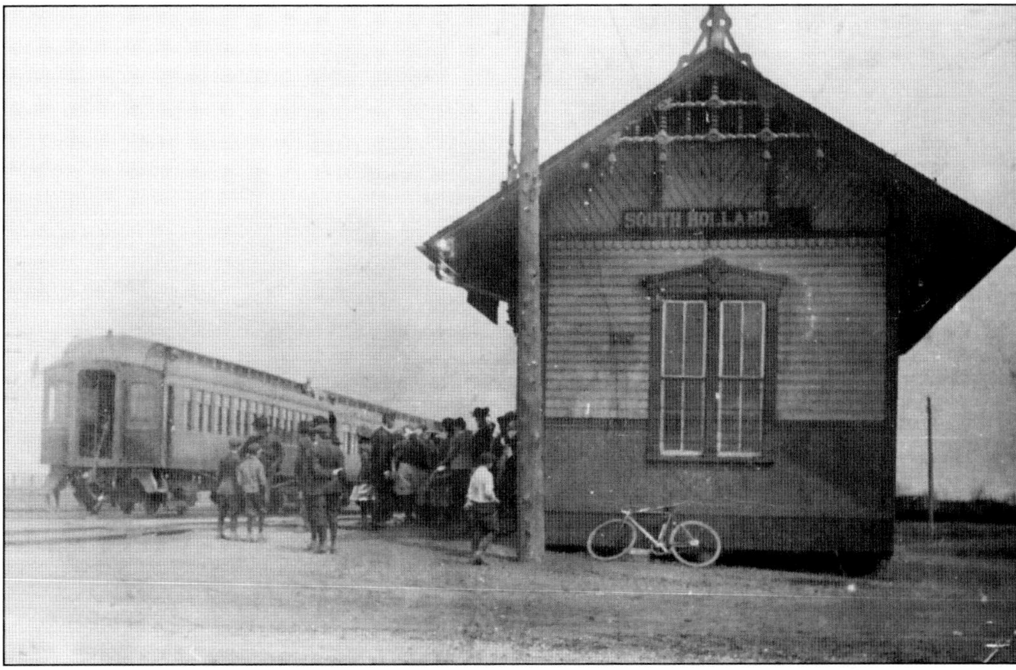

The congregation of the Reformed Church of South Holland is gathered here at the depot to say goodbye to Reverend Harmiling. This station burned down around 1910. The C&EI station agent, Jake Meeboer, then used a boxcar for his office, the freight house, and the passenger waiting room until a replacement was built. (Courtesy of the South Holland Historical Society.)

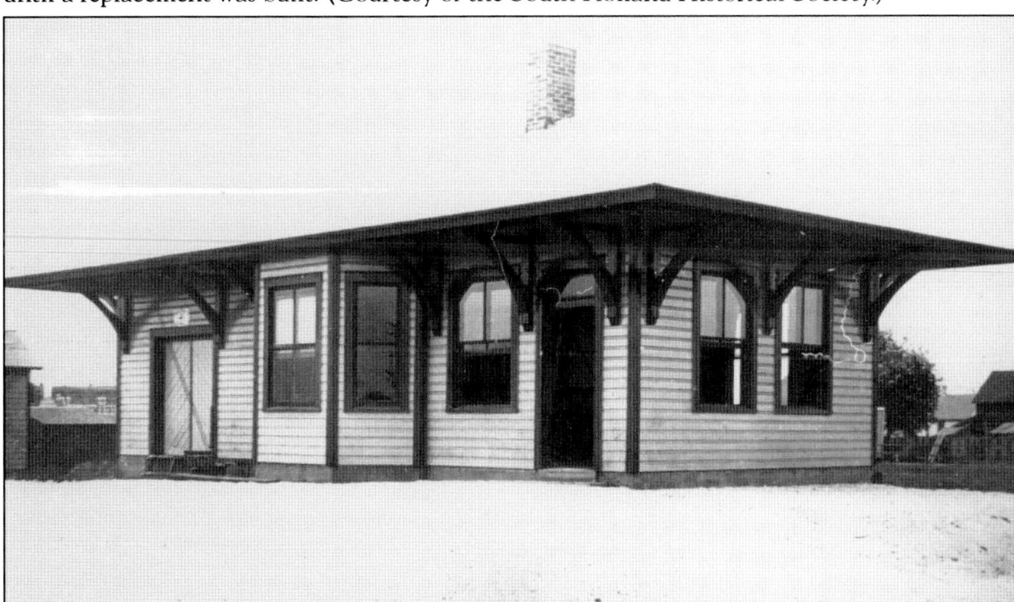

Within a year, a new building was put up. Typical of the shed type of station building, the agent's desk and office were in the bay window so he could observe approaching trains. The freight depot was behind the double doors. Shipment pick-ups and drop-offs were done from the front of the building. Merchandise was loaded onto the train from the track side. (Courtesy of the South Holland Historical Society.)

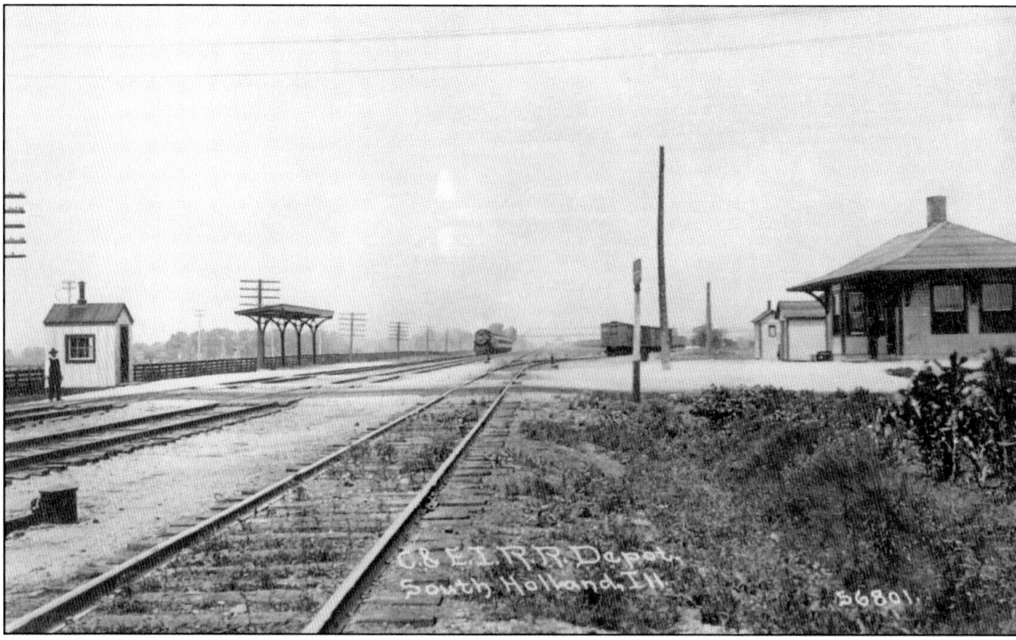

A wide-angle view shows the new station to the right, with a watchman's shanty and a small passenger shelter on the left. The site was located a few blocks north of today's US Route 6–162nd Street crossing, which was at grade back then. In the distance, behind the station, are the C&EI's team tracks. (Courtesy of the South Holland Historical Society.)

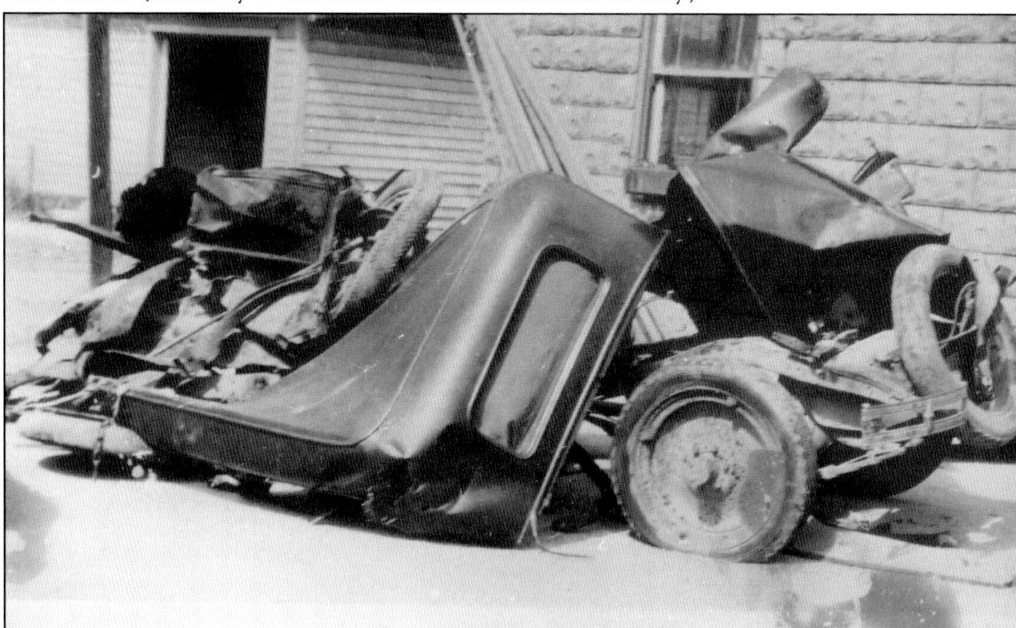

Above is the result of loosely protected at-grade street and rail crossings. The Kampen family's car was struck by a train at 162nd Street in May 1933. On their way home from a Bearcats baseball game, Mr. and Mrs. Thomas Kampen and their daughter, Ruth Joanne, were killed. Their son, Howard, was not in the car—he had ridden his bike to and from the game. (Courtesy of the South Holland Historical Society.)

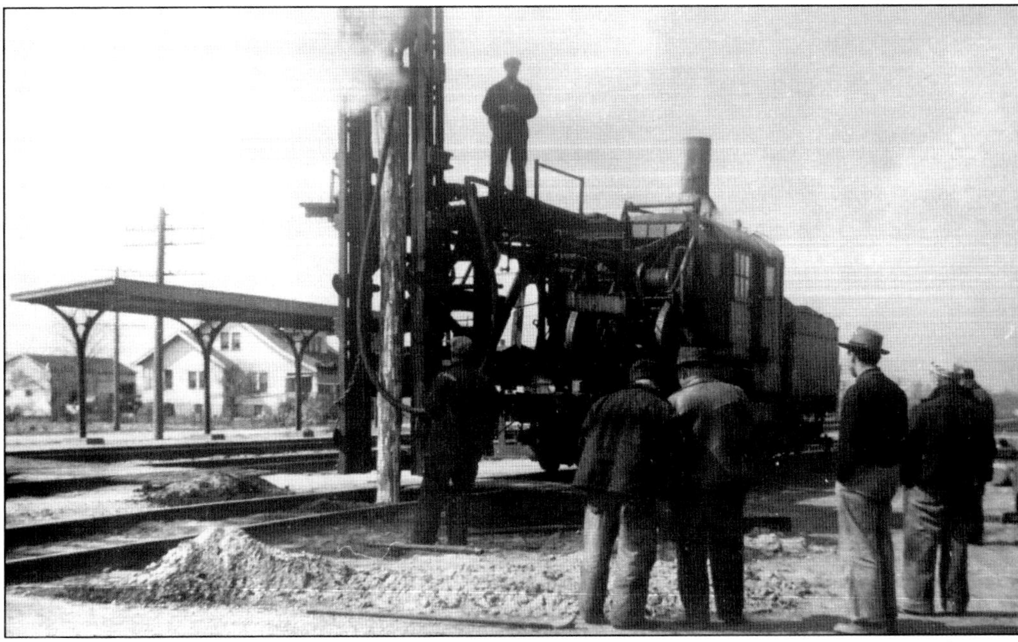

Possibly as a result of such awful accidents, the C&EI began to fix the situation. Here, workers are shown driving the first piling for an overpass across 162nd Street in 1940. The pile driver came in on a railroad flatcar and was driven by steam. (Courtesy of the South Holland Historical Society.)

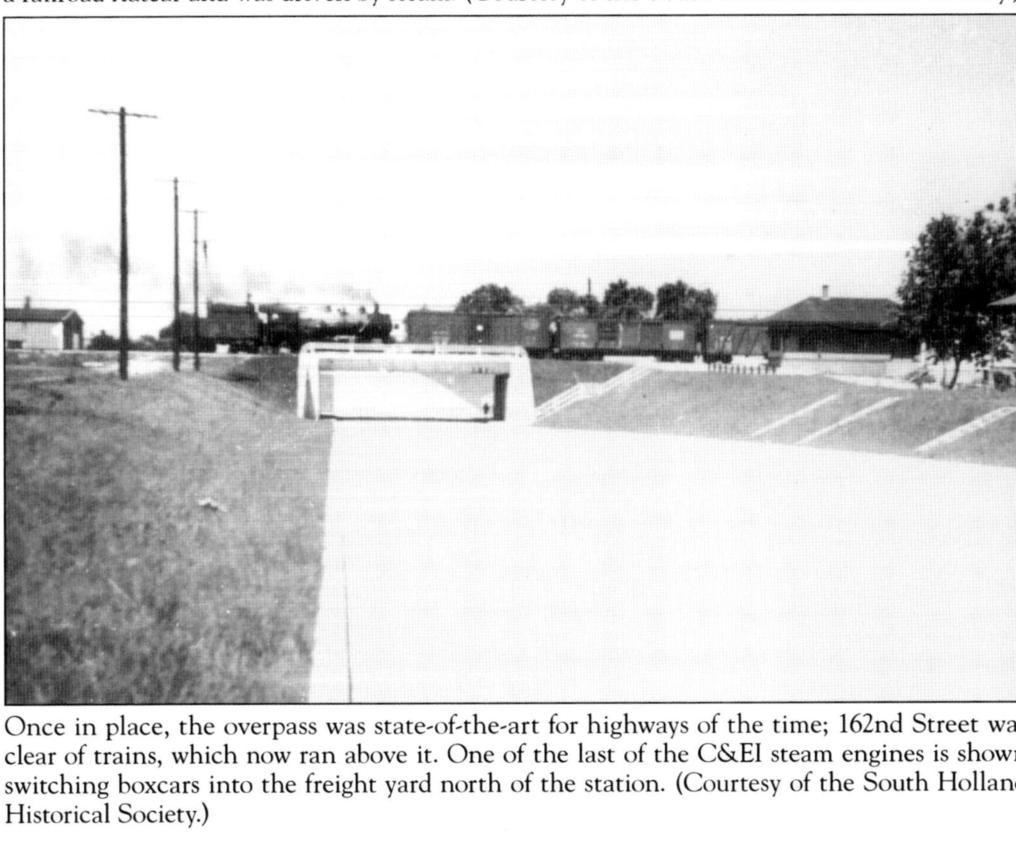

Once in place, the overpass was state-of-the-art for highways of the time; 162nd Street was clear of trains, which now ran above it. One of the last of the C&EI steam engines is shown switching boxcars into the freight yard north of the station. (Courtesy of the South Holland Historical Society.)

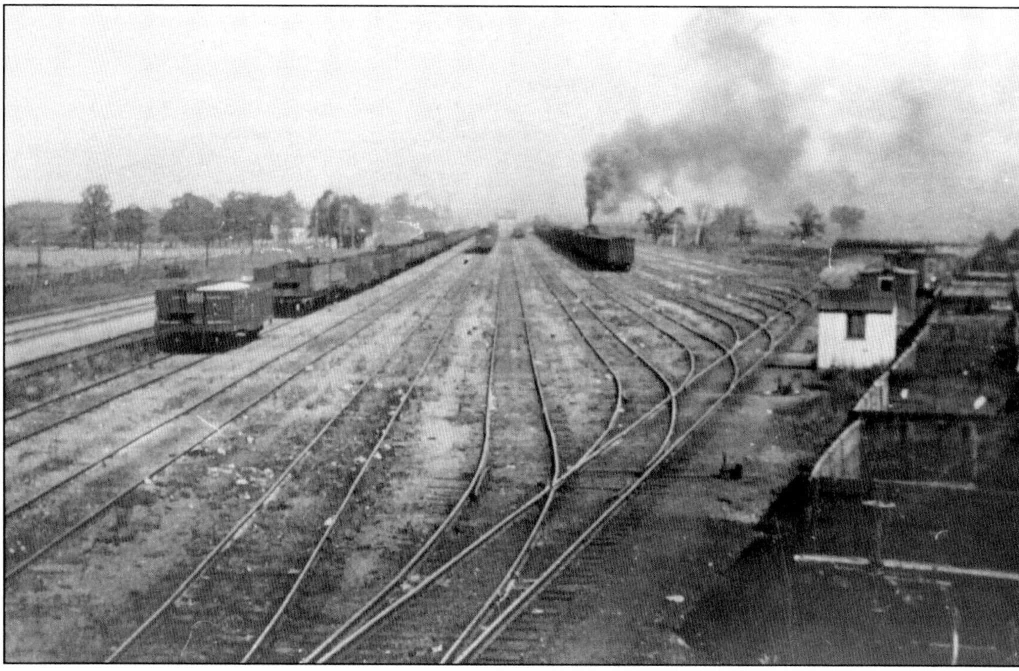

The engine moving cars in this scene over the team tracks may be the same one as in the previous photograph. Wooden hopper cars with hand-operated brakes were still being used for shipping, as seen on the right. South Holland truck farmers shipped their produce from this siding just across the street from the Wausau Lumber Company. (Courtesy of the South Holland Historical Society.)

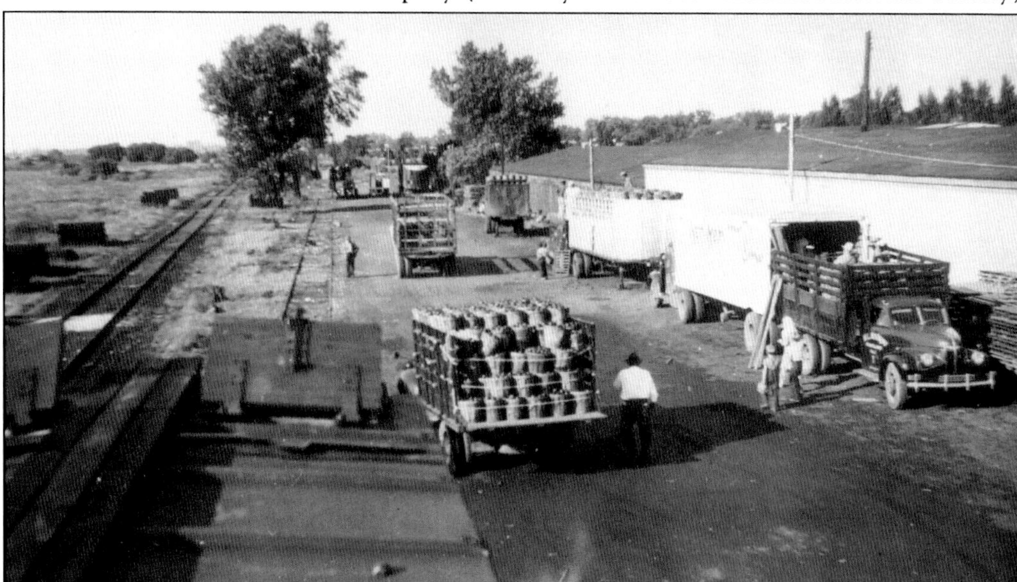

An enterprising photographer climbed to the top of a refrigerator car to take this photograph of produce, probably tomatoes, being readied for shipment at South Holland. Most of the farms just beyond Chicago's city limits were truck farms that provided food mainly for the Chicago market. South Holland, however, shipped onion sets across the nation. (Courtesy of the South Holland Historical Society.)

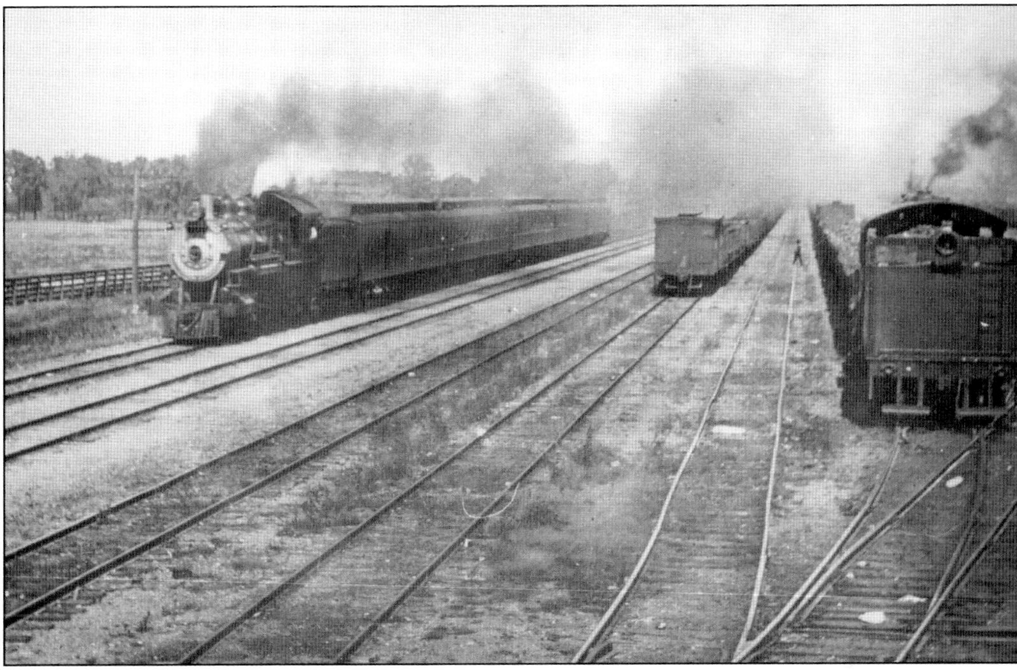

This is the "2:20" coming in from Chicago at the South Holland depot with five passenger cars. Woodlawn Avenue would be to the left, along with De Young's Grove, which was a popular picnic spot for locals and people from the city. (Courtesy of the South Holland Historical Society.)

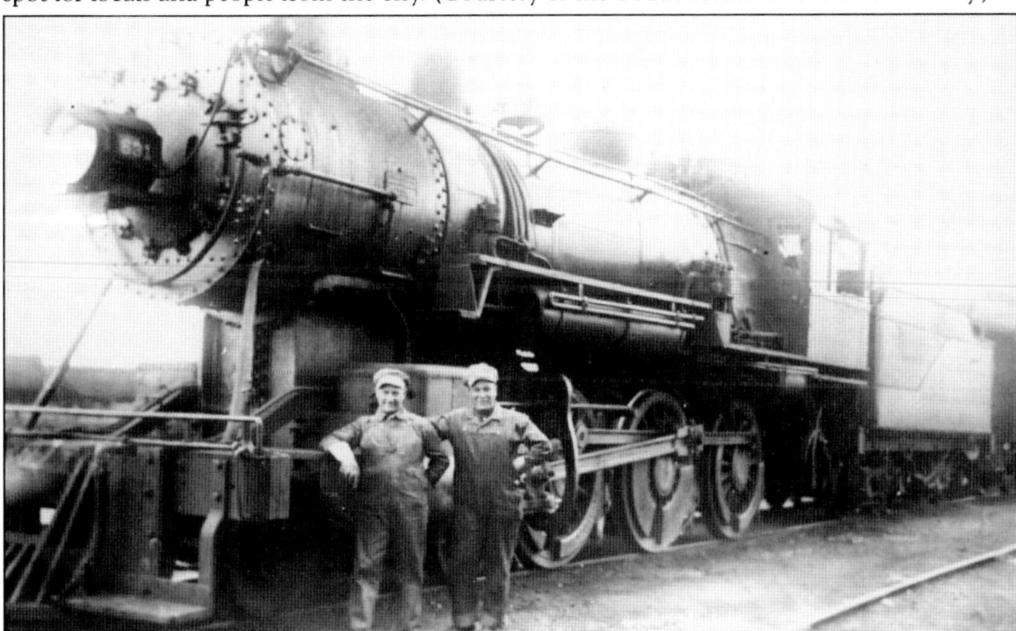

Jake Mossell of South Holland, shown on the left, was the engineer assigned to Chicago & Eastern Illinois Railroad's 4-6-0 Ten Wheeler-type No. 631. The unidentified man on his right was his fireman, the person responsible for shoveling coal into the firebox and making sure that the engineer had enough steam to keep the train on schedule. (Courtesy of the South Holland Historical Society.)

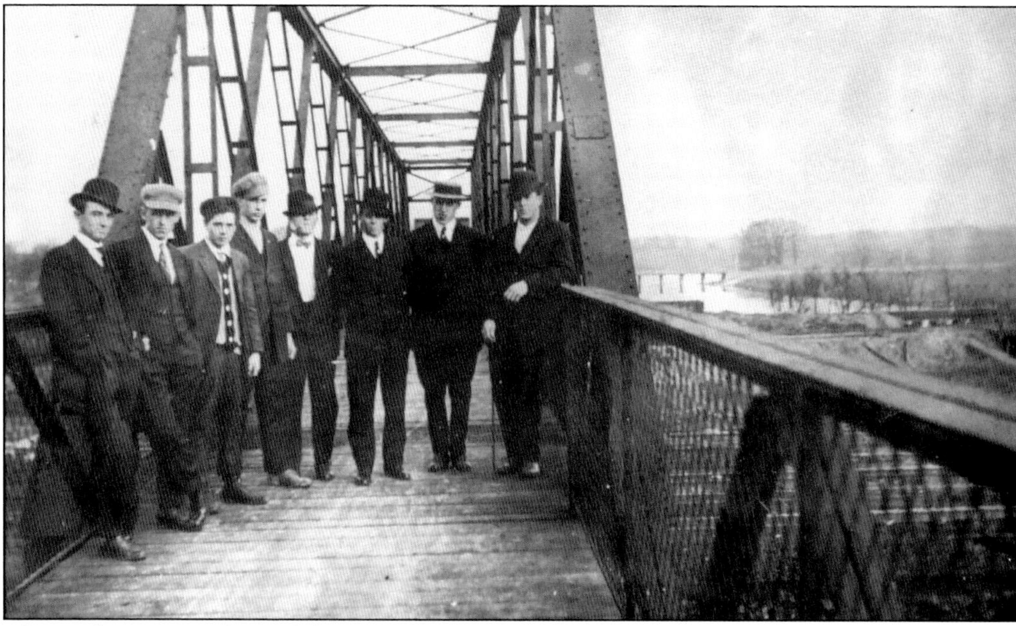

This pedestrian viaduct of the C&EI was built in 1911 north of the Little Calumet River. At 601 feet long, it crossed 21 sets of tracks. A South Holland teacher once counted 104 steps to the top. In 1946, the C&EI petitioned the Illinois Commerce Commission for its removal due to poor condition and lack of use. It was torn down in 1947. (Courtesy of the South Holland Historical Society.)

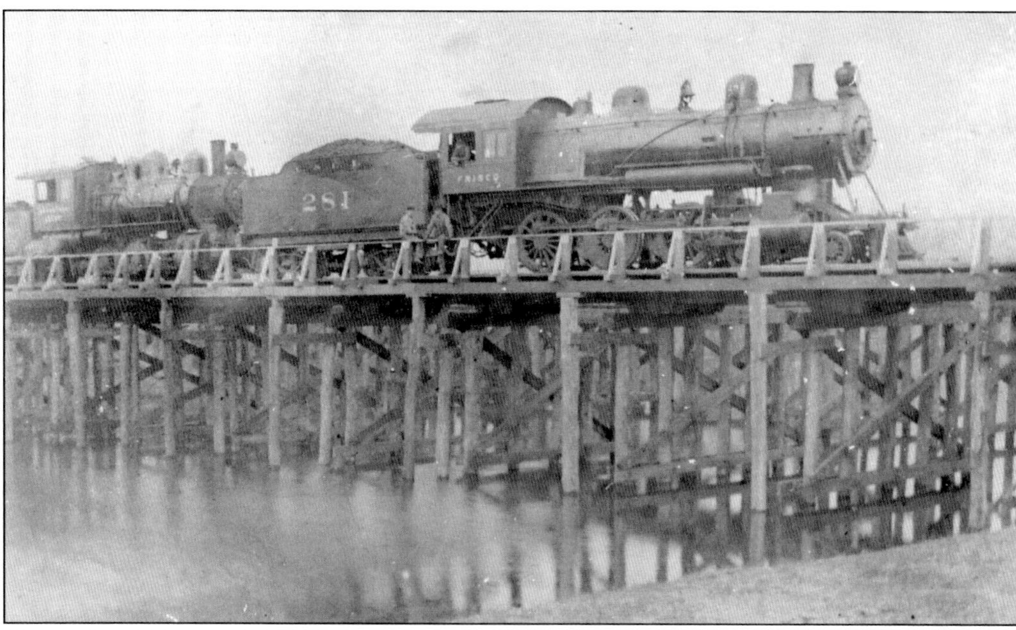

This is the C&EI trestle bridge crossing the Little Calumet River near Woodlawn Avenue on the west side of South Holland. The front locomotive, however, belonged to the Frisco line, which owned the C&EI from 1902 to 1914. As rolling stock became heavier and faster, lightweight wooden bridges like this were replaced with iron or steel trestles. (Courtesy of the South Holland Historical Society.)

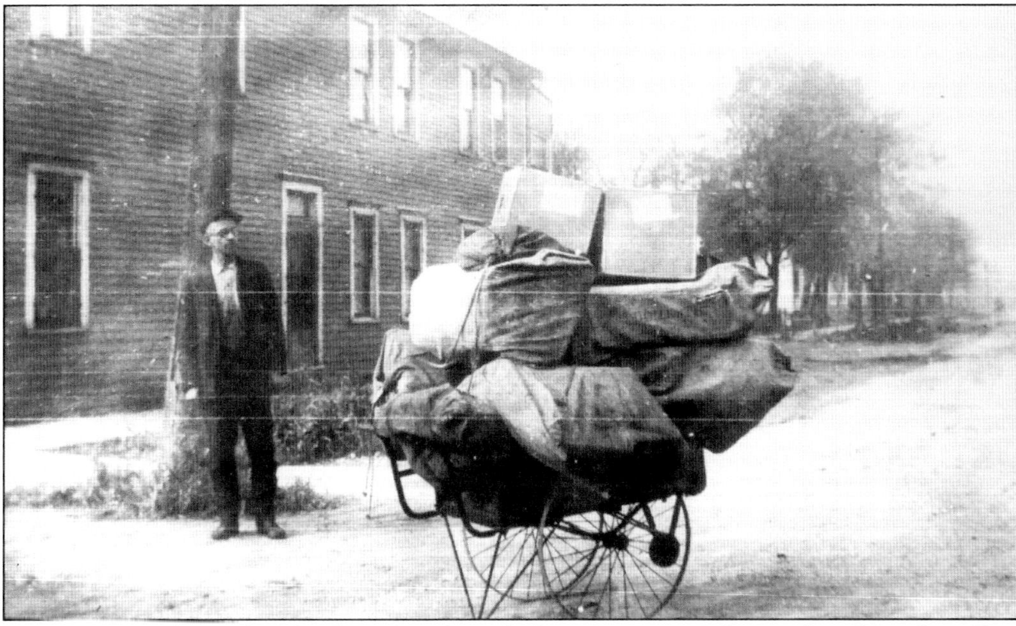

Not everyone who worked for the railroads worked on the trains. Ed Van Kley of South Holland is shown here with the mail cart he operated between the C&EI depot and the South Holland Post Office. The Burns general store was behind him on South Park Avenue. (Courtesy of the South Holland Historical Society.)

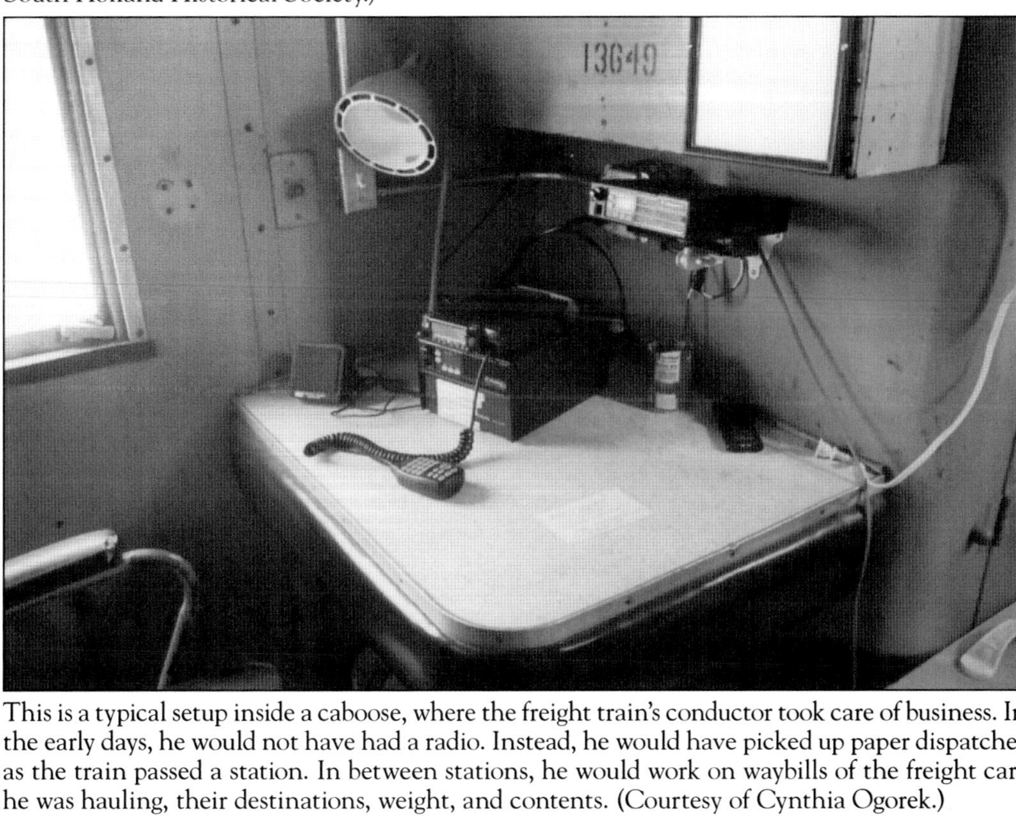

This is a typical setup inside a caboose, where the freight train's conductor took care of business. In the early days, he would not have had a radio. Instead, he would have picked up paper dispatches as the train passed a station. In between stations, he would work on waybills of the freight cars he was hauling, their destinations, weight, and contents. (Courtesy of Cynthia Ogorek.)

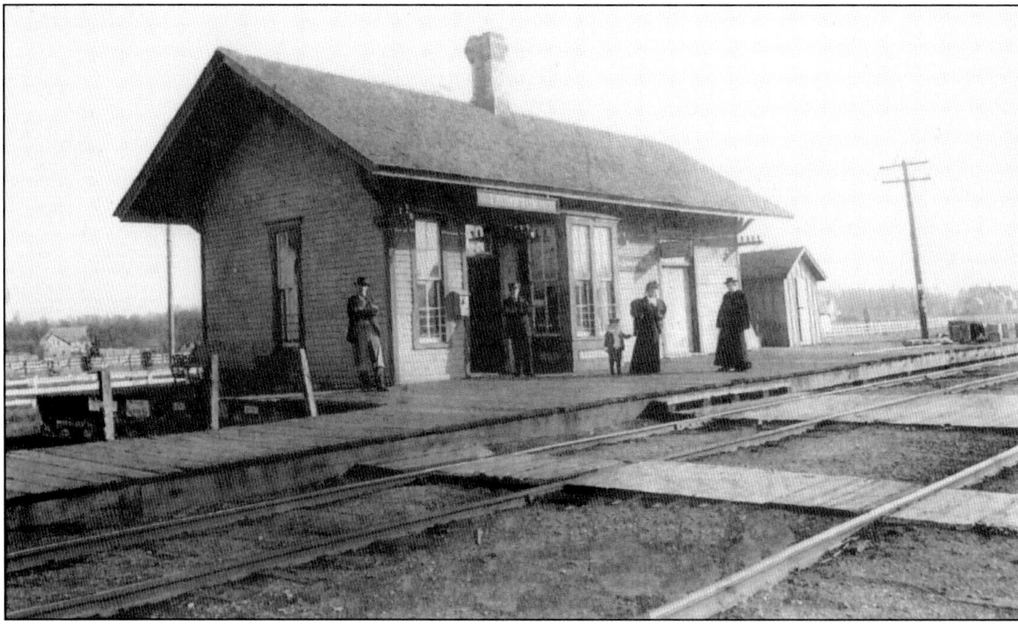

South of Englewood Avenue and Forty-Seventh Street, stations on the C&WI and the C&EI were small affairs, because until 1889, most of the route was not in Chicago. The C&EI passed through dozens of small settlements, villages, and towns on its way to southern Illinois. This wood-framed station was located in Thornton, the next town south of South Holland. (Courtesy of the Village of Thornton Historical Society.)

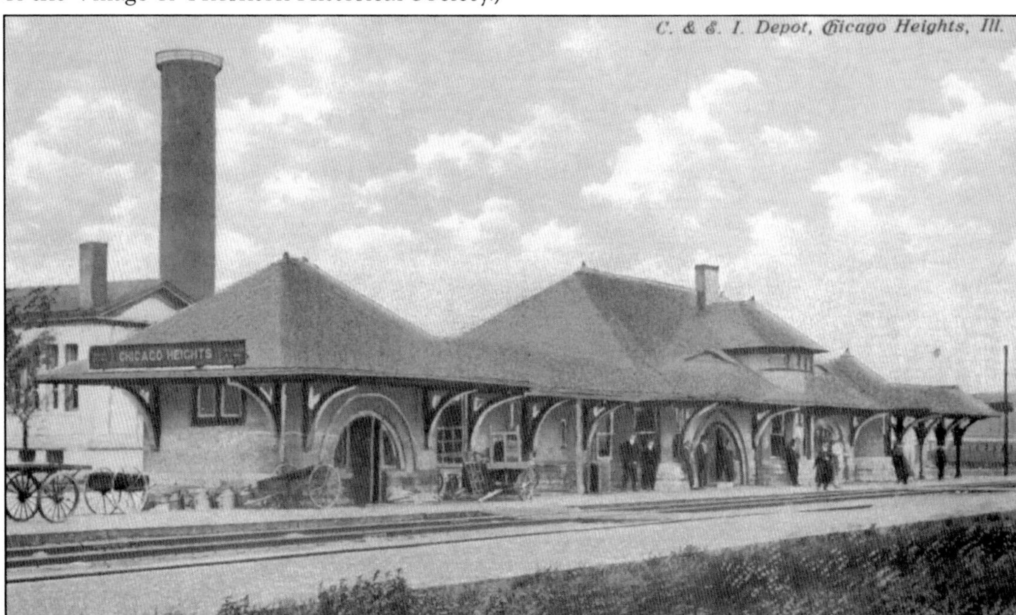

The biggest and last of the stations in south Cook County was here at Chicago Heights. It was built of Bedford limestone and hydraulic pressed brick. The roof was slate, and the interior ceiling was Georgia pine. Chicago Heights was a full-service station, with agent's quarters, baggage room, freight house, and separate waiting rooms for women and men. (Courtesy of S.H. Knox & Company.)

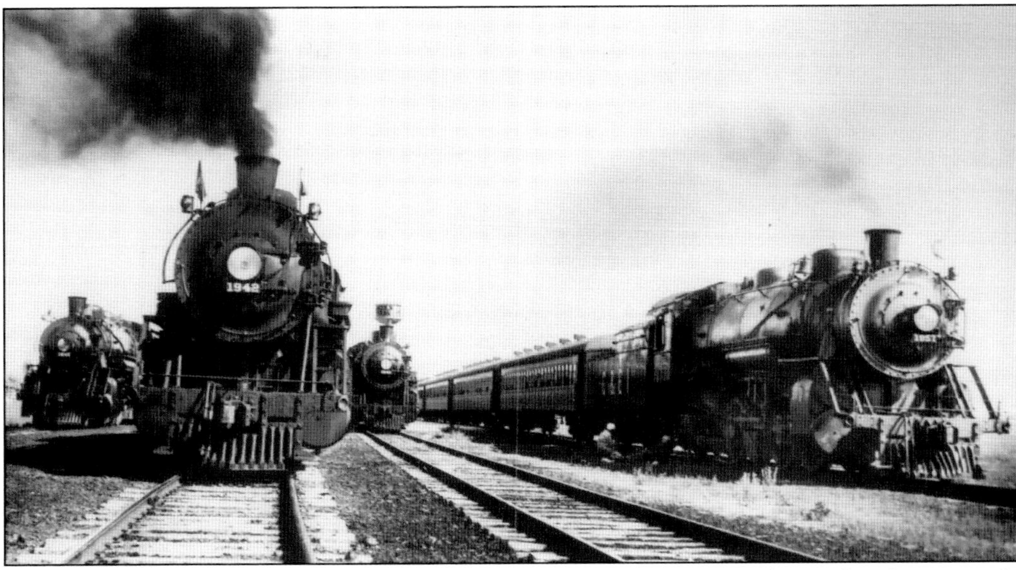

Four Chicago & Eastern Illinois Railroad passenger trains are shown on the tracks adjacent to the Lincoln Fields (later Balmoral) Race Track just south of Crete, Illinois, on race day in May 1939. The four 1900-class 2-8-2 freight engines and their day coaches shuttled track patrons between Dearborn Station in downtown Chicago and Lincoln Fields, a distance of about 31 miles. All passengers were required to purchase round-trip tickets.

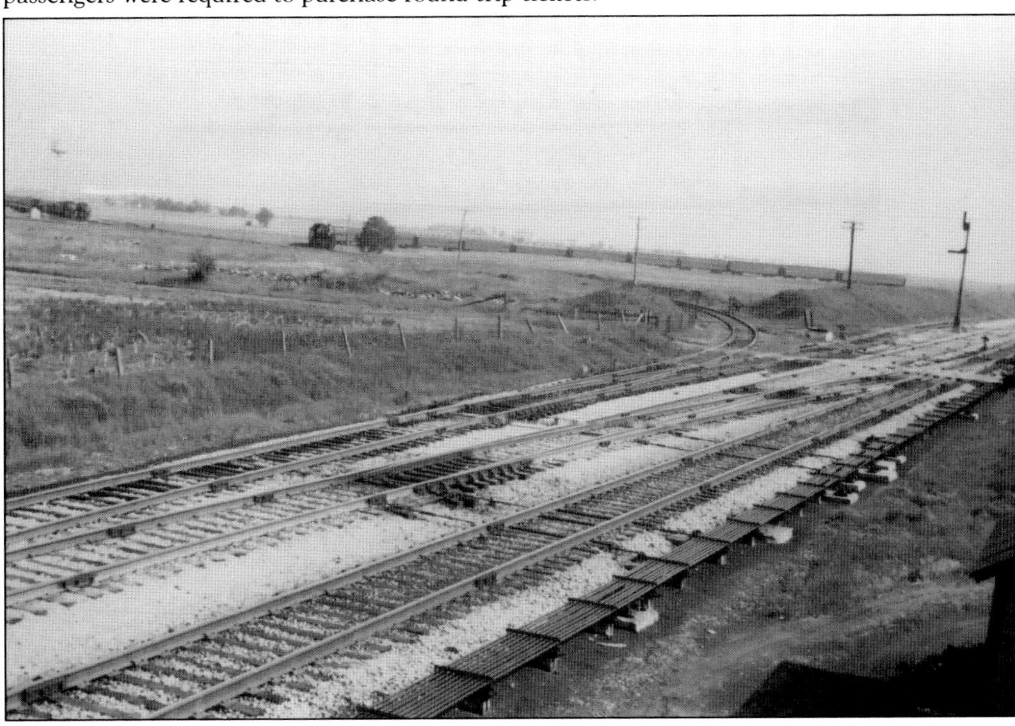

This view shows the north end of the balloon tracks adjacent to the race track. Such a configuration allowed arriving southbound trains to diverge to the left from the main line into the park, then head back north after the races were over. One train can be seen in the background on the balloon track, and two more trains can be seen on the left, backed in at the racetrack platforms.

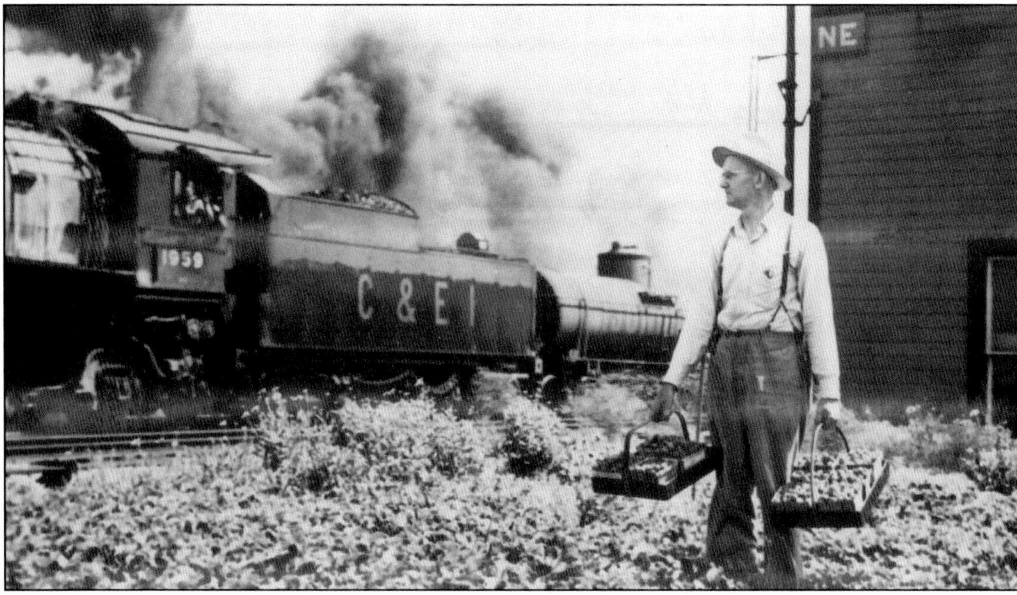

M.C. Murphy was the tower operator at the C&EI's northeast tower near Lincoln Fields. He is shown here tending to the strawberry patch in his World War II Victory Garden in July 1943 as a northbound C&EI freight passes by. He also raised onions in the same garden. Considering the extent of the garden and the way the berries were boxed, he was probably taking them to market.

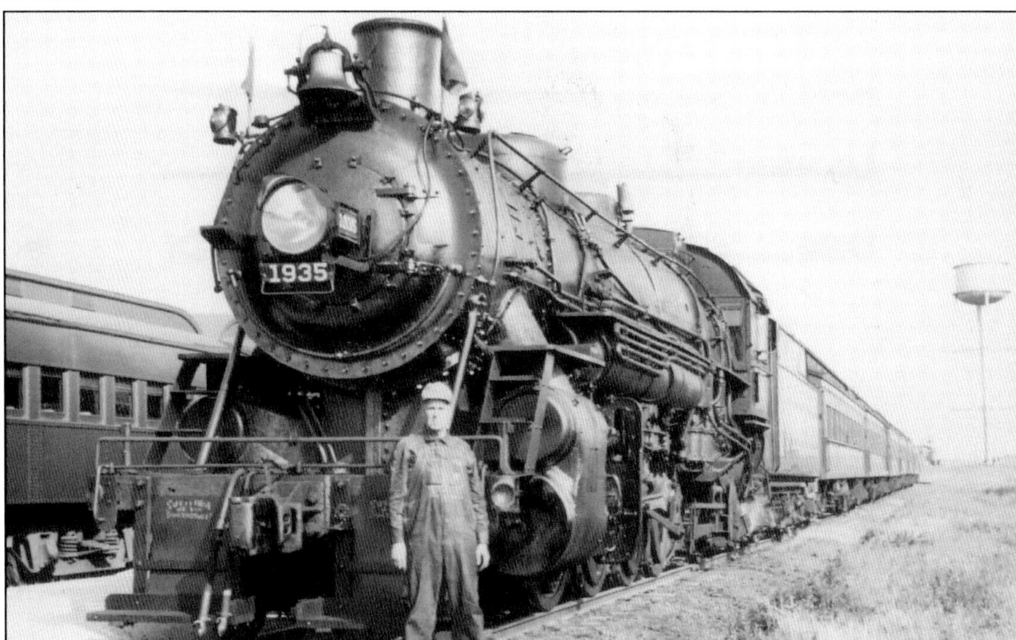

Chicago & Eastern Illinois Railroad's No. 1935 was a 2-8-2 Mikado-type freight locomotive, so hauling six day coaches from Dearborn Station to the race track south of Crete, Illinois, was easy work for it. The two green flags displayed on the front of the locomotive were there to indicate that another section of the train was following. The layover at Lincoln Fields allowed plenty of time for photographs such as this one.

Four

Other Owners, Tenants, and the Main Line

After the two subsidiaries of the C&WI were formed—the Main Branch (through South Chicago to the Indiana state line) and the Belt Railway of Chicago—three of the owner lines, the Wabash, the Erie and the Monon, entered Illinois from Hammond at Burnham/Hegewisch. A fourth owner, the Grand Trunk Western (GTW), cut northwest from Valparaiso, Indiana, and circled around the south and southwest sides of Chicago to a connection with the C&WI at Forty-Ninth Street. The opening of this route from the Indiana state line through the southeast side of what would soon become part of the city of Chicago heralded the second phase of Calumet Region railroading. The GTW made its debut in 1880, followed by the Erie in 1881, the Monon in 1884, and the Wabash in 1895. The C&WI's most famous tenant was the Atchison, Topeka & Santa Fe Railroad, which served Southern California and cities eastward to Chicago. The Santa Fe, even by its name, was the glamour tenant of the terminal at Dearborn Street, because it catered to Hollywood's elite and business moguls from Chicago and New York. It came onto the C&WI from the west at Twenty-First Street. The Chesapeake & Ohio was a short-lived tenant that entered the Main Line through Hammond.

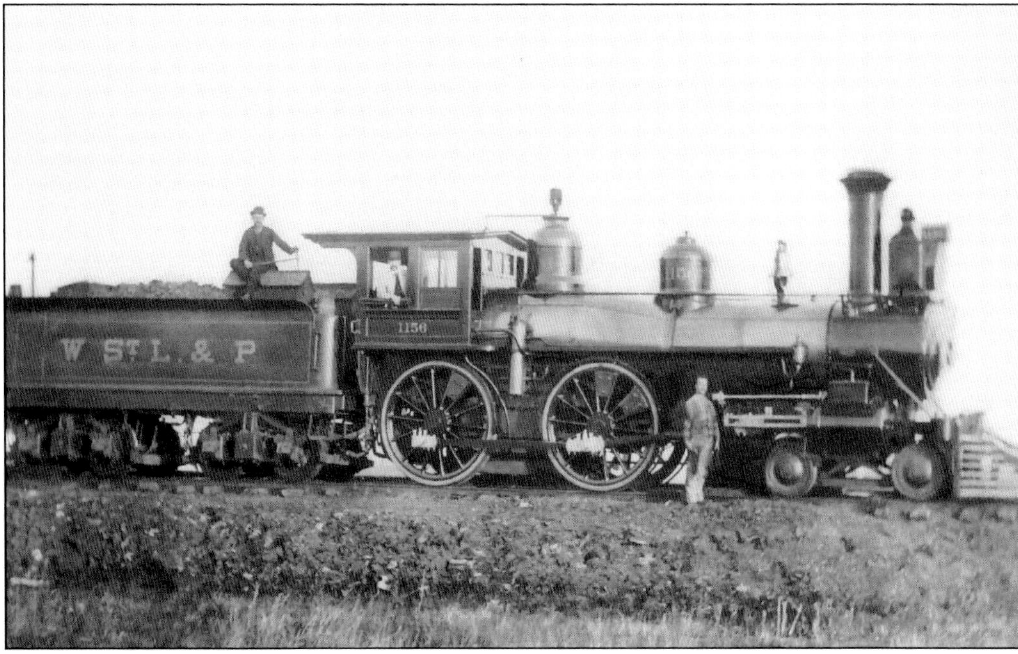

The Wabash, St. Louis & Pacific Railroad class D2 4-4-0 American-type No. 1156 was built by the Mason Machine Works of Taunton, Massachusetts, in September 1870. The steam locomotives with a 4-4-0 wheel arrangement were the mainstay of the railroad industry from the 1850s until the 1900s, when larger and heavier locomotives became more commonplace. The 1156 was retired by the Wabash and scrapped in 1912.

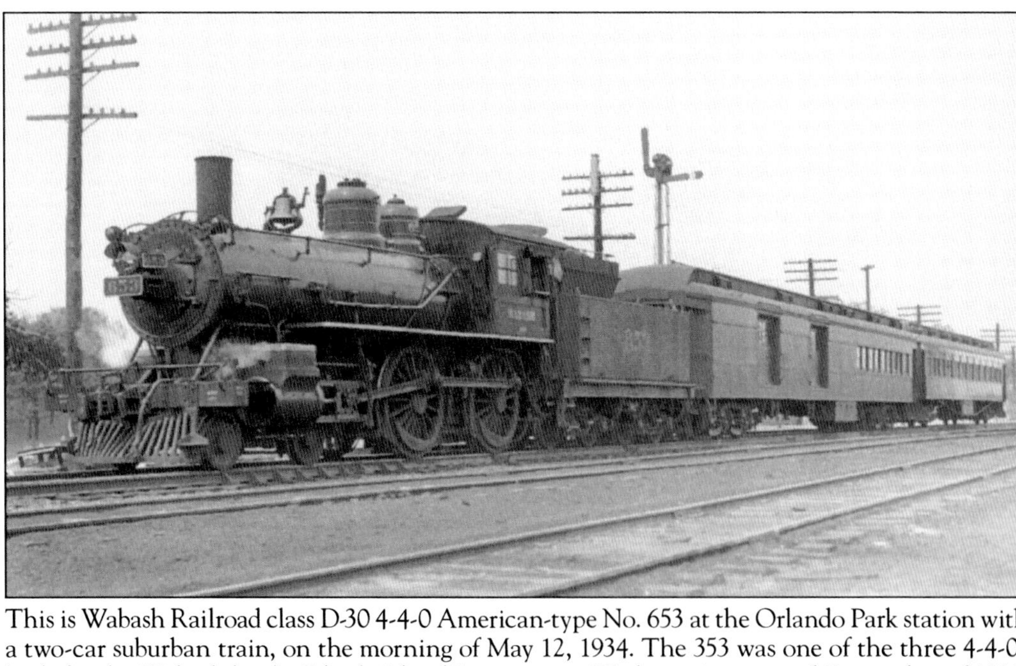

This is Wabash Railroad class D-30 4-4-0 American-type No. 653 at the Orlando Park station with a two-car suburban train, on the morning of May 12, 1934. The 353 was one of the three 4-4-0s built for the Wabash by the Rhode Island Locomotive Works in August and September of 1899. It was scrapped in June 1936, little more than two years after this photograph was taken.

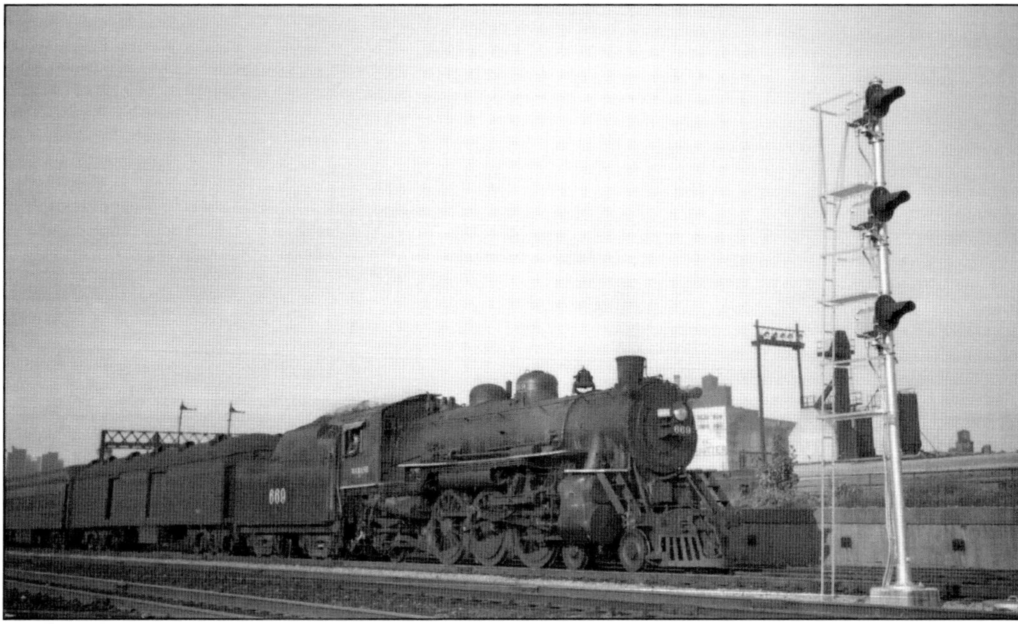

Wabash Railroad class J-1 4-6-2 Pacific-type No. 669 is pictured with train No. 11, the southbound *Banner Blue* at Sixteenth Street on the Chicago & Western Indiana tracks in Chicago on October 27, 1952. This train was reequipped with an EMD E8A diesel locomotive just three days later, on October 30, 1952.

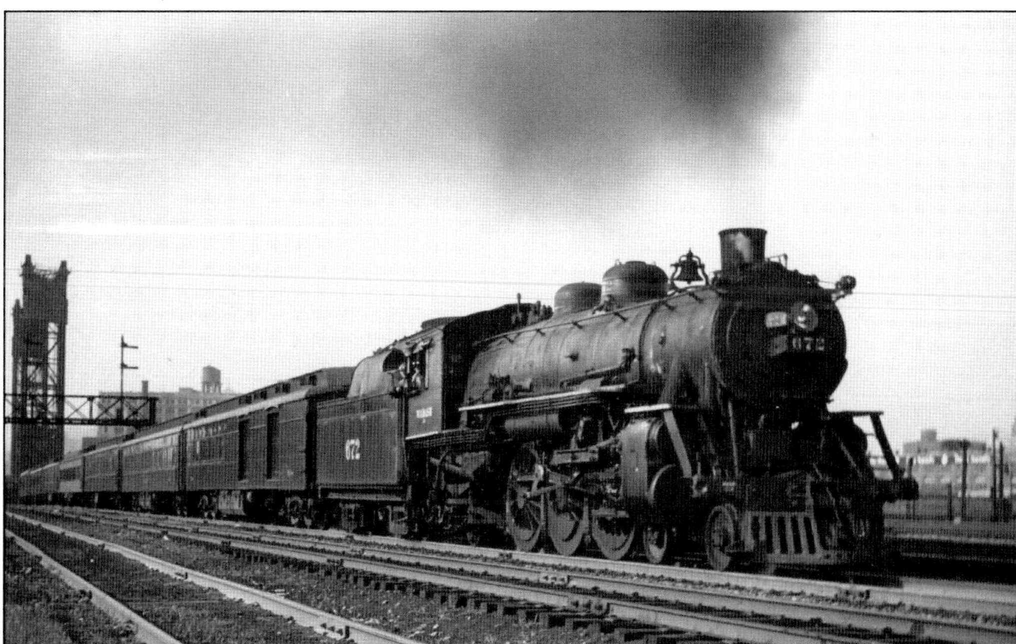

This is the Wabash Railroad's train No. 21, the seven-car *Bluebird* bound for St. Louis. This train featured deluxe reclining chair cars, a dining car, a Pullman parlor-lounge car, and a Pullman observation-drawing room parlor car. It is shown here on the C&WI tracks at Twenty-First Street being pulled by class J-1 4-6-2 Pacific-type No. 672.

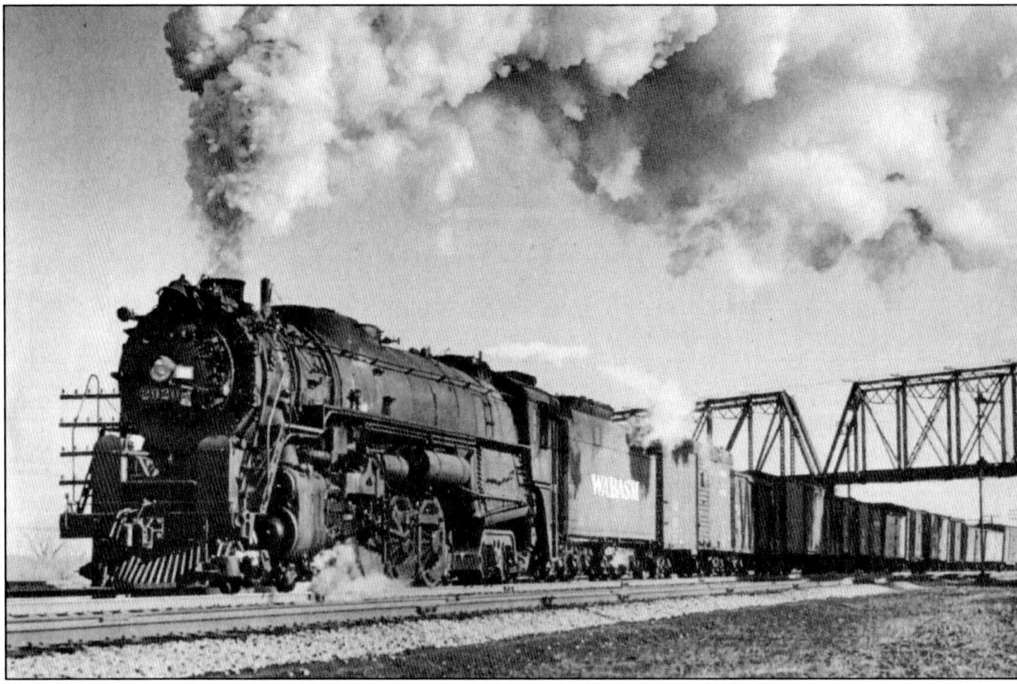

Shown here around 1930 is the Wabash 4-8-4 Northern-type No. 2920. The four-wheel trailing truck on a model such as this allowed for a bigger fire box within the locomotive. It was built for dual service, to power either fast passenger trains or heavy freights. In this publicity shot, No. 2920 may be posed near Englewood and shot from below eye-level to emphasize the company's tagline, "Wabash Dependable Freight Service."

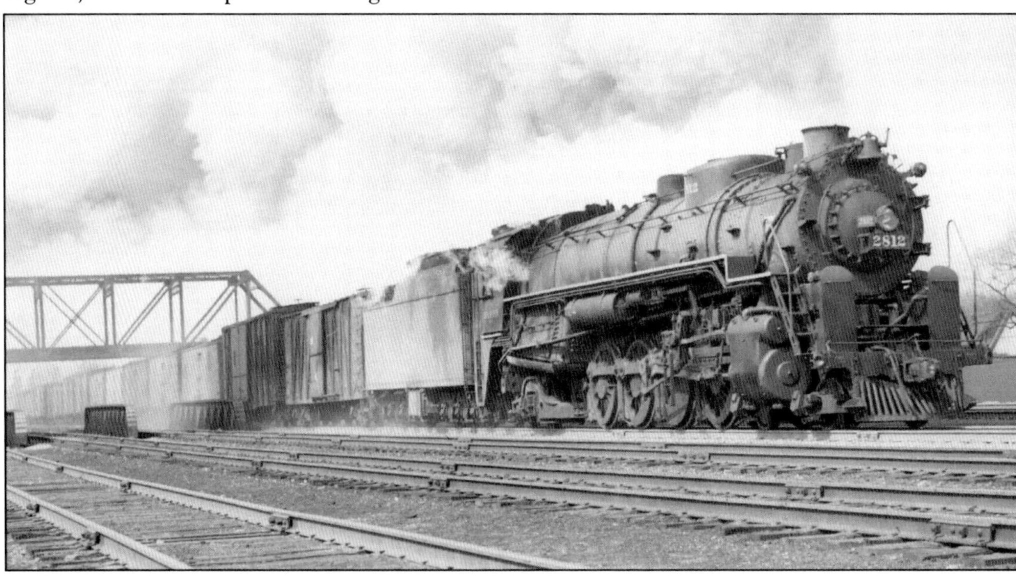

The Baldwin Locomotive Works of Eddystone, Pennsylvania, built 25 class M 4-8-2 Mountain-type freight locomotives for the Wabash Railroad in January and February 1930. This is No. 2812, southbound with a manifest freight train on the Chicago & Western Indiana Railroad tracks at Englewood on the South Side of Chicago. They were retired from service in 1953, when new diesel locomotives replaced them.

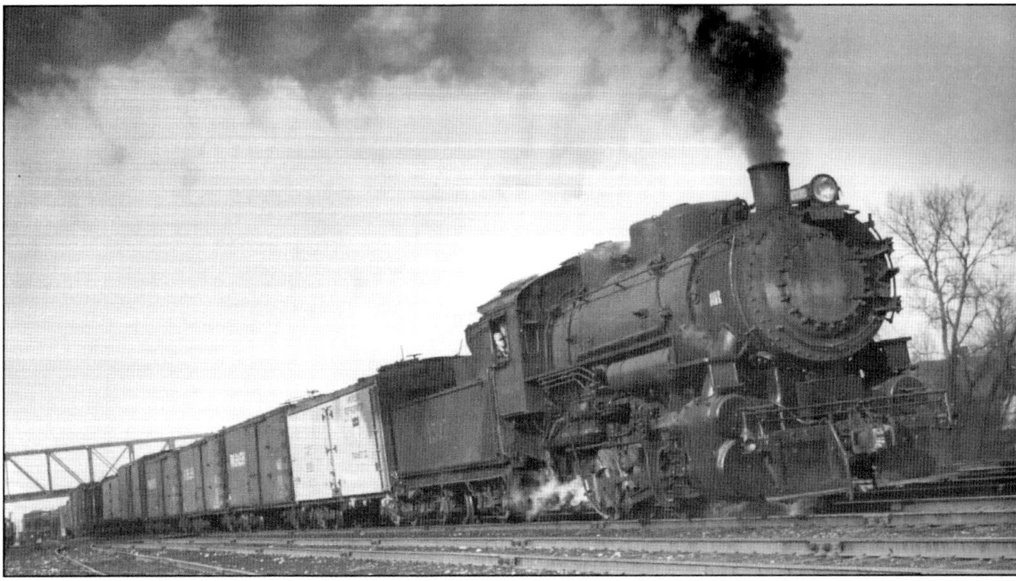

A Wabash Railroad class C-4 0-8-0 switch engine is seen here making a freight transfer run on the Chicago & Western Indiana Railroad tracks at Englewood on the South Side of Chicago. This group of 25 switch engines was built by the Lima Locomotive Corporation of Lima, Ohio, in 1926. They were well suited for moving heavy trains for short distances. They were all retired in the early 1950s.

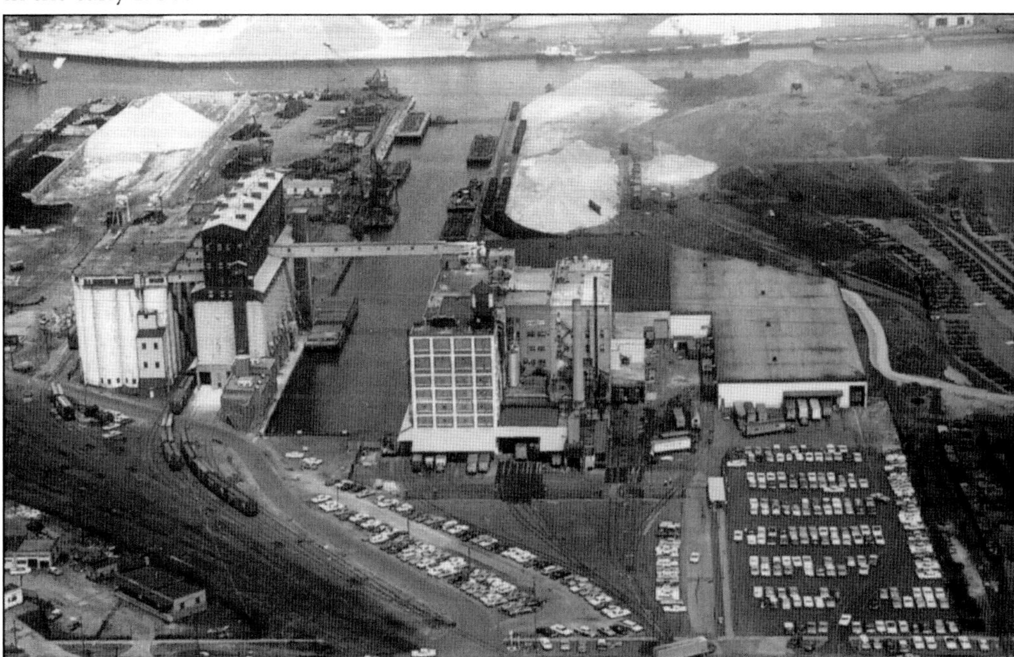

Many of the grain elevators that sprouted along the Calumet River were built by railroads and then sold to grain distributors. The Rialto Elevator (later General Mills) was built by the Wabash line and located along tracks that were owned by the Belt Railway of Chicago, a subsidiary of the C&WI. Wabash cars were spotted at the elevator by the BRC. (Courtesy of the Southeast Chicago Historical Society.)

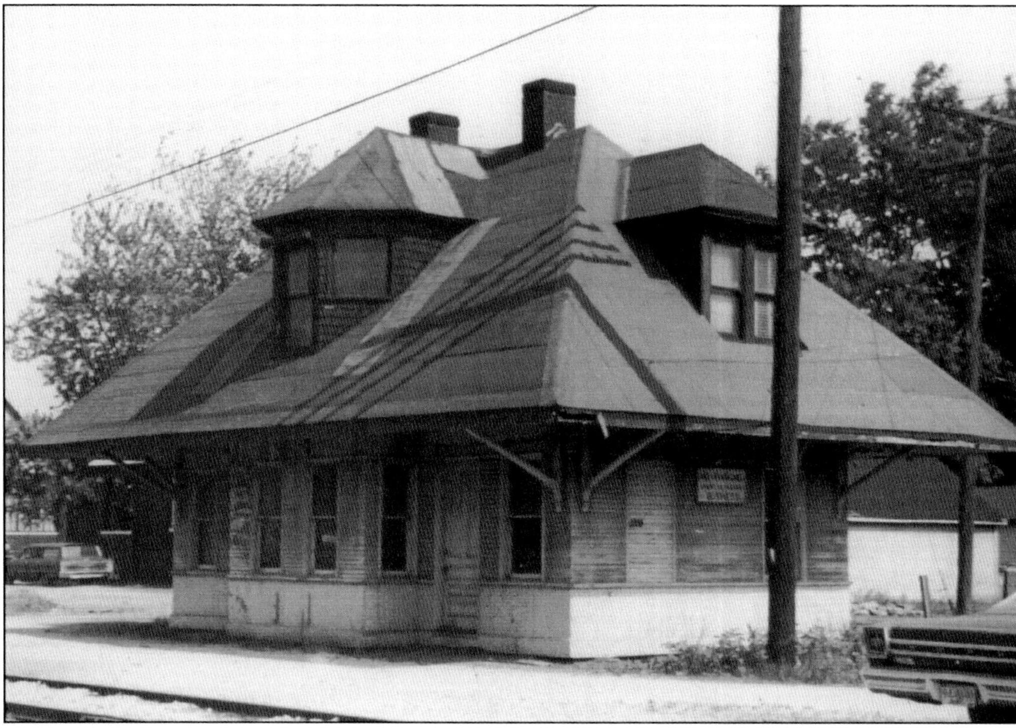

After moving north from downtown Hammond in 1892, the Wabash used the right-of-way of the Baltimore & Ohio and the Indiana Harbor Belt Railroad from Gary to the Illinois state line. It then built this station at the southeast corner of Hohman Avenue and Hudson Street. The Wabash route across northern Indiana was never as profitable as its route from Chicago to St. Louis. (Courtesy of Hammond Public Library.)

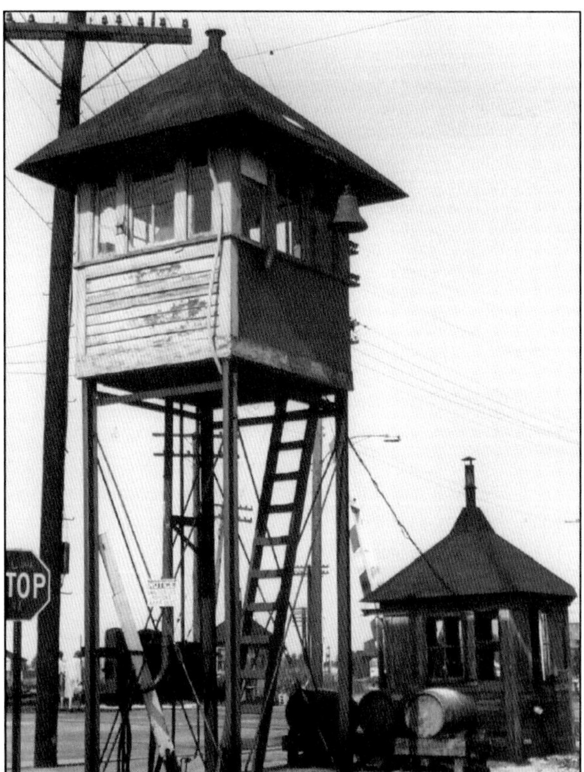

This is the controlling tower at Willow Court and Hohman Avenue in downtown Hammond. It controlled the movements of the Monon and Erie Railroads, which passed by in a northwest-southeast direction to the right of it in this photograph. The flagman's shanty is the peaked-roof building beneath it. That man's job was to control vehicular traffic when trains were coming through. (Courtesy of Hammond Public Library.)

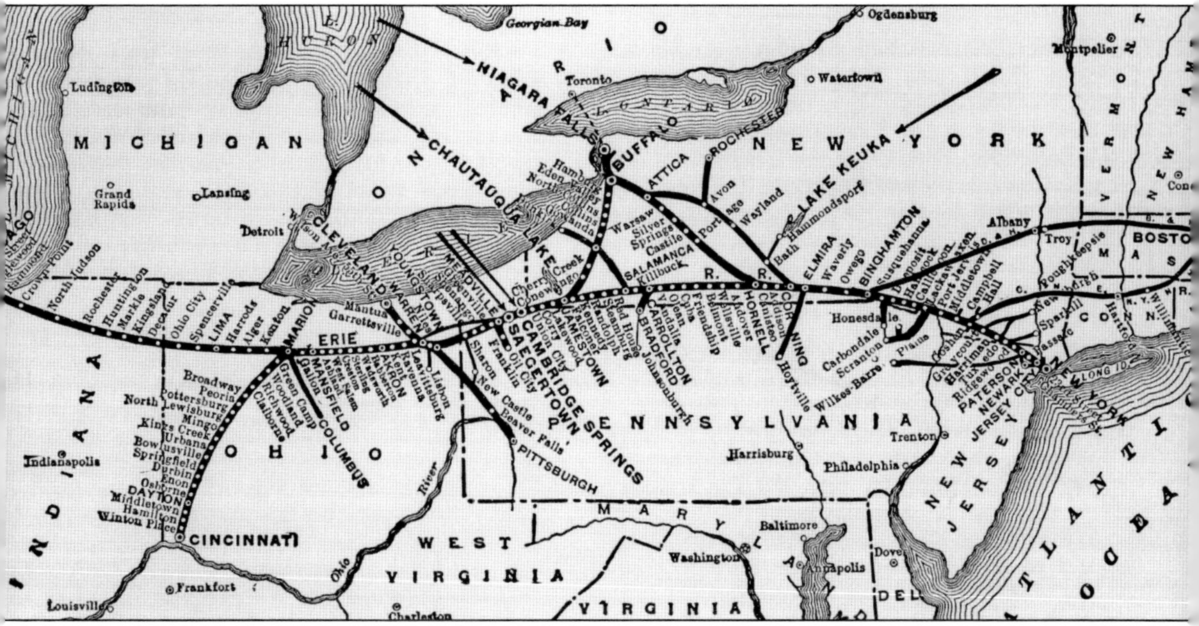

Since the late 1860s, the Erie Railroad had been trying to gain access to Chicago. In the mid-1870s, it bought the old Atlantic & Great Western, sometimes known as the Great Broad Route because it used a six-foot-gauge track, as did the Erie. This purchase got it to Marion, Ohio, and from there, in 1880, the Erie completed a 250-mile right-of-way called the Chicago & Atlantic to the Illinois state line at Hammond, Indiana. The Erie then bought into the Chicago & Western Indiana and finally had its Chicago terminal. With this new route, the Erie offered an evening limited express train from New York to Chicago that took 28 hours. The Erie was known for a comfortable ride, and the *Limited* used Pullman cars. For Chicago passengers, there were hotel, sleeping, parlor, and smoking cars. It was not the shortest route between New York and Chicago, but it was one with very low grades. The Erie collected passengers and freight in towns that the Pennsylvania and New York Central ignored. (Courtesy of Cynthia Ogorek.)

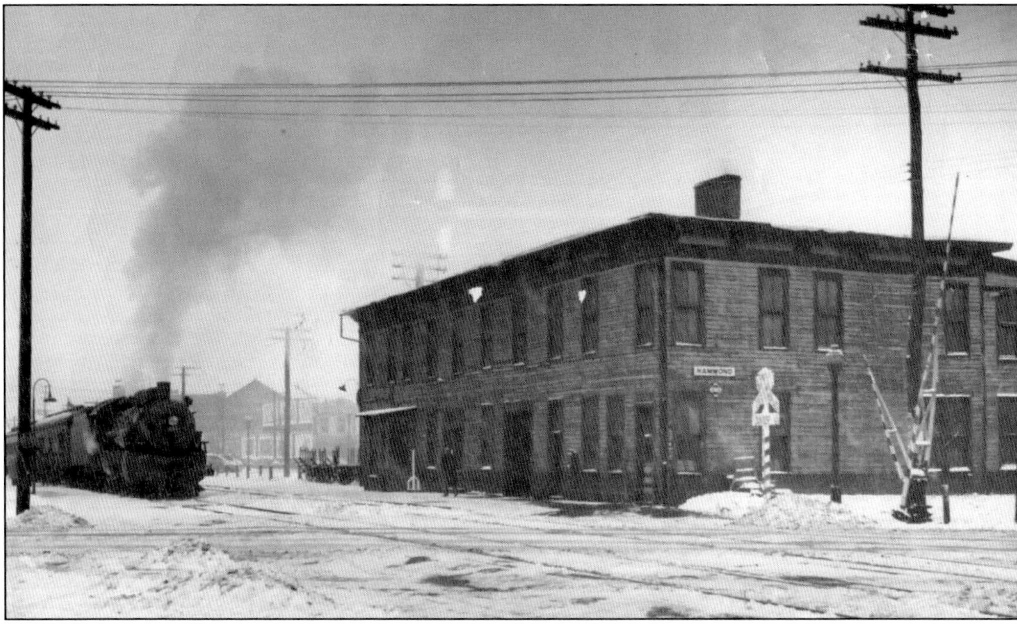

Twenty-one miles from Dearborn Station, the Erie made its connection with the C&WI at Hammond. The Chicago & Erie station in Hammond, at 133 Sibley Street in 1919, had been the property of the Chicago & Atlantic. The two-story frame building housed the Atlantic Hotel, lunch and dining rooms, and a kitchen. The passenger depot was originally in another building south along the tracks. (Courtesy of Hammond Public Library.)

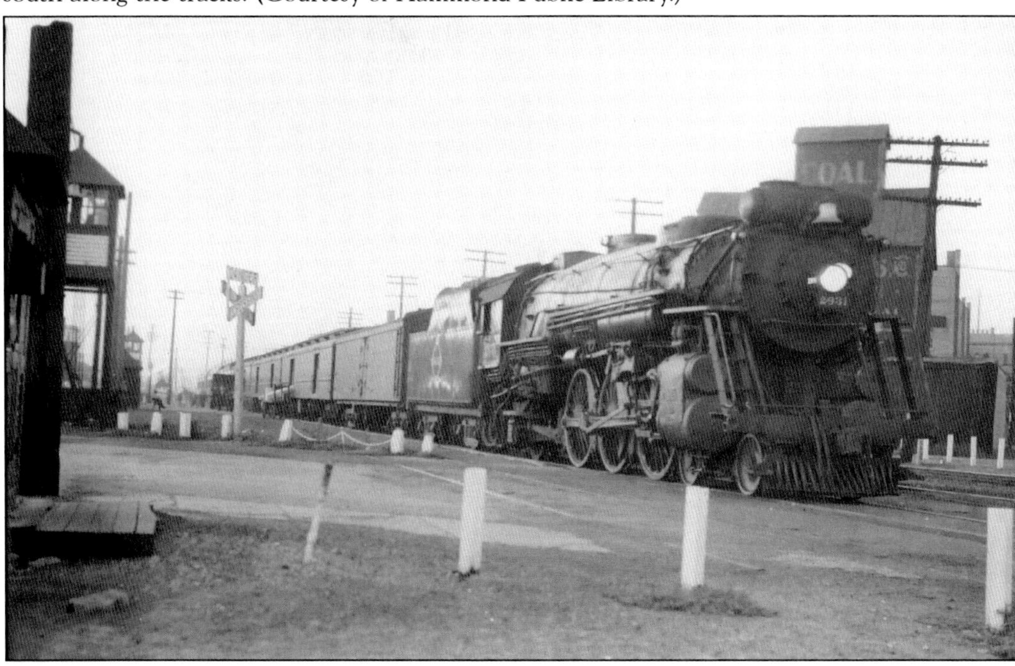

One of the Erie Railroad's awesome K-5 4-6-2 Pacific-type locomotives pulled through Hammond on a regular schedule with the Erie's train No. 6, the *Lake Cities*. This train operated daily between Dearborn Station in Chicago and Jersey City, New Jersey, where passengers boarded a ferryboat that took them across the Hudson River to New York City.

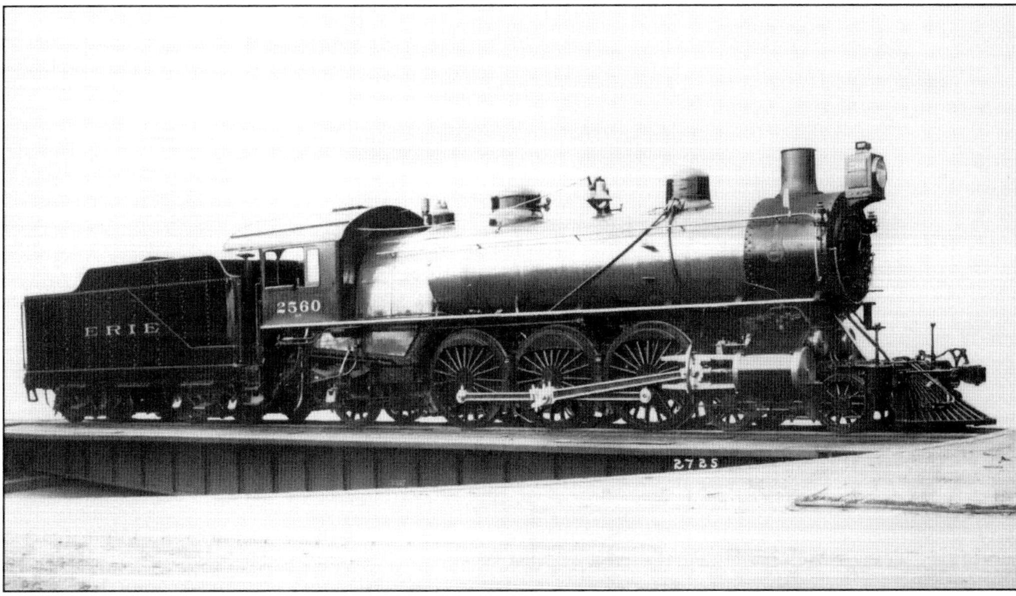

This is a publicity photograph of Erie Railroad class K-1 4-6-2 Pacific-type No. 2560 as it rolled off of the production line of the Baldwin Locomotive Works in Eddystone, Pennsylvania, in 1908. Originally this was main-line passenger train power, replacing older and less powerful 2-6-2 and 4-6-0 locomotives. It later was downgraded to lesser trains as larger Pacific-type locomotives came onto the Erie's locomotive roster.

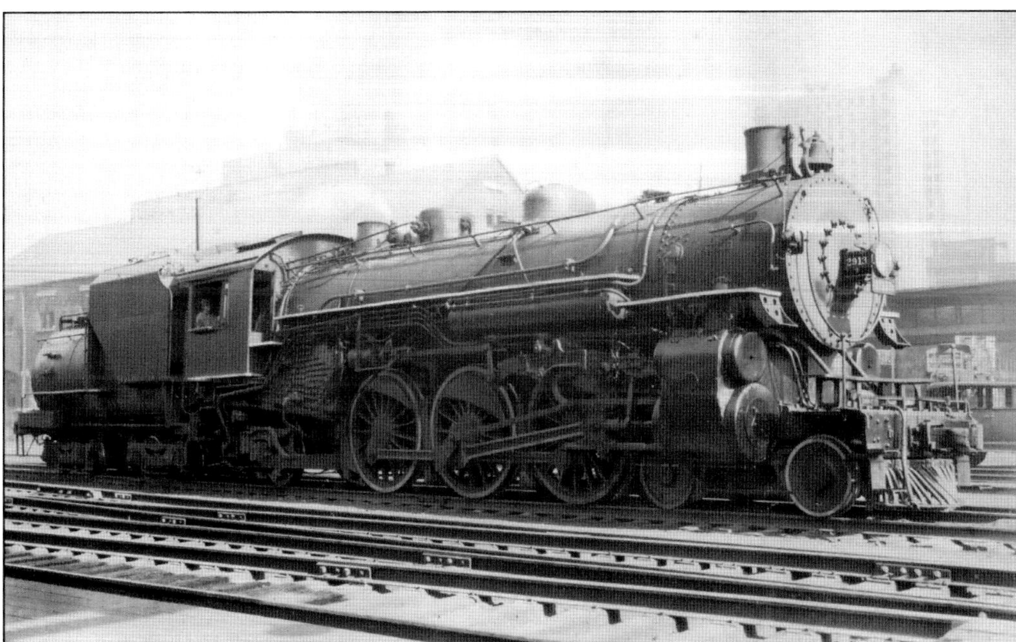

In 1923, the American Locomotive Company in Schenectady, New York, constructed 10 class K-2-A 4-6-2 Pacific-type locomotives for the Erie Railroad, numbered 2905 through 2014. The locomotives were equipped with mechanical coal stokers and Vanderbilt tenders that used cylindrical water tanks. Shown here on October 27, 1927, is Erie Railroad 4-6-2 No. 2913 backing into Dearborn Station in Chicago, where it will couple on to an eastbound train.

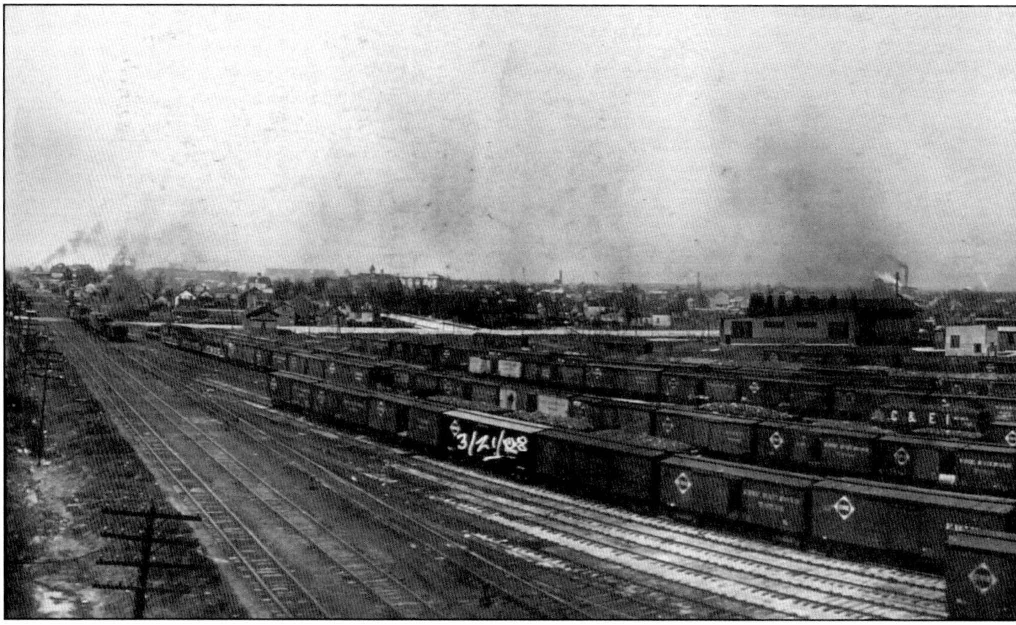

This aerial view shows the extent of the Erie freight yard in South Hammond around 1928. By mid-20th century, the Erie had become primarily a freight carrier, generating some 85 percent of its revenue by hauling coal, timber, minerals, agricultural products, milk, and meat—both dressed and on the hoof—between Chicago and Hoboken, New Jersey, for markets in New York City. Trains were made up daily in this yard for the cross-country run. (Courtesy of Hammond Public Library.)

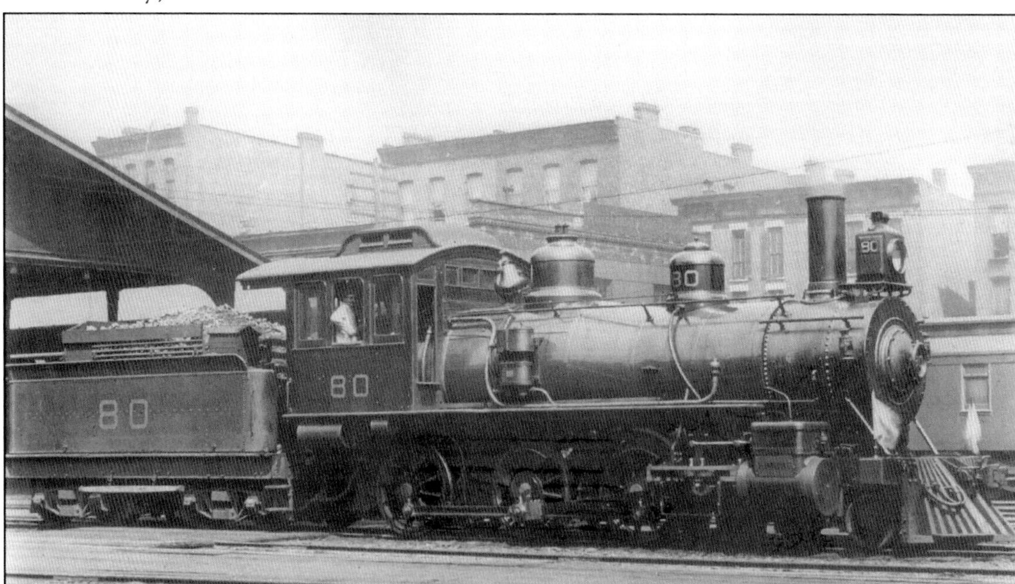

The Chicago, Indianapolis & Louisville Railroad (CI&L, later the Monon) class G-5 4-6-0 Ten Wheeler-type No. 80 was at Dearborn Station when this photograph was taken in 1918. Built by the Rogers Locomotive and Machine Works of Patterson, New Jersey, in June 1890, No. 80 remained in revenue service until July 1936, even though the C&IL had acquired several, more suitable, 4-6-2 Pacific-type locomotives for passenger service since 1905.

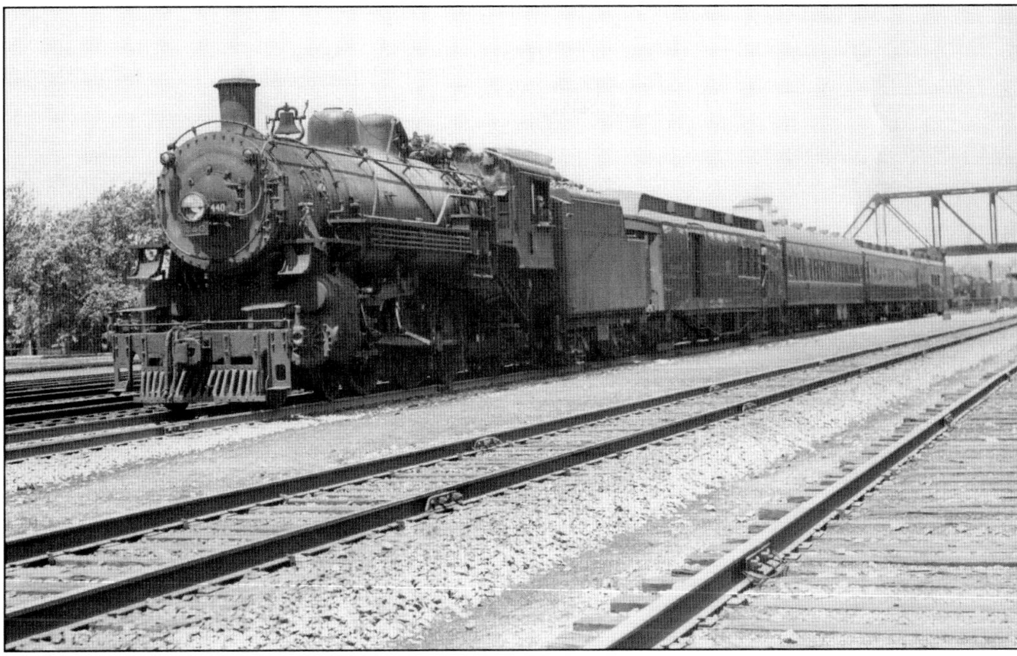

The American Locomotive Company built Monon Railroad's class K-5 4-6-2 Pacific-type No. 440 at its former Brooks Locomotive plant in Dunkirk, New York. It is pausing here at the C&WI's Englewood Station in June 1940 with a passenger train headed for Dearborn Station. The 440 was retired in April 1948. (Courtesy of Sid Davies.)

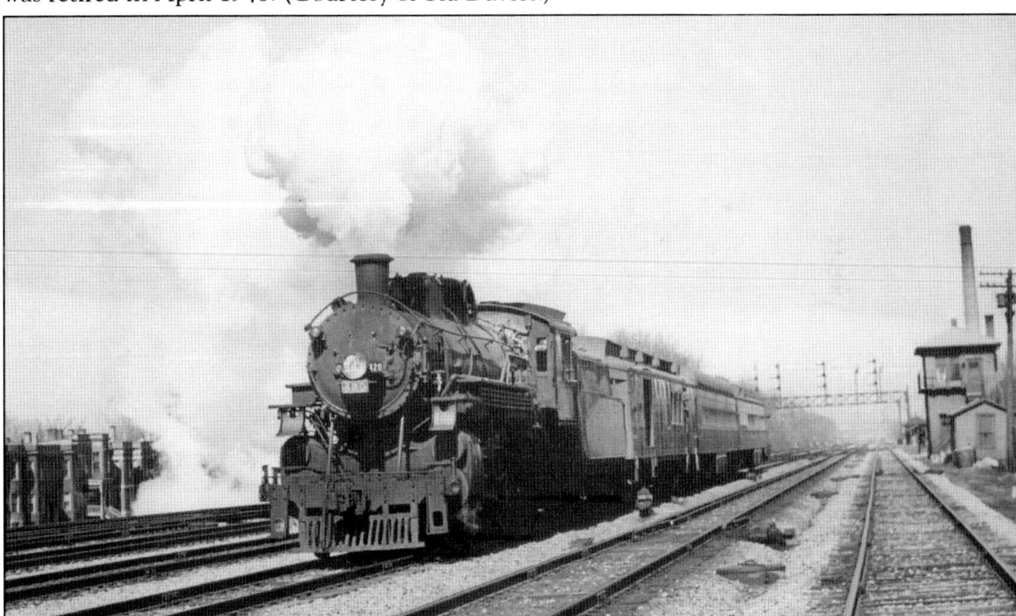

Monon Railroad class K-3 4-6-2 Pacific-type No. 420 is southbound with a three-car passenger train passing the Chicago & Western Indiana Railroad's interlocking tower at Seventy-Fourth Street in Chicago's Gresham neighborhood. The 420 was built by the American Locomotive Company's Brooks Locomotive plant in Dunkirk, New York, in June 1909, and it remained in service on the Monon until June 1947, when it was retired.

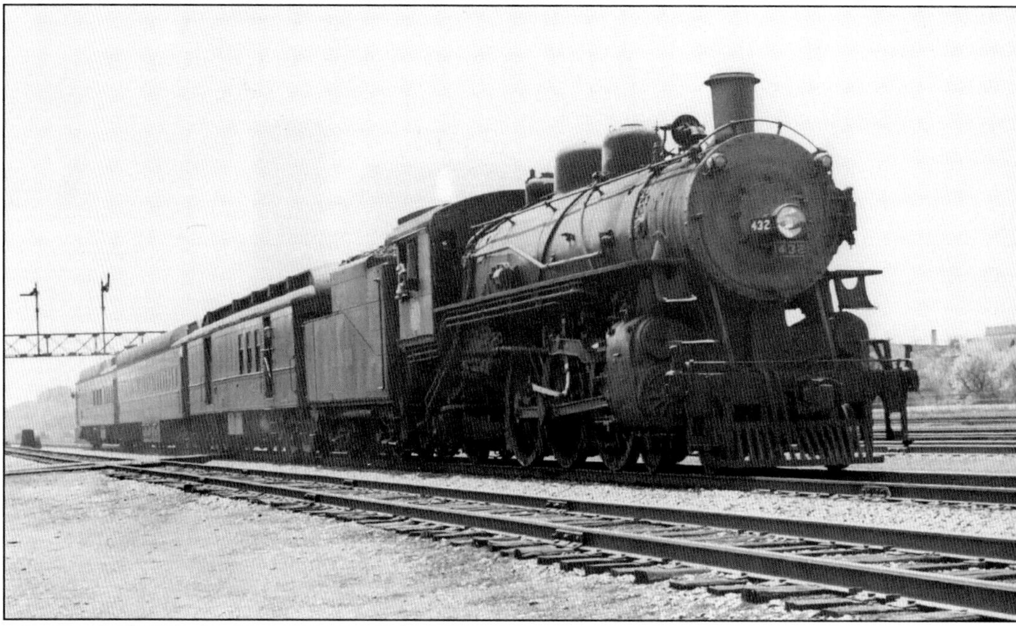

Monon Railroad class K-4 4-6-2 Pacific-type No. 432 didn't have to work very hard to keep this three-car train on the advertised schedule back in June 1940. A combination mail-baggage car and two passenger coaches were more than adequate for the Monon's passenger business. The train is shown here on the Chicago & Western Indiana Railroad's tracks near Seventy-Eighth Street. (Courtesy of Sid Davies.)

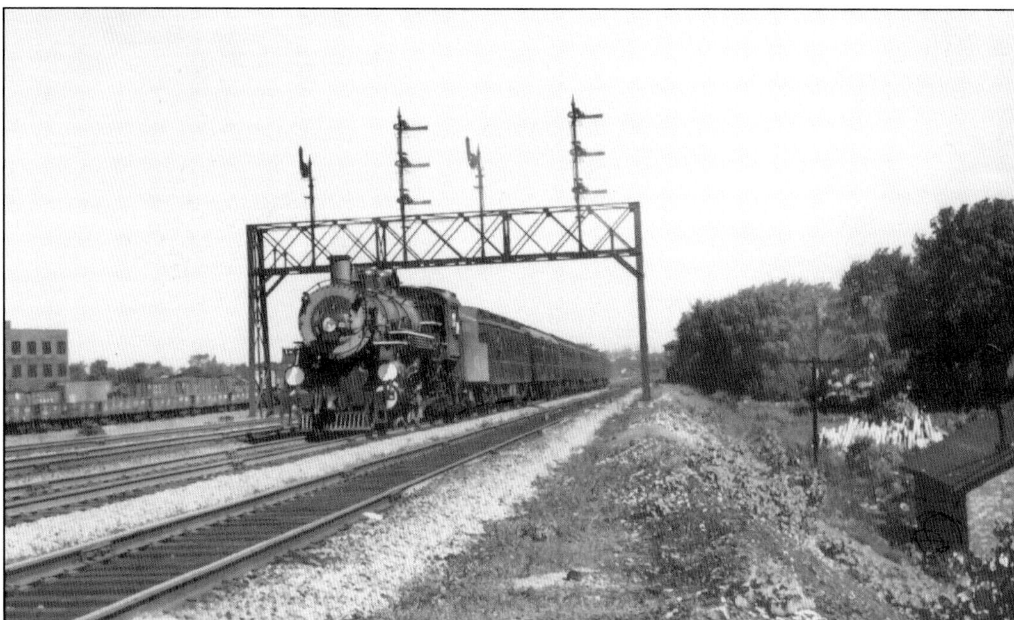

A five-car Monon passenger train is shown here in August 1948 headed southbound behind a 4-6-2 Pacific-type locomotive on the Chicago & Western Indiana Railroad's tracks at Eighty-Second Street, nine miles south of Dearborn Station. It is passing under the semaphore signal bridge that controls train movement on these busy tracks.

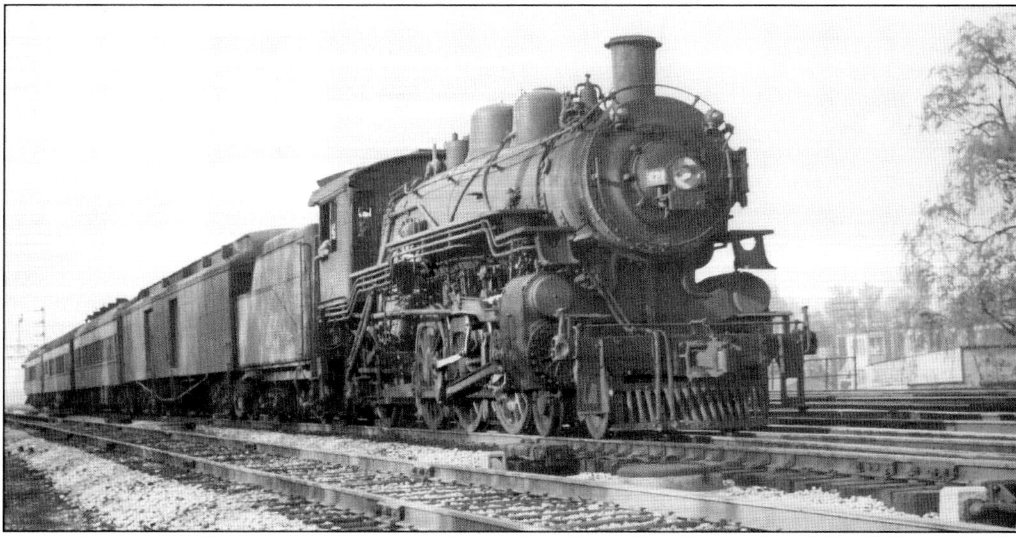

The Monon's Pacific-type passenger locomotives were well suited for the 183-mile run between Chicago and Indianapolis and the 324-mile run between Chicago and Louisville, Kentucky. This is class K-3 Pacific-type No. 421 on the Chicago & Western Indiana Railroad's tracks near Eighty-First Street with a four-car passenger train in May 1940. (Courtesy of Sid Davies.)

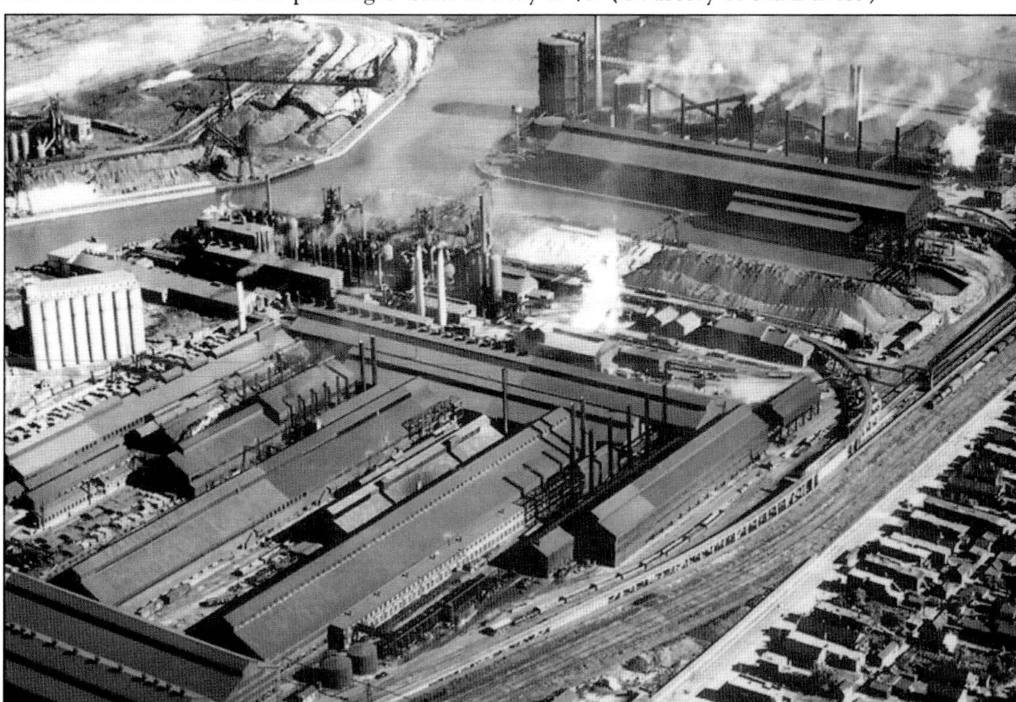

Wisconsin Steel, at 104th and Torrence Avenue in Chicago, was served exclusively by the Chicago West Pullman and Southern Railroad (CWP&S). So the Monon, which hauled coal from Kentucky for Wisconsin's coke plant, transferred its coal cars to the Belt Railway of Chicago, and the BRC transferred them to the CWP&S. For the first half of the 20th century, there was no agreement between the C&WI owner roads and the CWP&S that allowed a direct transfer. (Courtesy of the Southeast Chicago Historical Society.)

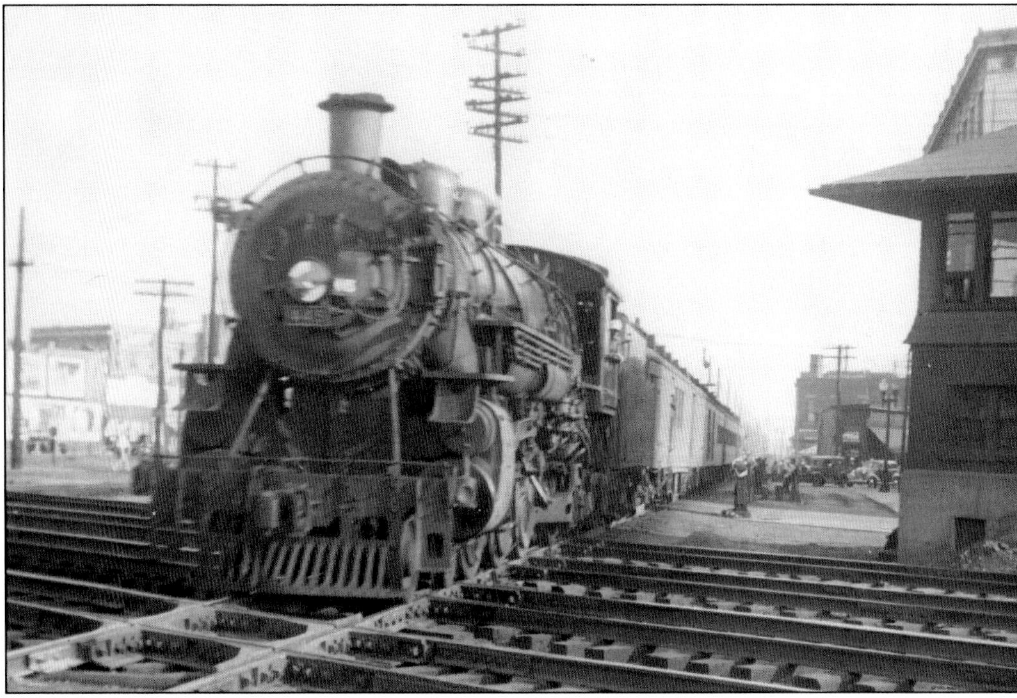

This is Monon Railroad's class K-5a 4-6-2 Pacific-type No. 445 with a passenger train at Hammond Hohman Avenue interlocking tower in August 1936. The multiple railroad lines that intersected in Hammond regularly caused traffic delays. In another view of the intersection, a crew in 1974 is repairing the tracks, switches, and signals. The flagman's shanties were still around, and the Hohman interlocking tower can be seen on the left in the background. The tracks on which the crew is working were for the Indiana Harbor Belt and the former Michigan Central. The Monon and Erie right-of-ways crossed them at an angle, with the bridges in the distance carrying those railroads over the Grand Calumet River. (Above, courtesy of Sid Davies; below, courtesy of Hammond Public Library.)

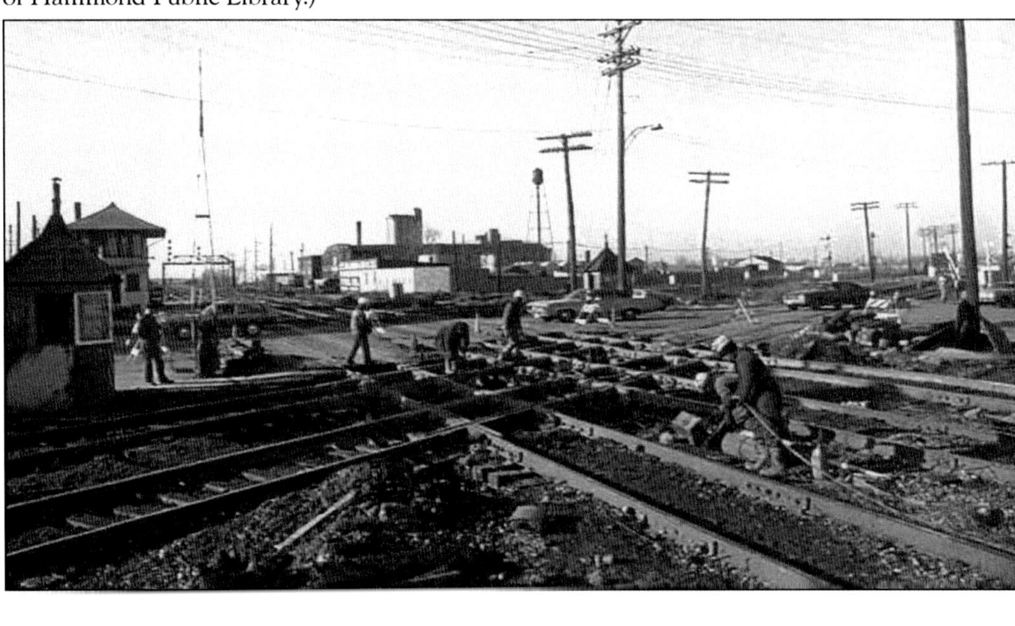

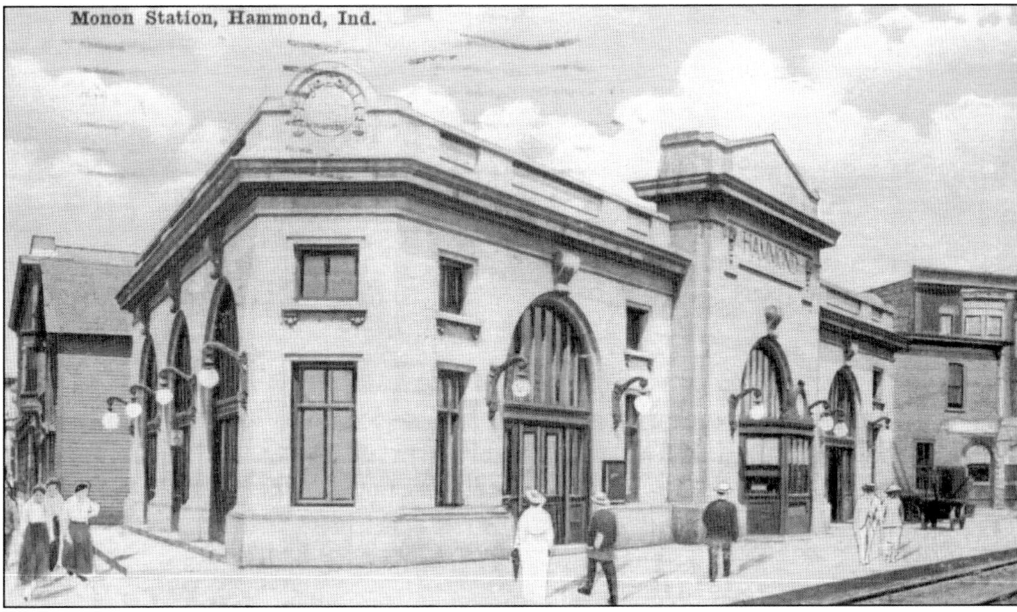

The Monon passenger station in downtown Hammond was located at 121 Sibley Street (old street numbering) in a triangle-shaped building. The line's freight depot was located about two blocks away on Fayette Street behind St. Joseph's Church. The city directory of 1889 proudly announced that the Monon offered "direct, continuous and unbroken passenger and freight communications . . . to all important points southeast to the Atlantic seaboard." (Courtesy of Hammond Public Library.)

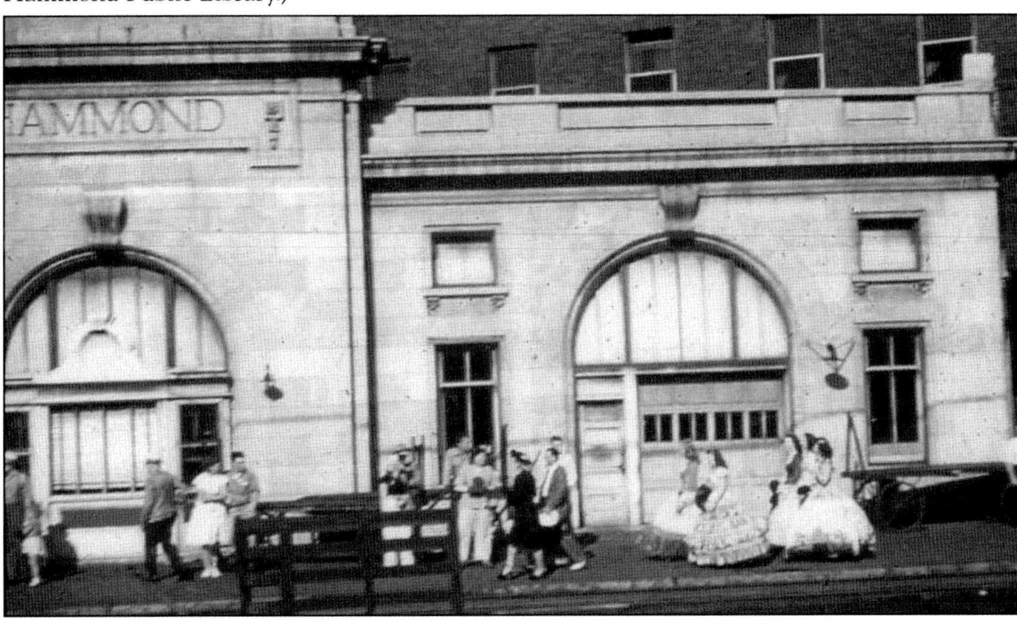

The first Hammond Monon freight house was attached to the passenger station. It was no longer active by 1947, when the "Hoosier Line" celebrated its 100th anniversary. The "Belles of the Monon," in their ruffles and hoop skirts, are walking in front of it on their way to meet the centennial train drawn by the *William Mason*. Coming in on the train were the Monon show troupe and John W. Barriger, president of the line. (Courtesy of Hammond Public Library.)

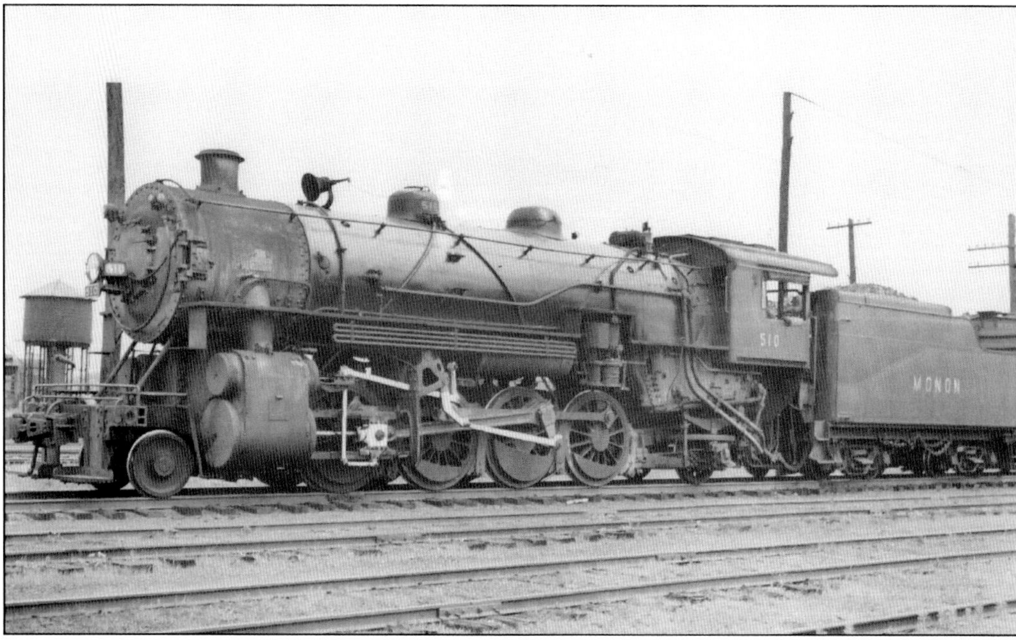

This is one of the Monon Railroad's 55 class J 2-8-2 Mikado-type freight locomotives at Hammond in June 1936. These engines were all purchased between 1912 and 1929 and remained in service on the Monon until the late 1940s, when they were replaced with new diesel freight locomotives. (Courtesy of C.T. Felstead and William Raia.)

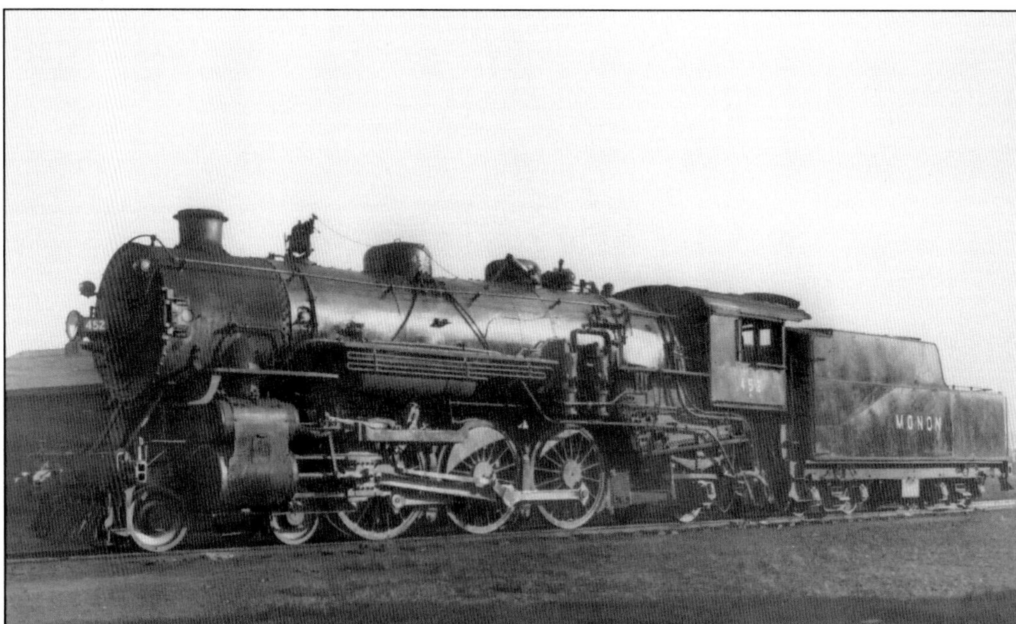

Monon Railroad class K-6 4-6-2 Pacific-type No. 452 was ready for its next assignment back in July 1937, when this photograph was taken in Hammond, Indiana. The 452 was built by the American Locomotive Company at its former Brooks Locomotive plant in Dunkirk, New York, in November 1916. It was the very last steam passenger locomotive purchased by the Monon. (Courtesy of Paul Eilenberger.)

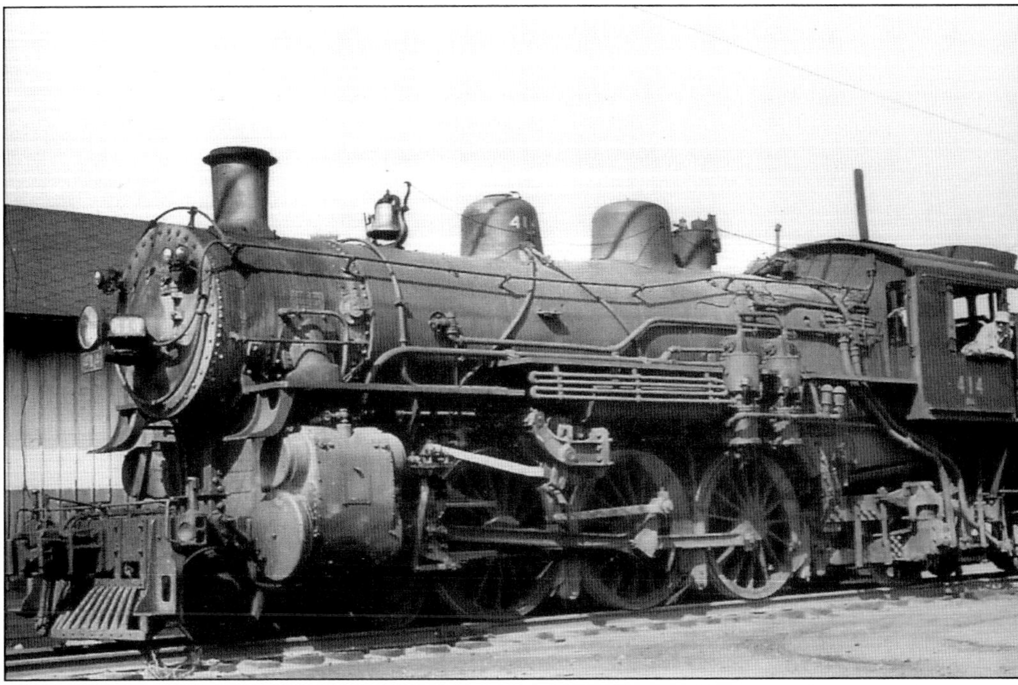

Monon Railroad 4-6-2 Pacific-type No. 414 was standing by in Hammond waiting for its next assignment when this photograph was taken in 1939. The fireman has already replenished the supply of coal and water and is leaning out of the cab window.

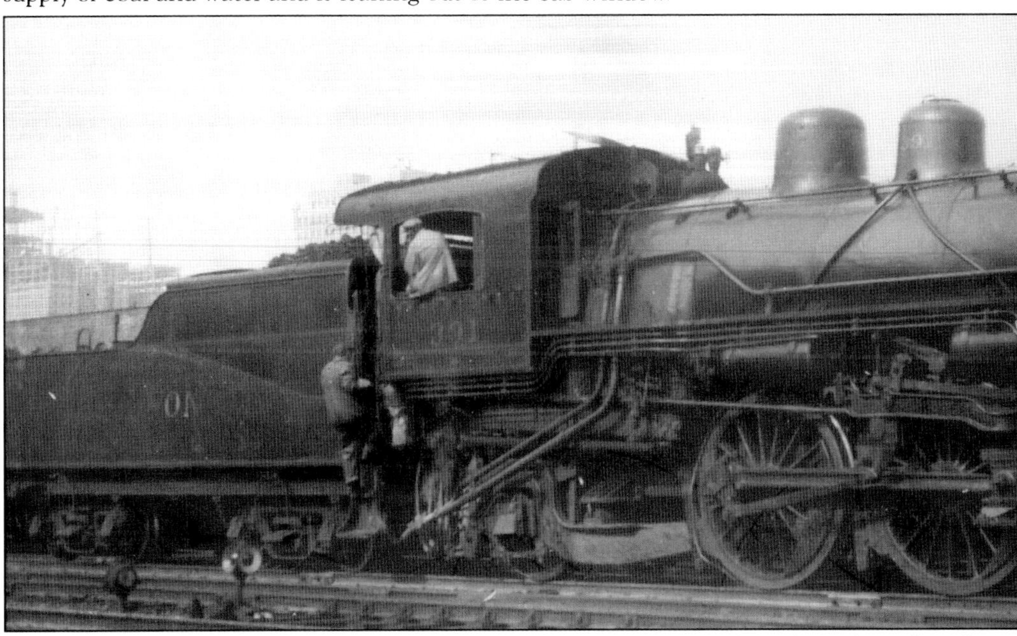

A steam locomotive required two men to run it. The engineer sat in the cab on the right side and operated the throttle, the brakes, the whistle, and the bell. The fireman, shown here climbing in to the cab of Monon Railroad class I-1a 4-4-2 Atlantic-type No. 391, was responsible for shoveling coal into the firebox and making sure that the engineer had enough steam available to pull the train.

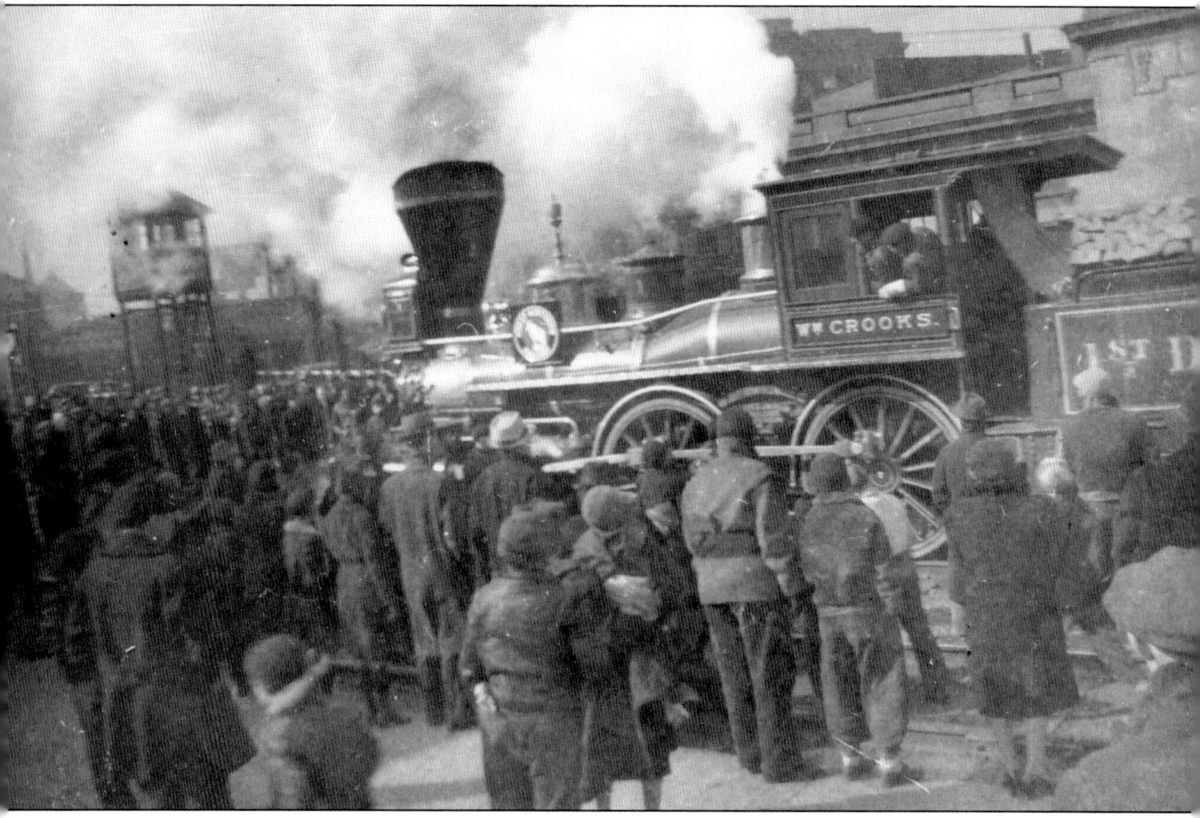

On its way to display at the New York World's Fair of 1939, the *William Crooks*, owned by the Great Northern Railroad, passed through Hammond on the Erie right-of-way, although it was posed for this photograph in front of the Monon station. The engine was the first locomotive used in Minnesota and was named for the then chief engineer of the St. Paul & Pacific Railroad, upon which it ran. It arrived in St. Paul by barge on September 9, 1861, from the workshops of Smith and Jackson in Paterson, New Jersey. When it was built, it was also dubbed "No. 1," but the number of a locomotive was not as important as the name painted on the cab in those days. Meant for short, fast passenger runs across the prairies, the *William Crooks* had 63-inch driving wheels and 12-inch-by-22-inch cylinders. It weighed in at only 36,000 pounds. (Courtesy of Hammond Public Library.)

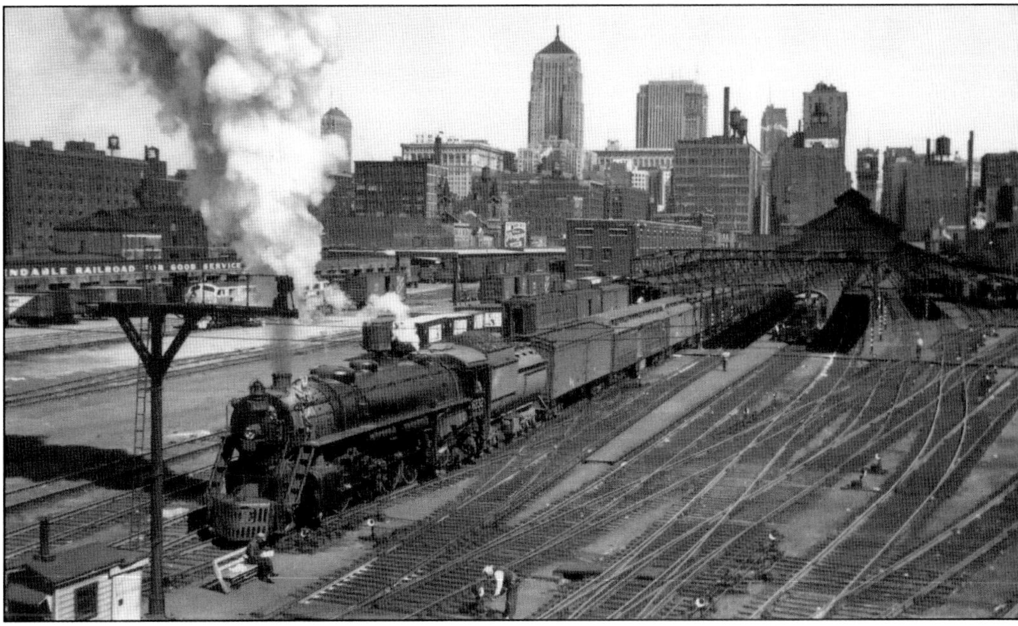

Grand Trunk Western Railway continued to operate their modern steam locomotives in passenger train service to and from Chicago well into the late 1950s, long after most other carriers had retired their vintage steam engines and switched to diesels. GTW class U-3 c-4-8-4 Northern-type No. 6332, shown here ready to depart from Dearborn Station, was built in 1942 by the American Locomotive Company.

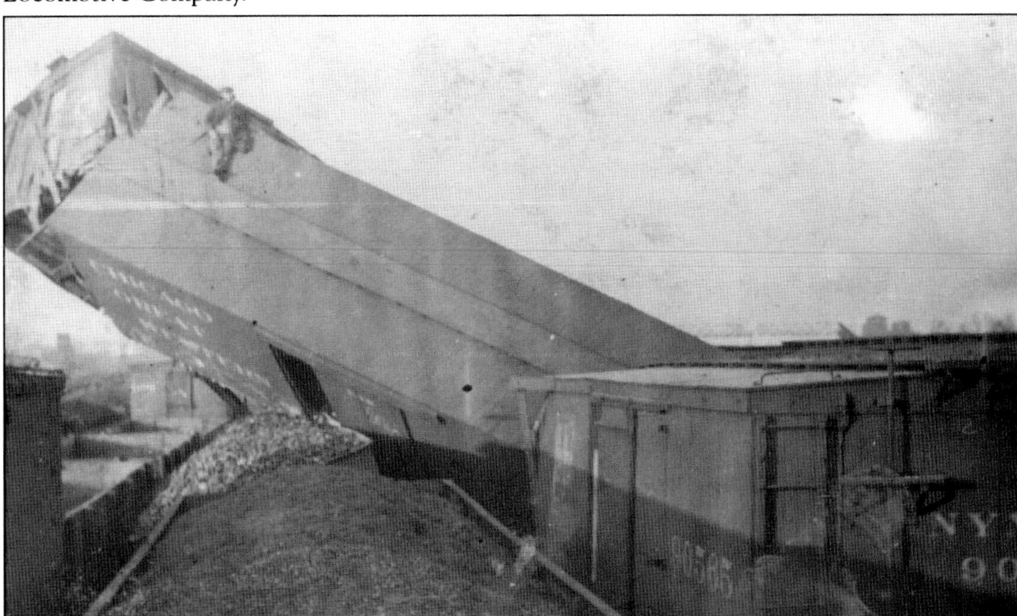

The hand brake wheels are clearly seen on these wooden freight cars involved in a wreck on the GTW near Chicago Road. A minimum of two brakemen were included in any freight crew. One rode on top of the cars at the rear and the other at the front of the train. No matter the weather, they trotted and jumped from car to car, turning each wheel by hand in order to stop the train. (Courtesy of the South Holland Historical Society.)

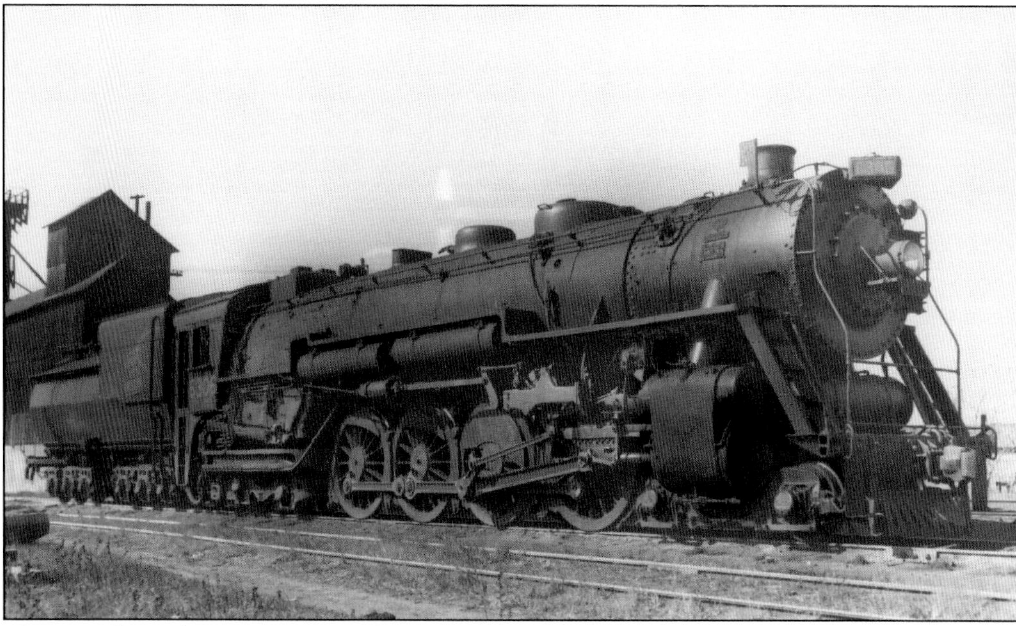

The Grand Trunk Western serviced its passenger train locomotives at its Elsdon Yard roundhouse, located near West Forty-Ninth Street and South Kedzie Avenue. GTW class U-3-a 4-8-4 Northern-type No. 6306 was laying over at the Elsdon Yard roundhouse in October 1939 when this photograph was taken. The American Locomotive Corporation of Schenectady, New York, built the 6306 in 1927.

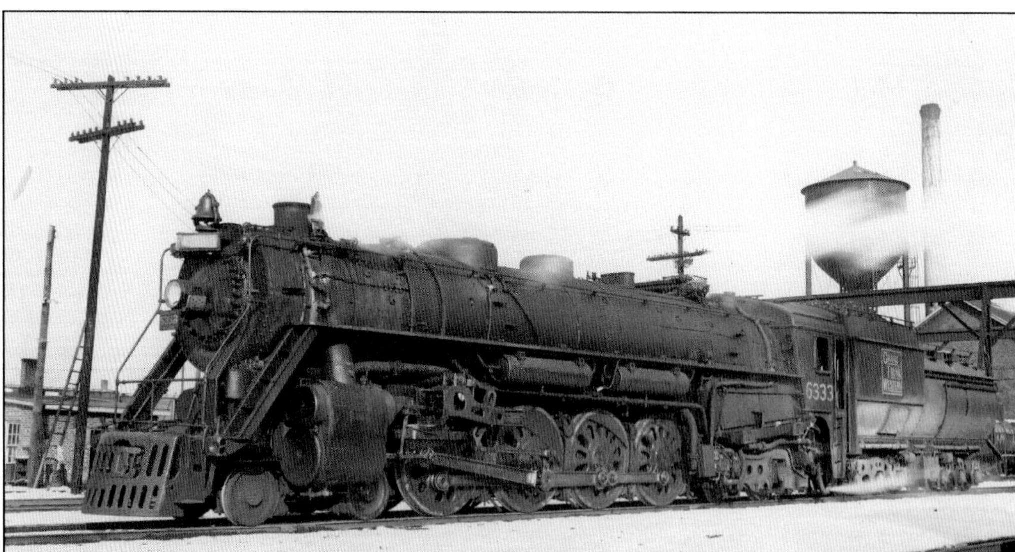

Visiting the Elsdon Yard roundhouse on November 19, 1955, is Grand Trunk Western class U-3-b 4-8-4 Northern-type No. 6333. The American Locomotive Corporation of Schenectady, New York, built this locomotive for the GTW in 1943, and it was one of very few new steam locomotives built in the United States during World War II. It saw regular service on the Grand Trunk Western to and from Chicago during the 1940s and 1950s.

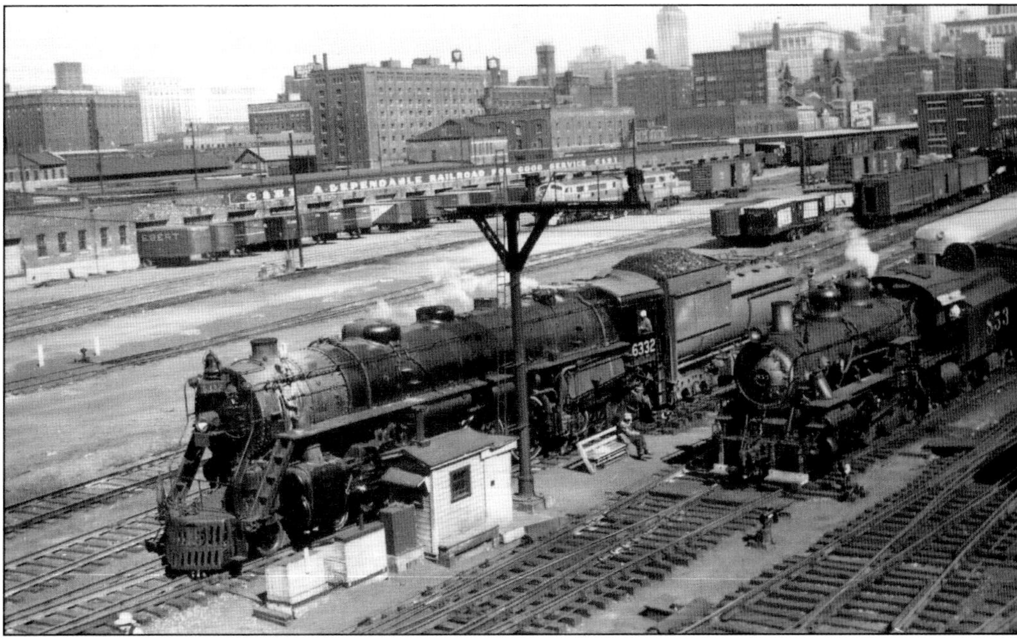

Grand Trunk Western class U-3-c 4-8-4 Northern-type No. 6332 is pictured at Dearborn Station on a sunny morning in the early 1950s, ready to couple onto GTW train No. 20, the *Maple Leaf*, scheduled to depart at 9:40 a.m. for Toronto. The American Locomotive Company of Schenectady, New York, built the 6332 in 1942. To the right is the Santa Fe's 0-8-0 switch engine No. 853, and in the background is a pair of Monon F3A diesel locomotives.

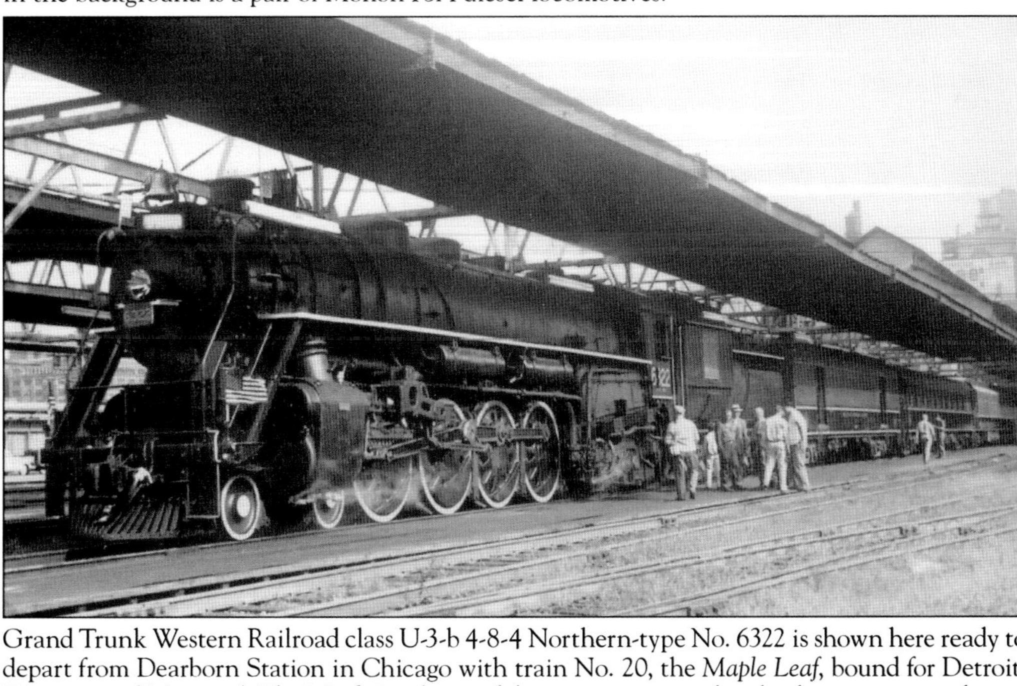

Grand Trunk Western Railroad class U-3-b 4-8-4 Northern-type No. 6322 is shown here ready to depart from Dearborn Station in Chicago with train No. 20, the *Maple Leaf*, bound for Detroit, Toronto, and Montreal. The *Maple Leaf* was a deluxe train equipped with a baggage car, reclining seat coaches, a dining car, parlor cars, and numerous sleeping cars. The American Locomotive Company built the 6322 for the GTW in 1943 at its plant in Schenectady, New York.

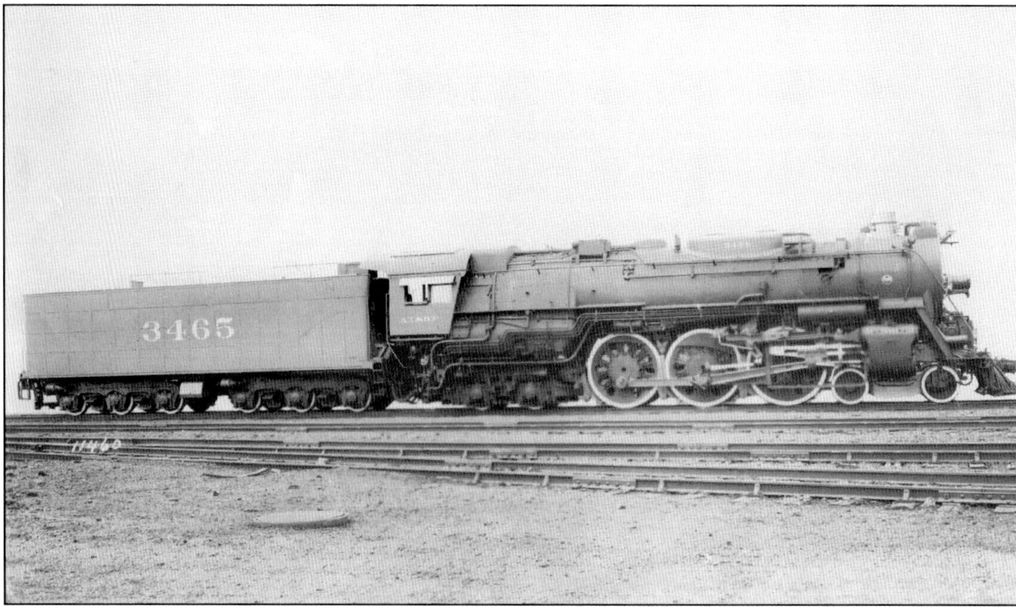

The Baldwin Locomotive Works of Eddystone, Pennsylvania, built six class 3460 4-6-4 Hudson-type locomotives for the Atchison, Topeka & Santa Fe Railroad in 1937 for use on passenger trains. No. 3465, shown here, was the last new 4-6-4 ever purchased by the Santa Fe. The locomotives were regularly assigned to Santa Fe trains No. 19 and No. 20, the streamlined, lightweight *Chief*, between Dearborn Station in Chicago and La Junta, Colorado.

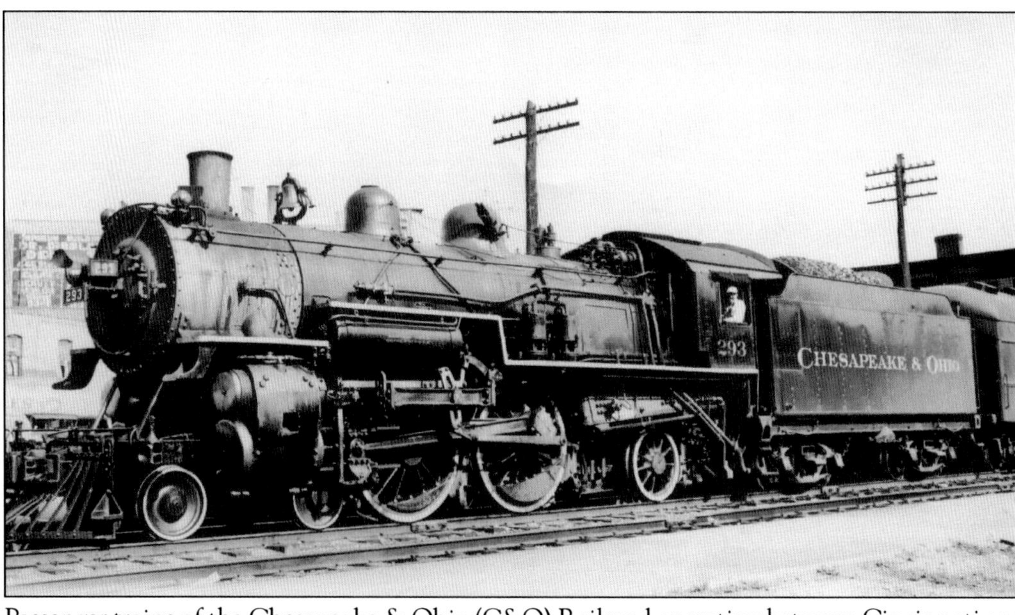

Passenger trains of the Chesapeake & Ohio (C&O) Railroad operating between Cincinnati and Chicago used the C&WI's tracks and Dearborn Station for a little over 14 years, beginning on December 1, 1910, and ending on March 1, 1925. Shown here is C&O class A-16 4-4-2 Atlantic-type No. 293 stopped at the station in Hammond with westbound passenger train No. 7. The American Locomotive Company built the 293 for the C&O in 1902.

Five

Streamline to Diesel on the Chicago & Western Indiana

As in all other industries, changes occurred on the railroads in the early 20th century. Steam power was dirty and inefficient. First wood, then coal, and water had to be stored at intervals along the routes, and trains had to stop to replenish supplies of both in order to continue running. Fashion also changed. By the 1930s, a style called "streamline" was being used in art, architecture, automobiles, furniture, clothing, and eventually in the design of railroad cars and locomotives. In order to successfully market train travel, railroads had to keep up with the times, but building a locomotive and matching or coordinating coaches was an expensive undertaking. So many companies simply covered the usual steam engine with a sleek "overcoat" and called it streamline. The era of streamlining also meant reducing the weight of passenger cars. While the C&WI itself plugged along through the 1920s, 1930s, and 1940s with its reliable, if homely, steam engines, some of its owner lines did try to glamorize their fleets. The streamlined steam locomotive era did not last long, though, and by the late 1940s, most of the lines had moved on to diesel locomotives and stainless steel coaches.

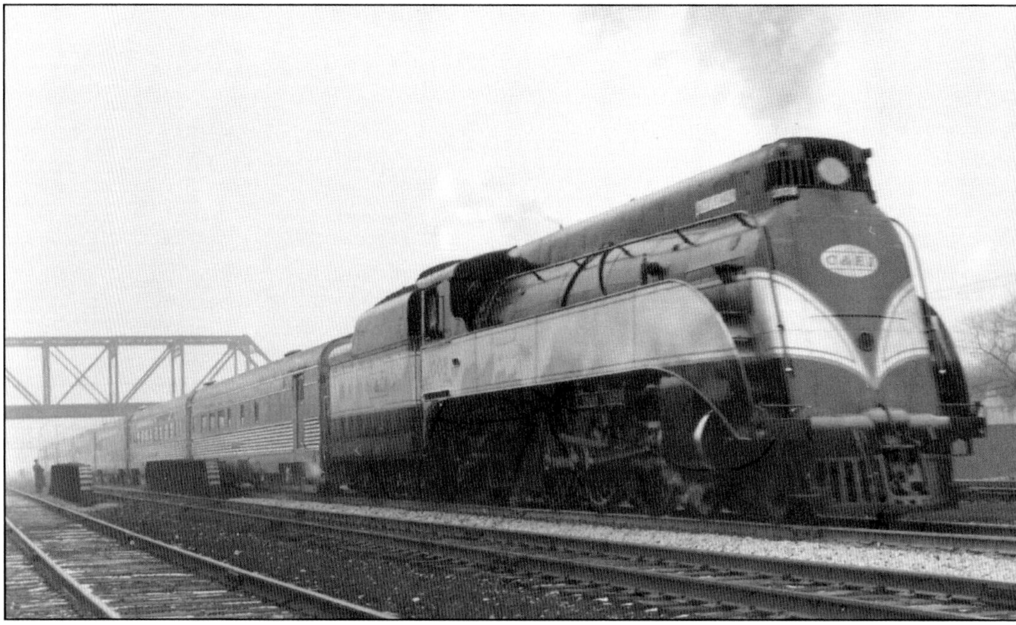

Chicago & Eastern Illinois Railroad's class P41 4-6-2 Pacific-type No. 1008 was built by the Baldwin Locomotive Works of Eddystone, Pennsylvania, in 1911. It received this streamlined shroud in November 1940 for use on the C&EI's new *Dixie Flagler* streamliner. This is the very first run of the new train passing through Englewood Station on December 17, 1940. (Courtesy of Sid Davies.)

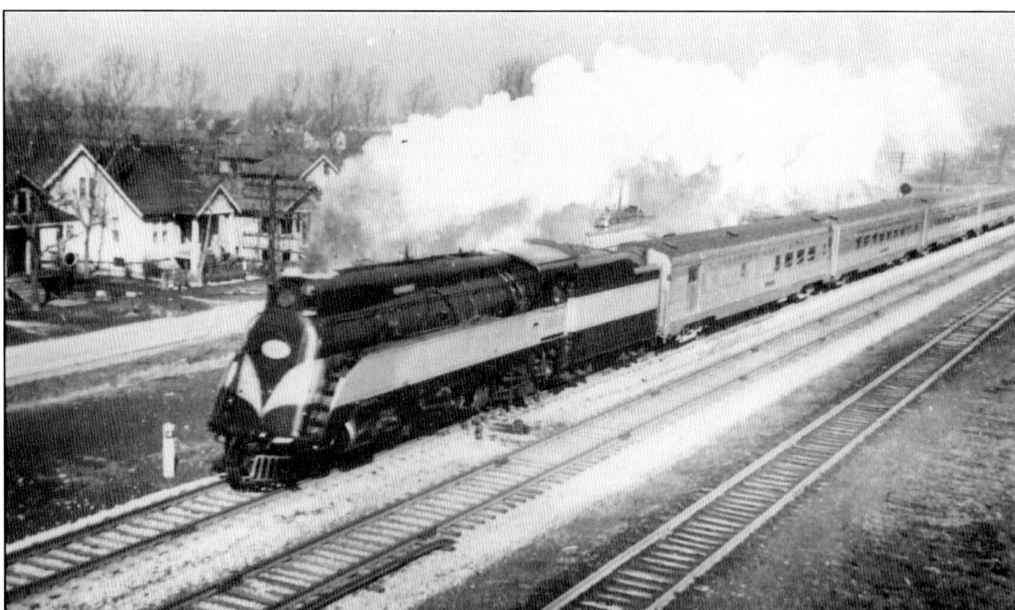

This is another view of the C&EI's streamlined class P41 4-6-2 Pacific-type No. 1008 with the *Dixie Flagler* just north of the South Holland Station. The *Dixie Flagler* was a deluxe all-coach streamlined train that operated every third day between Chicago and Miami. It was equipped with five reclining seat coaches, a dining car, and an observation-buffet-lounge car. (Courtesy of the South Holland Historical Society.)

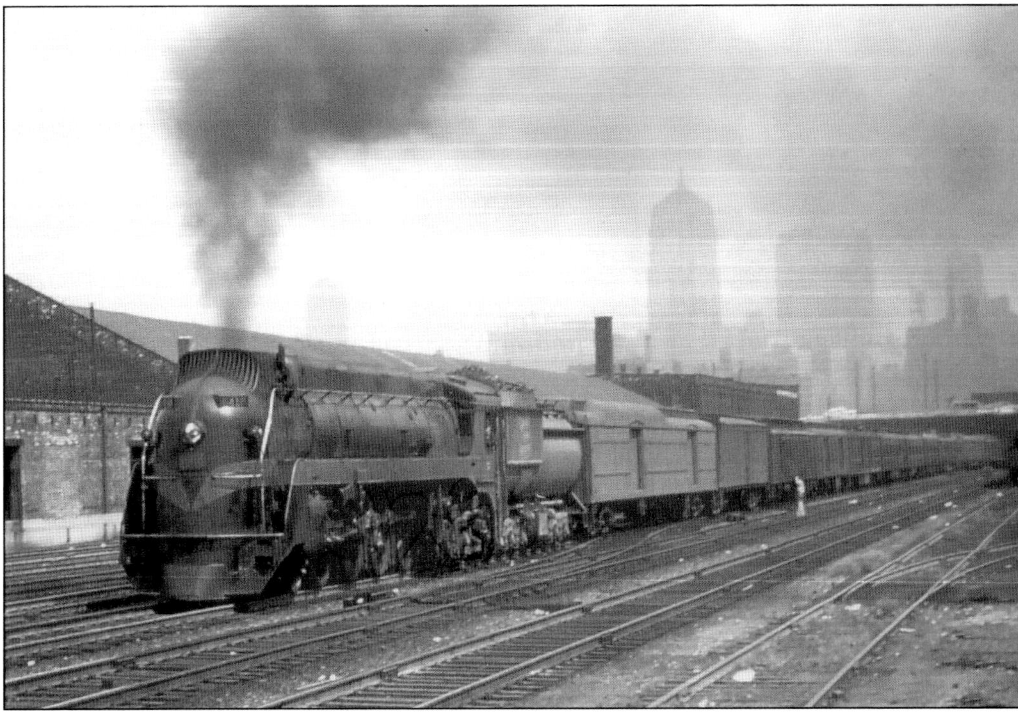

The Grand Trunk Western Railroad used its six relatively modern class U-4-b streamlined 4-8-4 Northern-type locomotives for its passenger trains operating between Port Huron, Michigan, and Dearborn Station in Chicago. The streamlining did not extend to the tender, which was in the Vanderbilt style with a cylindrical water tank. These locomotives were built by the Lima Locomotive Corporation in 1938 and remained in service until the late 1950s.

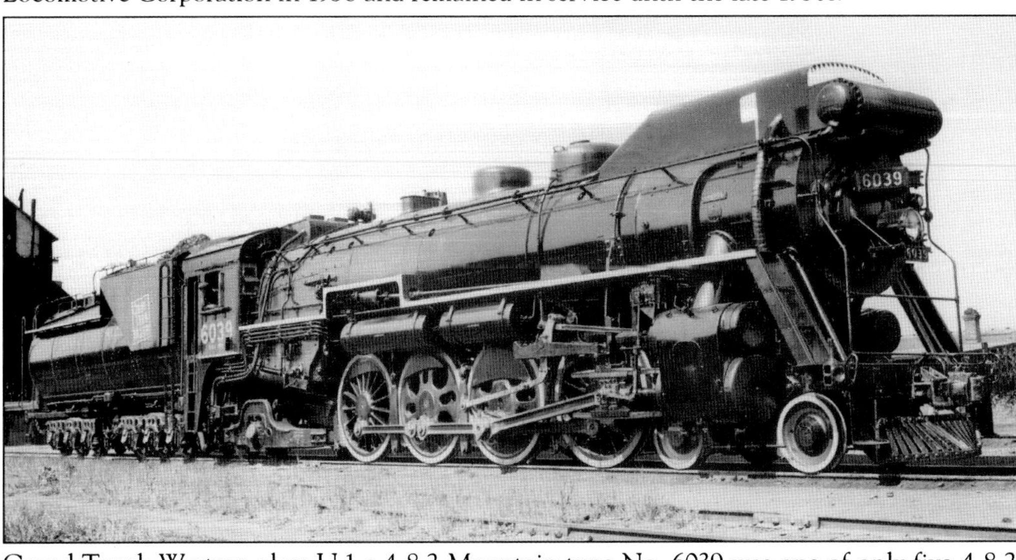

Grand Trunk Western class U-1-c 4-8-2 Mountain-type No. 6039 was one of only five 4-8-2s owned by the company. Built by the Baldwin Locomotive Works in 1925, it was equipped with 73-inch drivers and 26-inch-by-30-inch cylinders. When this photograph was taken at the Elsdon Yard roundhouse on September 21, 1944, it had been reequipped with disc drive wheels on its second and third drive axles.

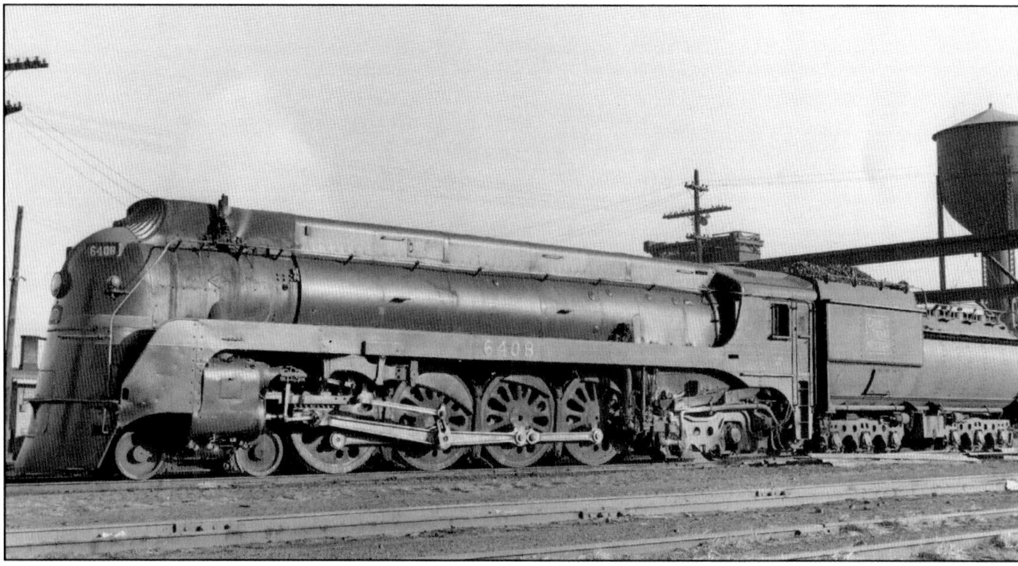

Grand Trunk Western class semi-streamlined U-4-b 4-8-4 Northern-type No. 6408 was laying over between assignments at the Elsdon Yard roundhouse on November 24, 1956, when this photograph was taken. The Lima Locomotive Corporation built the 6408 in 1938. It was equipped with 77-inch drive wheels and 24-inch-30-inch cylinders. This left-side view shows the position of the locomotive's whistle toward the front of the boiler.

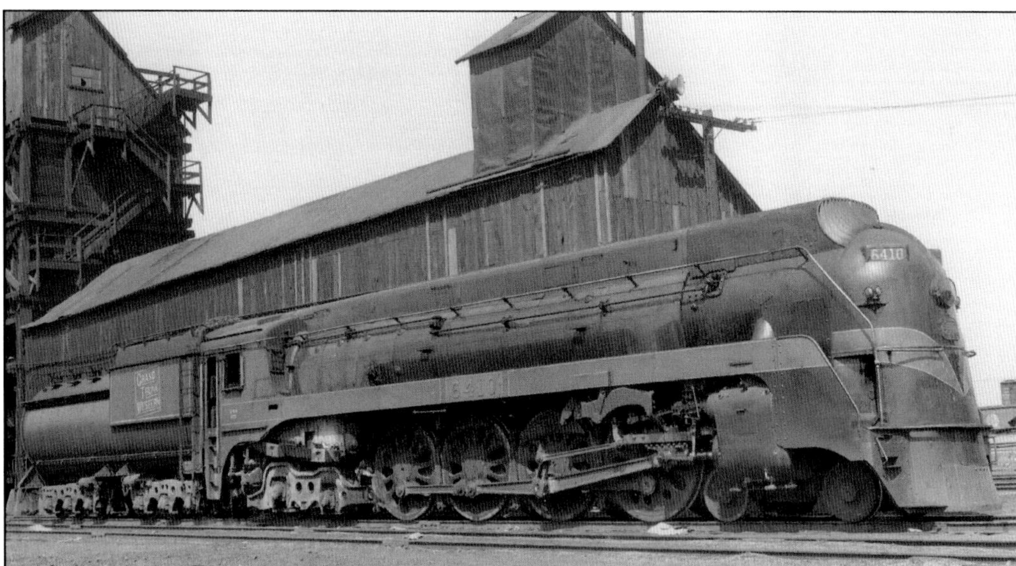

"Semi-streamlined" was the term used to describe the styling of Grand Trunk Western class U-4-b 4-8-4 Northern-type No. 6410. It was visiting the Elsdon Yard roundhouse on April 15, 1956, when this photograph was taken. The Lima Locomotive Corporation built the 6410 in 1938. Railroad engineers operated the locomotive throttle, brakes, whistle, and bell from the right side of the cab, shown here.

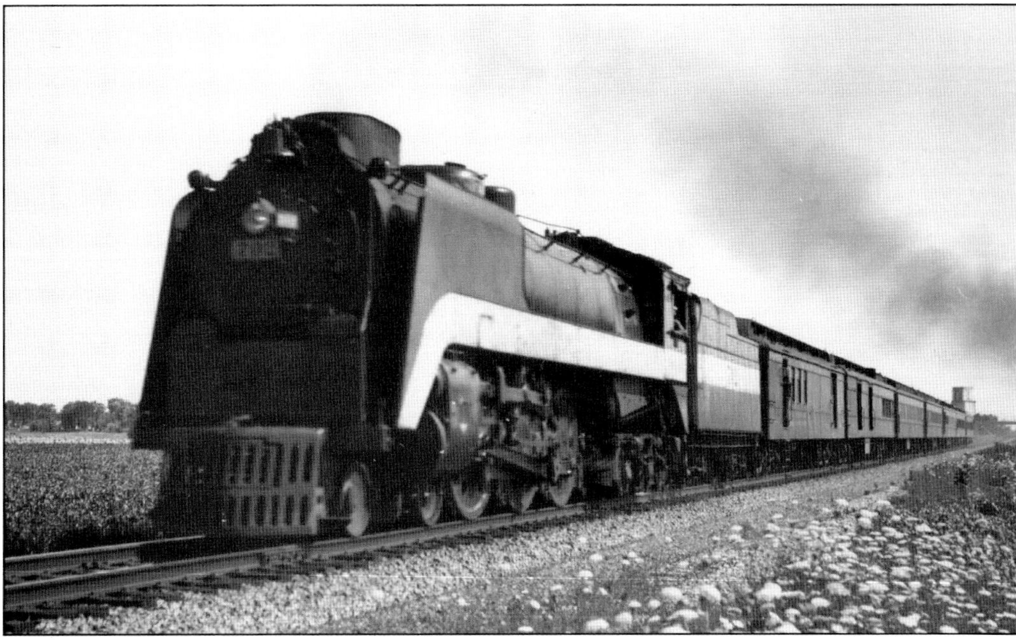

In the 1940s, the Wabash Railroad built five class P-1 semi-streamlined 4-6-4 Hudson-type passenger locomotives at its Decatur shops, using the boilers and tenders from retired class K-5 2-8-2 Mikado-type freight locomotives. They remained in revenue service until the mid-1950s. No. 702 is shown here at speed with train No. 10, the *Banner Blue*, en route from St. Louis to Dearborn Station in July 1947. (Courtesy of P. Stringham/William Raia Collection.)

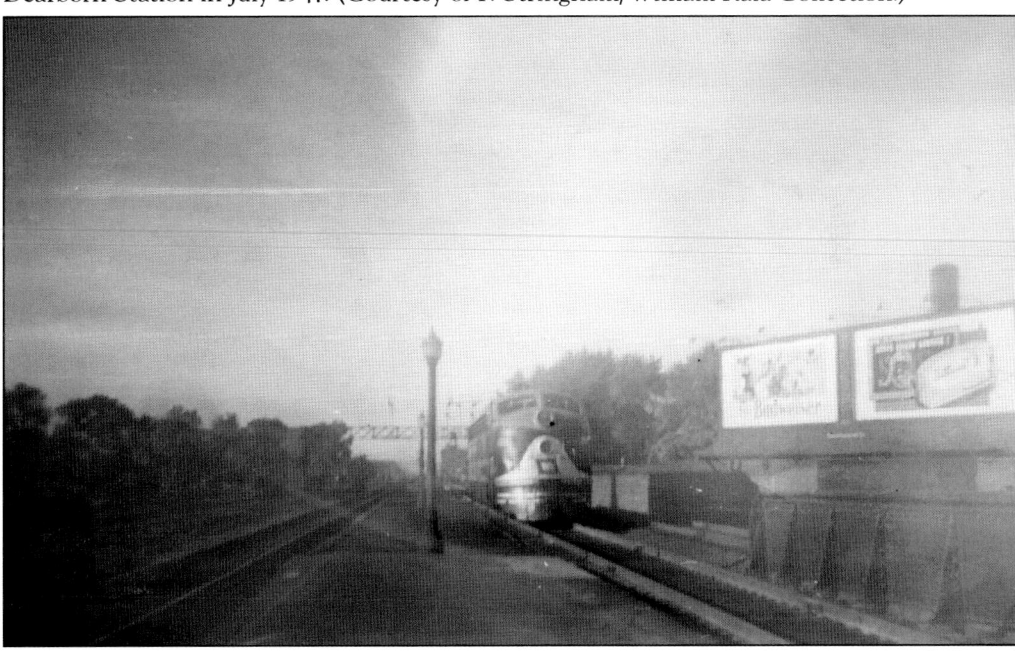

Another example of Bill Molony's early photograph efforts shows a Wabash diesel headed north toward Dearborn Station. It is pulling into the Englewood Station at Sixty-Third Street. Bill recalled that in the 1950s, there was still a drive-up ramp near Fifty-Seventh Street, built with beach sand when the tracks were elevated. It was used to haul milk cans up to the platform.

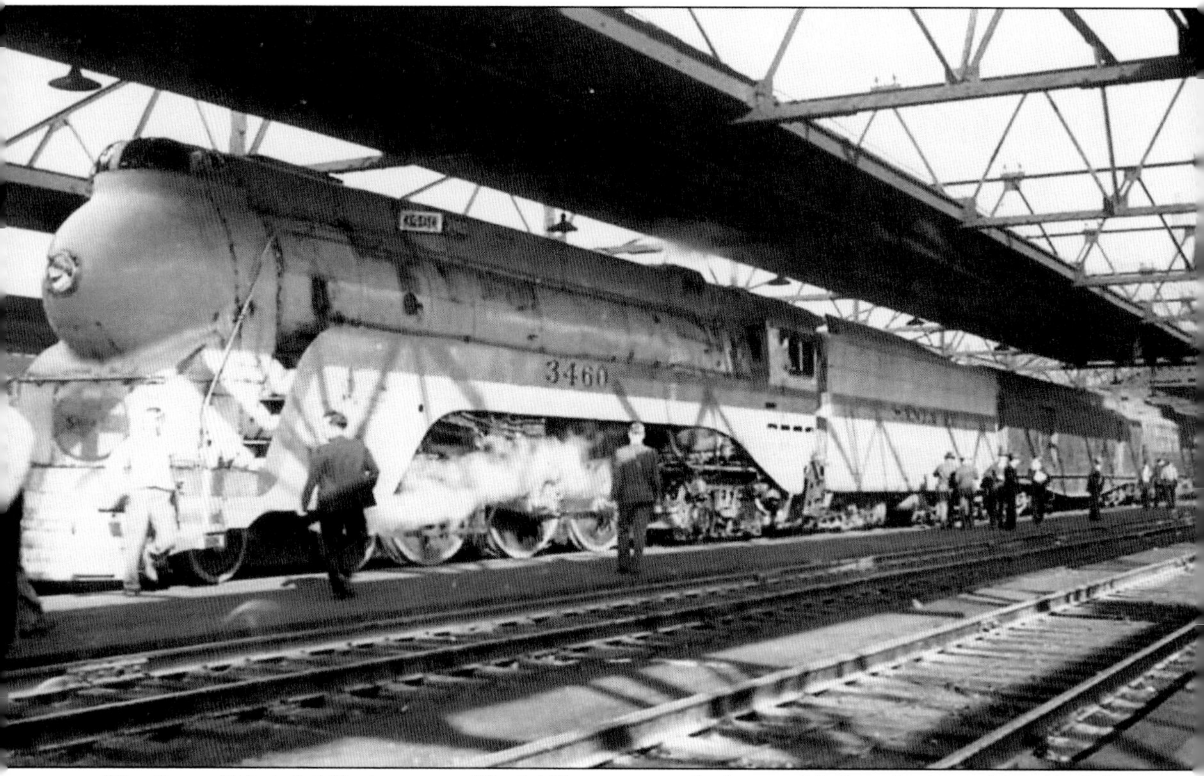

The Santa Fe's 4-6-4 Hudson-type No. 3460 was painted silver and light robin's-egg blue. Built by the Baldwin Locomotive Works in 1937 for service between Chicago and La Junta, Colorado, it was the Santa Fe's only streamlined steam locomotive and as such was featured extensively in the railroad's publicity. It is shown here—a little worse for wear—on a summer morning at Dearborn Station in Chicago, ready to depart with a heavyweight passenger train. The first car behind the engine is a heavyweight baggage car. Typically, the Santa Fe used coal-burning equipment between Kansas City and Chicago, switching to oil burners west of Kansas City because of the local availability of the two fuels in those regions. Santa Fe began buying diesels for passenger service in 1936, but the 3460-series locomotives were oil burners.

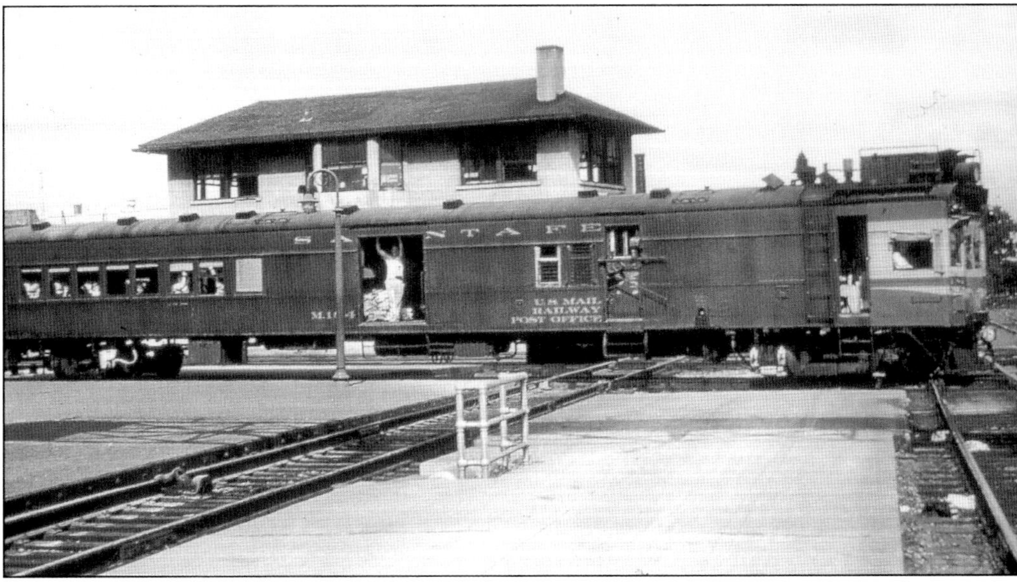

Atchison, Topeka & Santa Fe Railway diesel-electric motorcar No. M.184 operated as the nameless all-stops local passenger train between Dearborn Station in Chicago and Pekin, Illinois. Also known as a "doodlebug," it was built for the Santa Fe by the Pullman Car and Manufacturing Company in 1931. Its single 400-horsepower Caterpillar D-397 diesel engine powered two traction motors on the front truck. This single unit provided space for a railway post office, a compartment for railway express and baggage, and seating for 28 passengers.

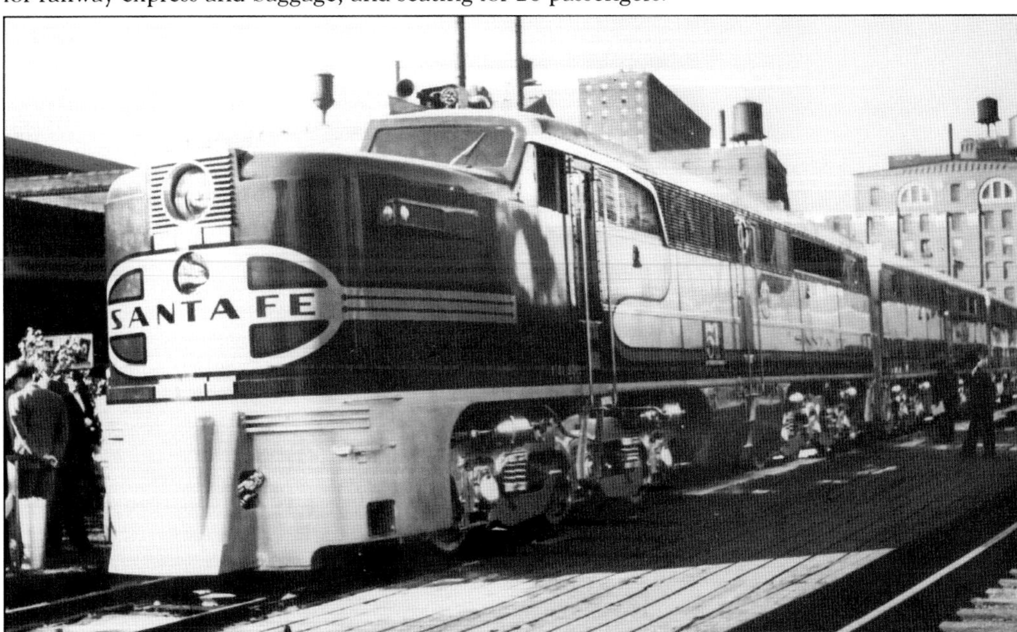

The Santa Fe Railroad exhibited its brand new American Locomotive Company class 51 PA-PB-PA streamlined passenger locomotives at the Chicago & Western Indiana Railroad's Dearborn Station in October 1946. The three units were originally rostered as No. 51L, No. 51A, and No. 51B but were later renumbered to 51L, 51A, and 51C. Each unit was equipped with ALCO's 244-series 16-cylinder prime mover rated at 2,000 horsepower.

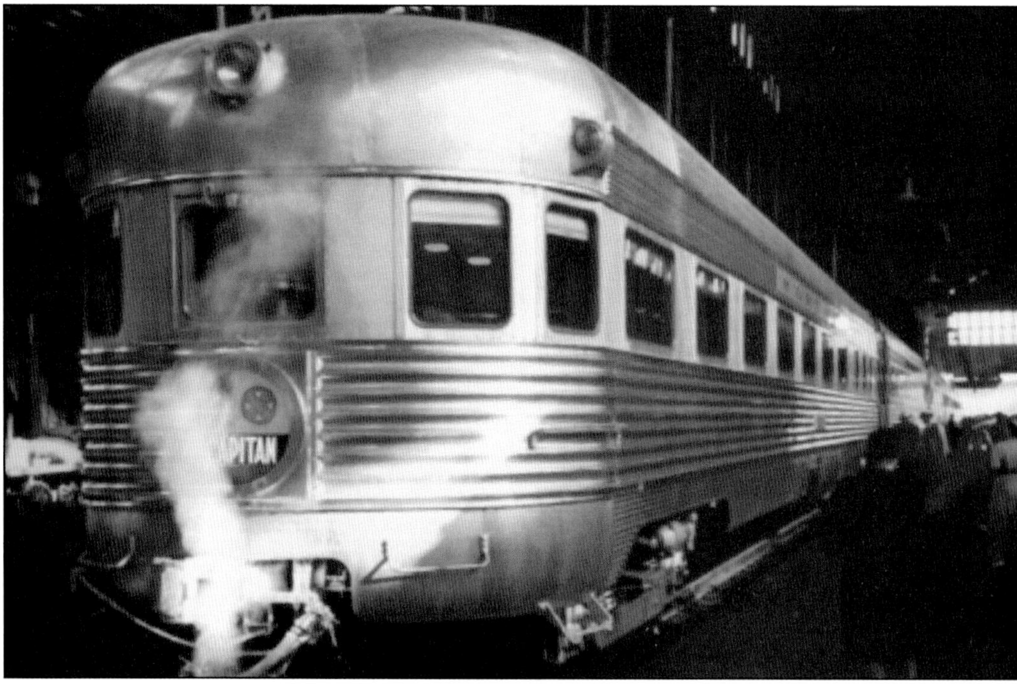

The Santa Fe put its new five-car *El Capitan* streamliner on exhibition at Dearborn Station in February 1938. The *El Capitan* was a deluxe extra-fare train for coach passengers only that operated twice a week between Chicago, Kansas City, and Los Angeles on the same fast schedule as the Santa Fe's premier, all-Pullman *Super Chief*. The Budd Company of Philadelphia constructed the train. (Courtesy of Richard J. Anderson.)

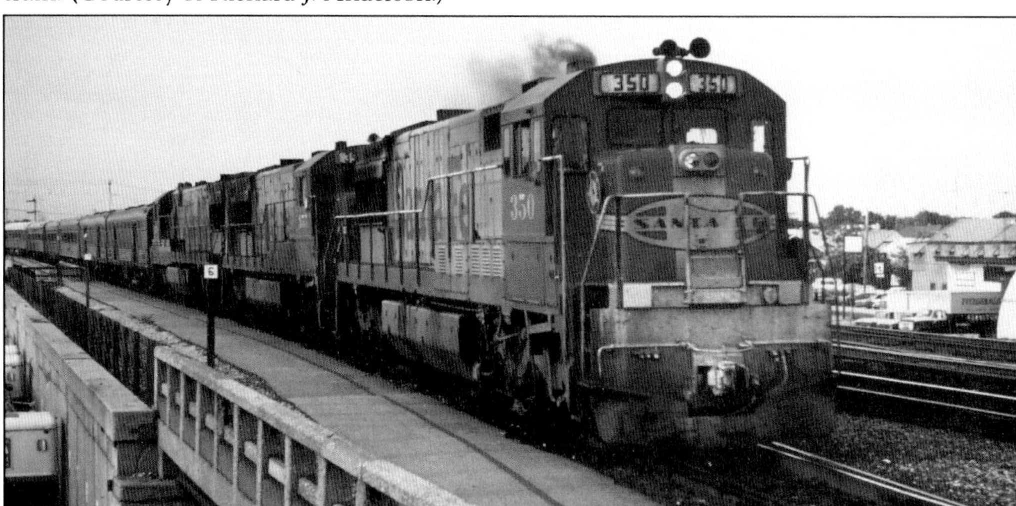

In 1966, the Atchison, Topeka & Santa Fe Railway purchased ten 2,800-horsepower U28CG passenger locomotives from General Electric Transportation. They were the first new passenger locomotives ordered by the Santa Fe since 1953 and were put in revenue service on long-distance passenger trains operating out of Dearborn Station. Shown here are three of the Santa Fe's U28CG locomotives arriving at Joliet Union Station from Dearborn with train No. 15, the westbound *Texas Chief* to Kansas City, Fort Worth, and Houston, in September 1969.

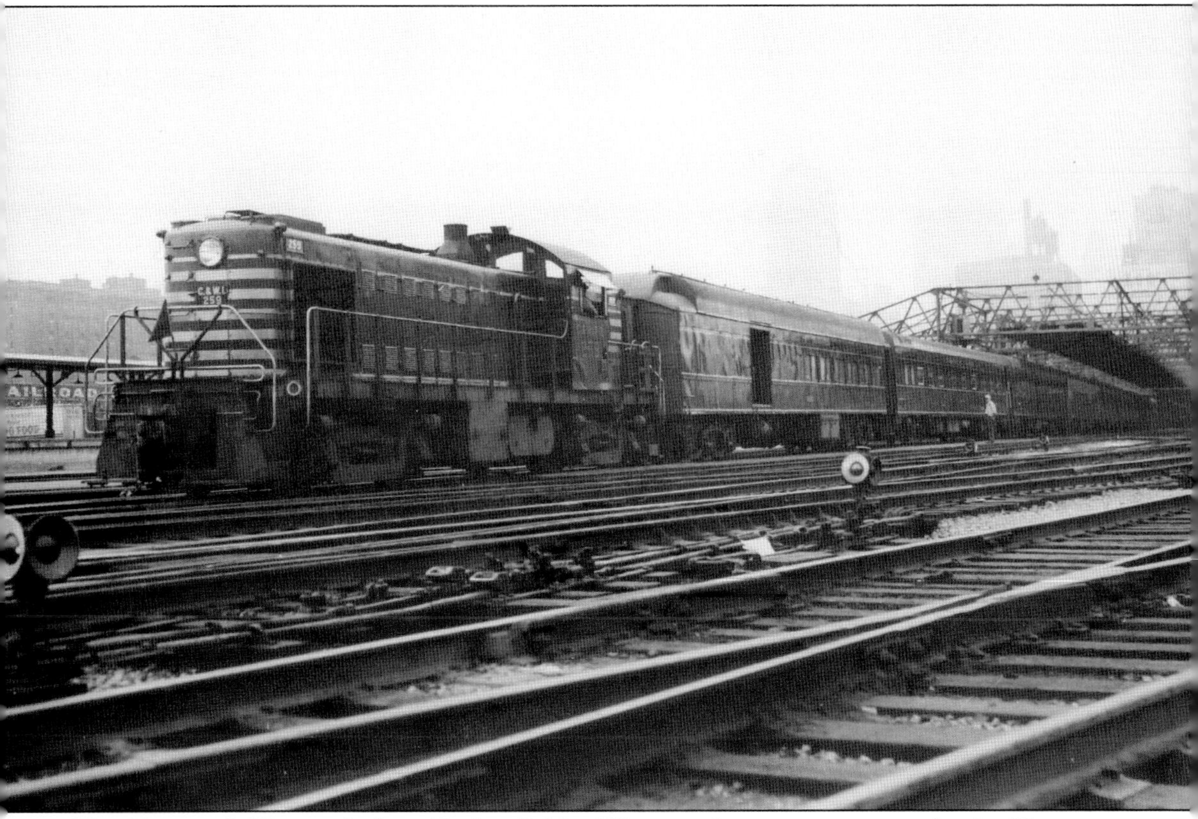

The Chicago & Western Indiana Railroad's No. 259 is switching passenger cars for the Chicago & Eastern Illinois Railroad at Dearborn Station in 1956. The 259 was one of 10 model RS-1 road switcher diesel locomotives that the C&WI purchased from the American Locomotive Company in 1949 and 1950. Each one was equipped with ALCO's six-cylinder 539 series prime mover, rated at 1,000 horsepower.

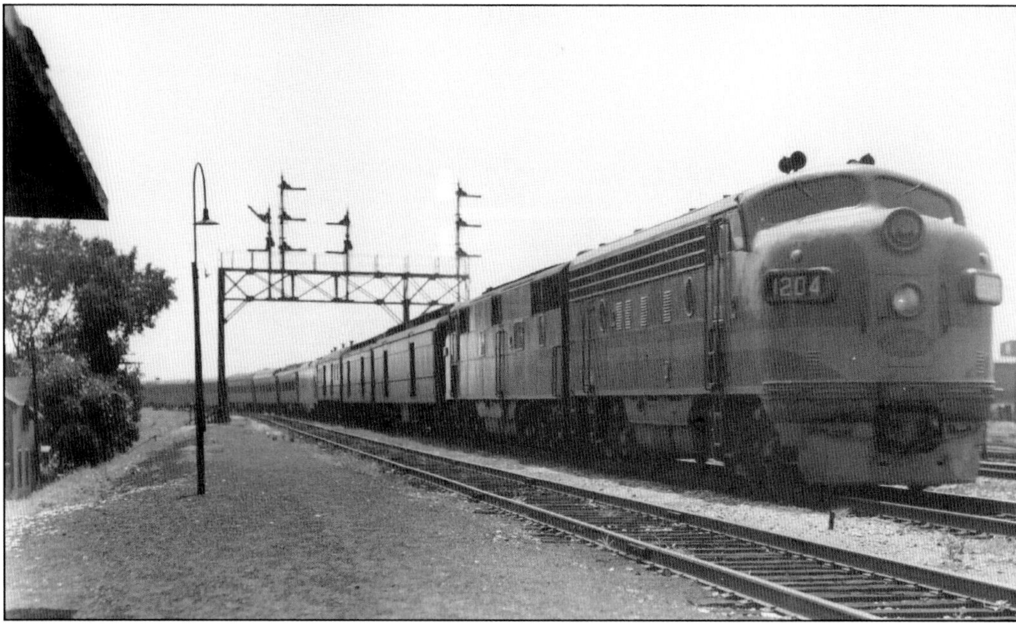

The Chicago & Eastern Illinois Railroad's train No. 92, the northbound *Dixie Limited*, is at the Chicago & Western Indiana Railroad's Englewood Station at Sixty-Third and Wallace Streets around 1948. Powered by the C&EI's E8A No. 1204 and a trailing E7A, the *Dixie Limited* operated daily between Jacksonville, Florida, and Chicago. It featured baggage, mail and express cars, coaches, a dining car, Pullman sleeping cars, and an observation lounge car.

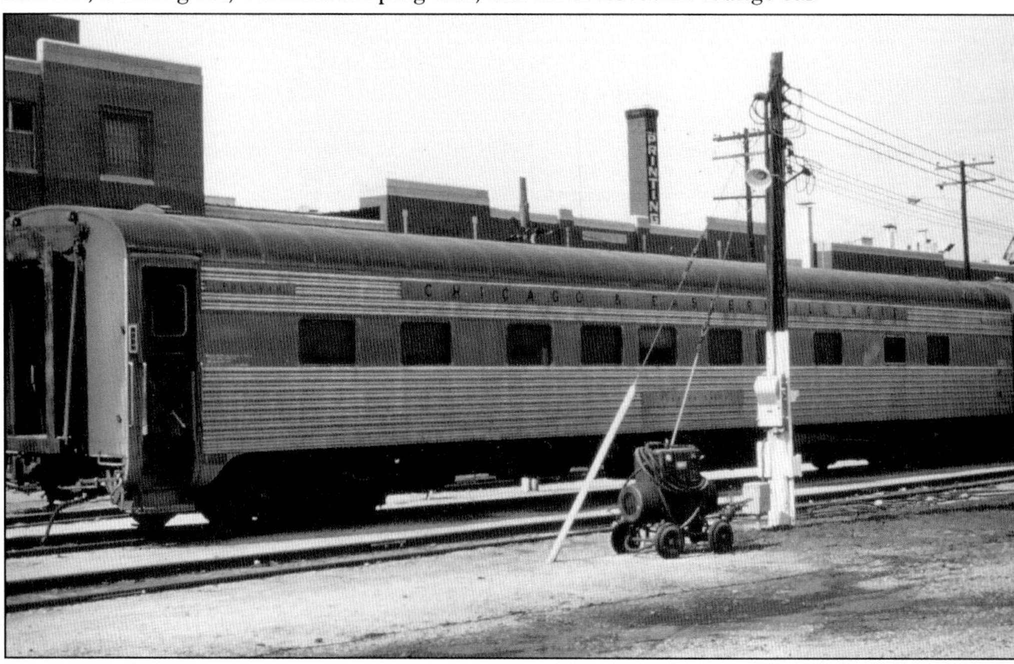

Streamlined cars like this one, being serviced at Dearborn Station, were used to equip the Chicago & Eastern Illinois Railroad's day trains that operated between Chicago and Evansville, Indiana, and Chicago and southern Illinois. The C&EI modernized its passenger car fleet in the post–World War II era with the purchase of 11 lightweight, stainless steel coaches.

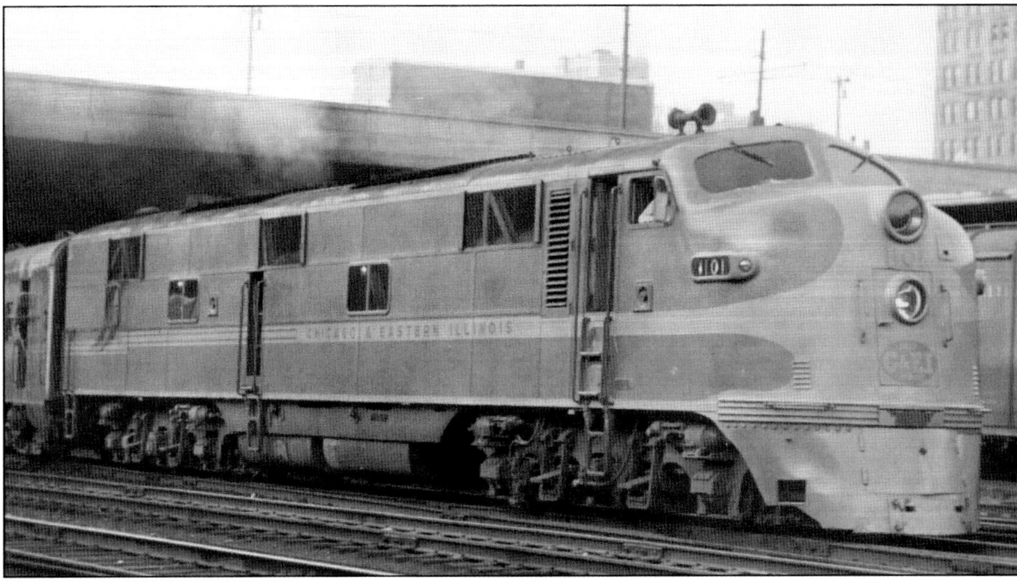

This is Chicago & Eastern Illinois Railroad's EMD E7A No. 1101 ready to depart from Dearborn Station in August 1948 with C&EI train No. 25, the southbound *Meadowlark* bound for Cypress in southern Illinois. This streamlined train was equipped with unreserved reclining seat coaches and a grill-lounge car but did not accept checked baggage.

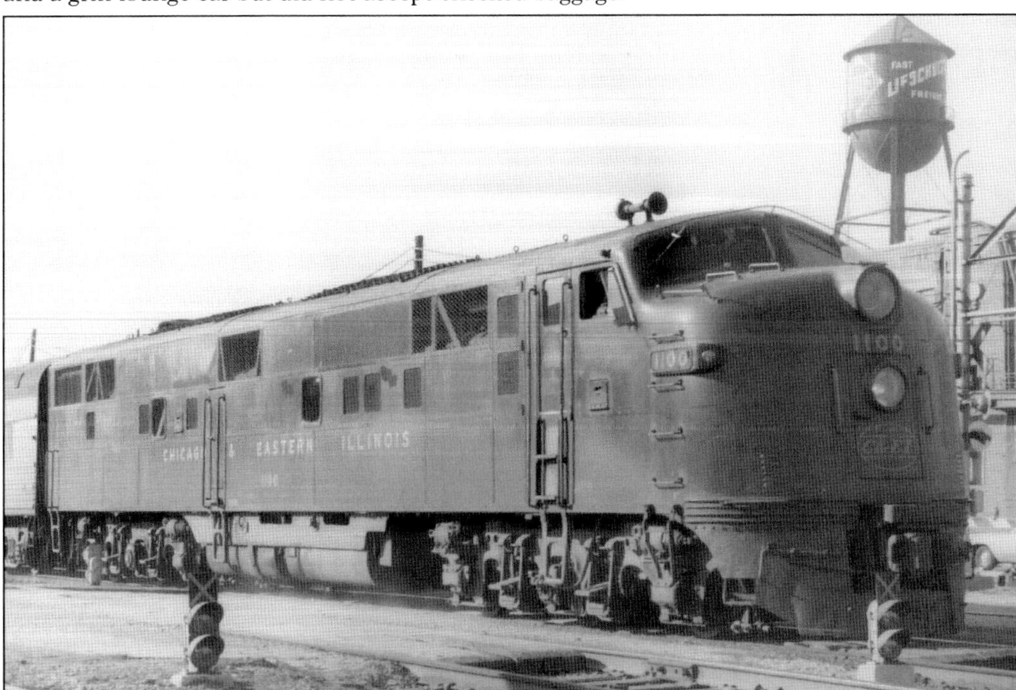

Chicago & Eastern Illinois E7A No. 1100, shown here at Dearborn Station in October 1966, was constructed by the Electro-Motive Division of General Motors (EMD) and delivered to the C&EI on May 15, 1946. This locomotive was powered by two of EMD's 12-cylinder 567A prime movers, rated at 1,000 horsepower each, and rode on EMD's standard three-axle A-1-A passenger car trucks.

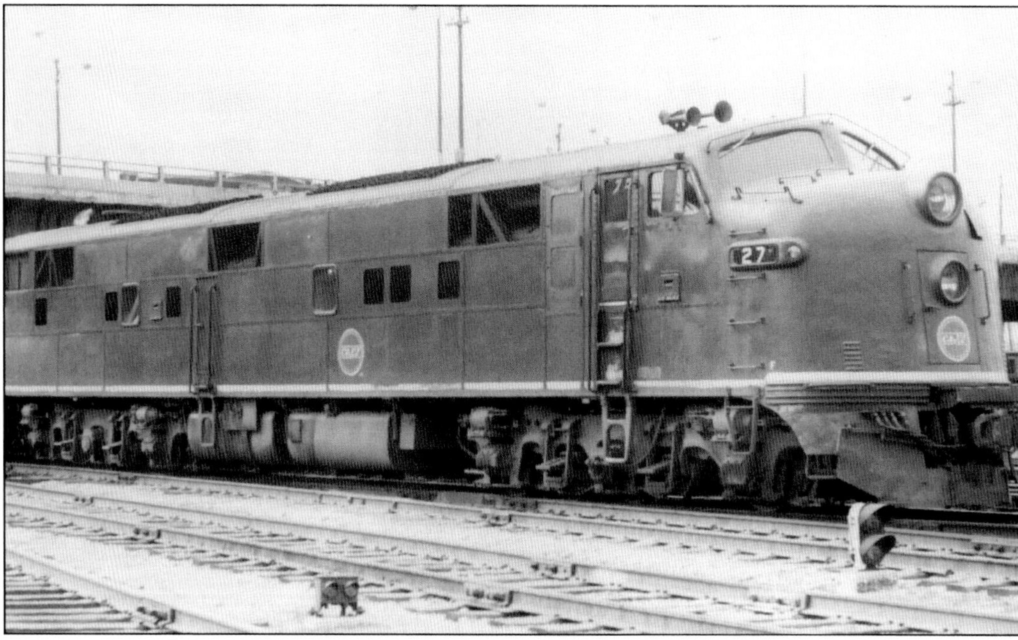

In May 1967, the Interstate Commerce Commission awarded the Missouri Pacific Railroad Company (MoPac) control of the Chicago & Eastern Illinois Railroad. One of the first actions of the MoPac was a locomotive renumbering program. C&EI E7A No. 1100, shown above, became C&EI No. 27. Show here at Dearborn Station in March 1969, it was later sold to the Louisville & Nashville Railroad and became L&N No. 798.

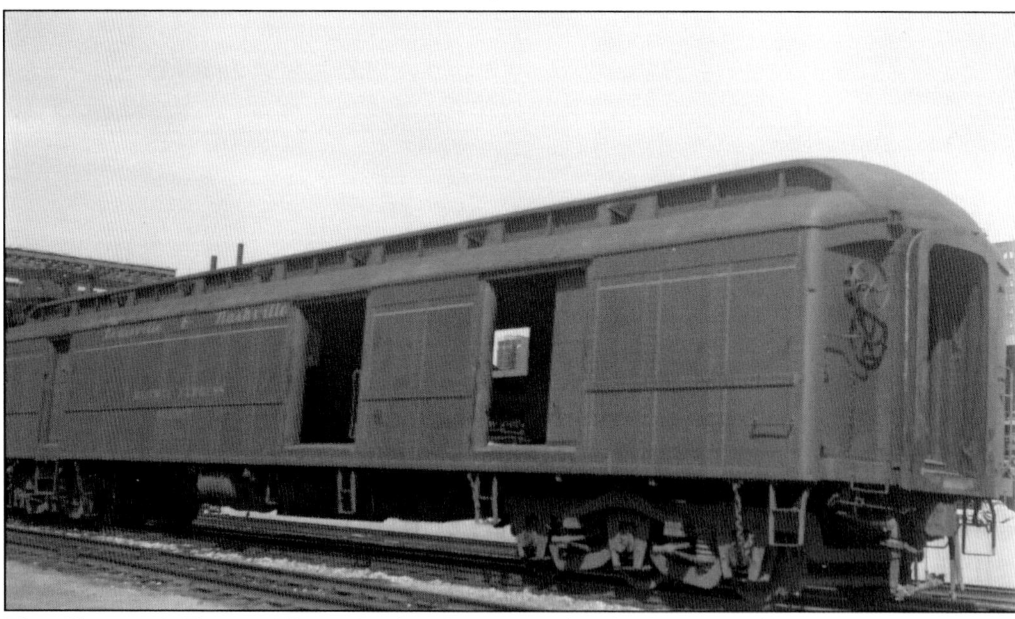

The Chicago & Eastern Illinois Railroad connected with the Louisville & Nashville Railroad at Evansville, Indiana, and it was not unusual for L&N passenger cars to operate into Dearborn Station in C&EI trains. Shown here is L&N heavyweight 70-foot Railway Express Agency and baggage car No. 1370 at Dearborn in Chicago in 1961. This car had originally been built as a Railway Post Office car.

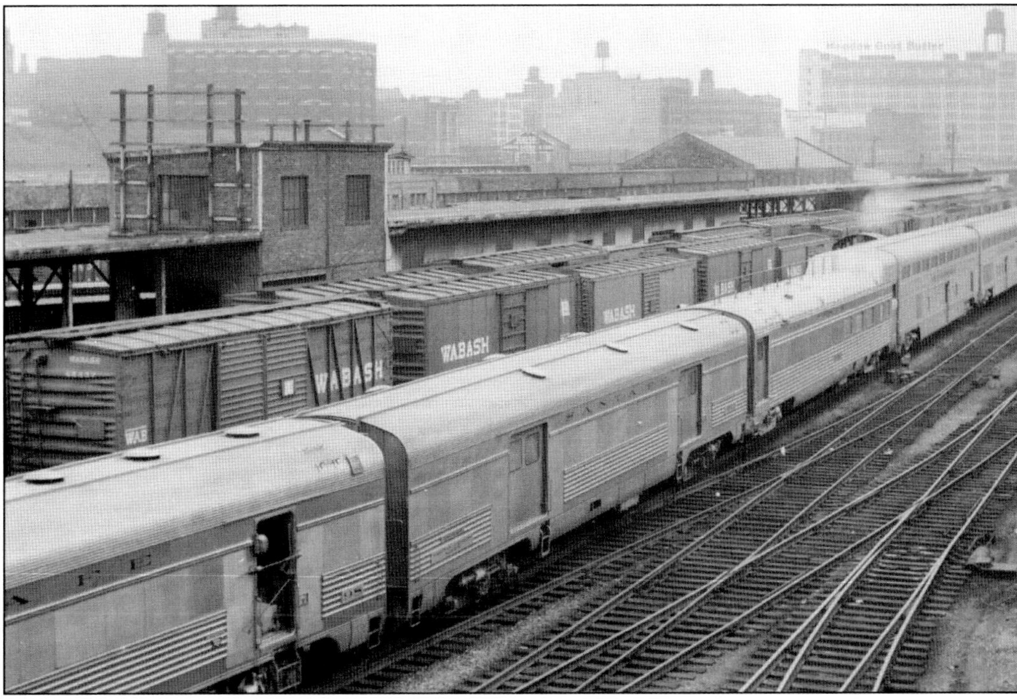

A group of Wabash Railroad boxcars were on a siding south of Roosevelt Road in the late 1950s when the Atchison, Topeka & Santa Fe Railway's train No. 22, the eastbound *El Capitan* was arriving in Chicago after its 2,226-mile trip from Los Angeles. Boxcars such as these were used by the Wabash for less-than-carload-lot freight shipments.

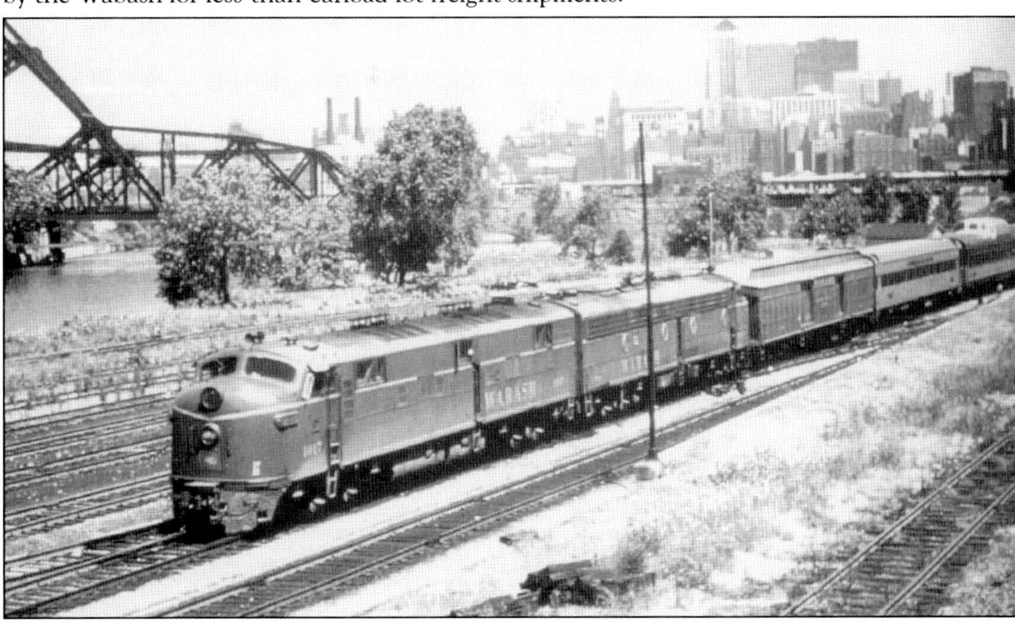

The Wabash Railroad's streamlined *Blue Bird* departed from Dearborn station at 4:25 p.m., arriving at St. Louis at 9:50 p.m. This deluxe train featured dome chair cars equipped with reclining seats, a "Coffee Shop Club" for coach passengers, a dining car with a cocktail lounge, a dome parlor-lounge car, and dome observation parlor car equipped with a drawing room.

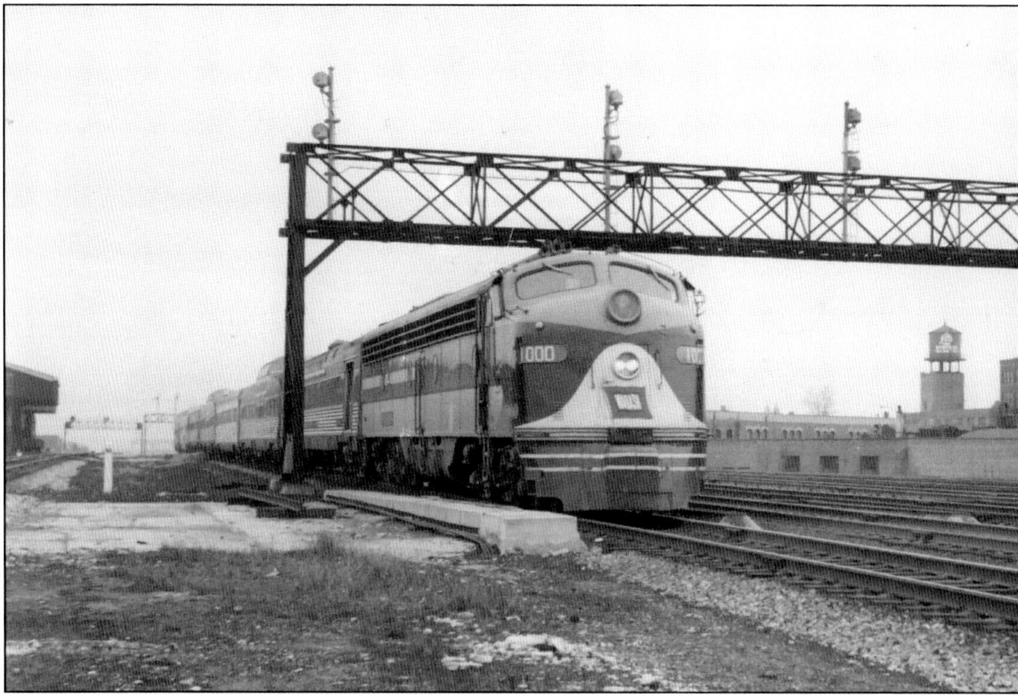

The Wabash Railroad's *Banner Blue*, shown here on the C&WI tracks northbound at Twenty-First Street, was its streamlined day train that operated between Chicago and St. Louis via Decatur in the post–World War II era. It offered checked baggage, reclining seat chair cars, and a dining-lounge car and also carried a Pullman sleeping car that continued on from St. Louis to Dallas and San Antonio over connecting railroads.

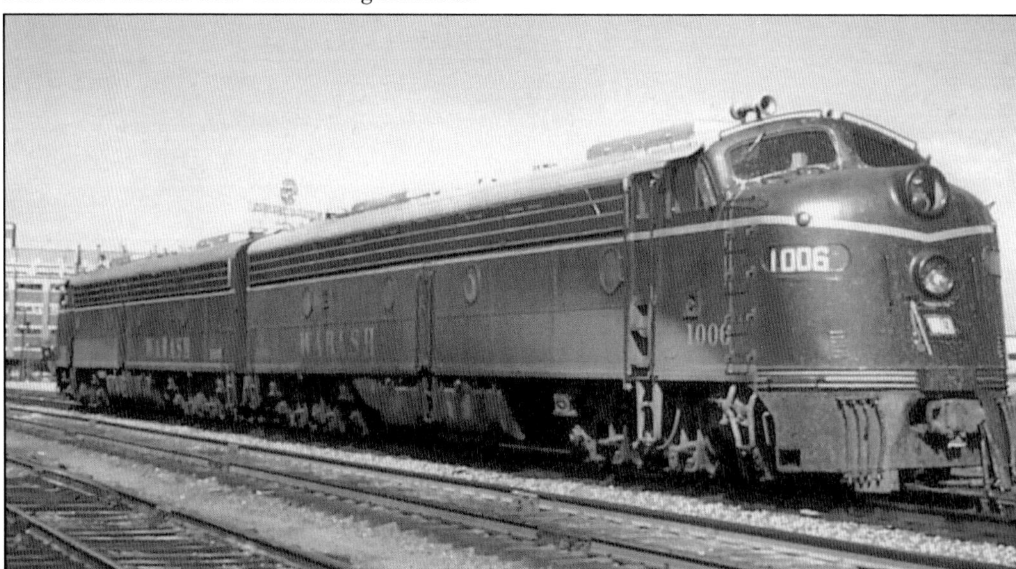

The Wabash Railroad purchased a total of 14 E8A diesel locomotives from the Electro-Motive Division of General Motors between 1949 and 1953 for use on its passenger trains. Wabash No. 1006 and one of its mates are shown in Chicago in this undated photograph. Each unit was equipped with two of EMD's 12-cylinder 567B diesel engines, rated at 1,125 horsepower each.

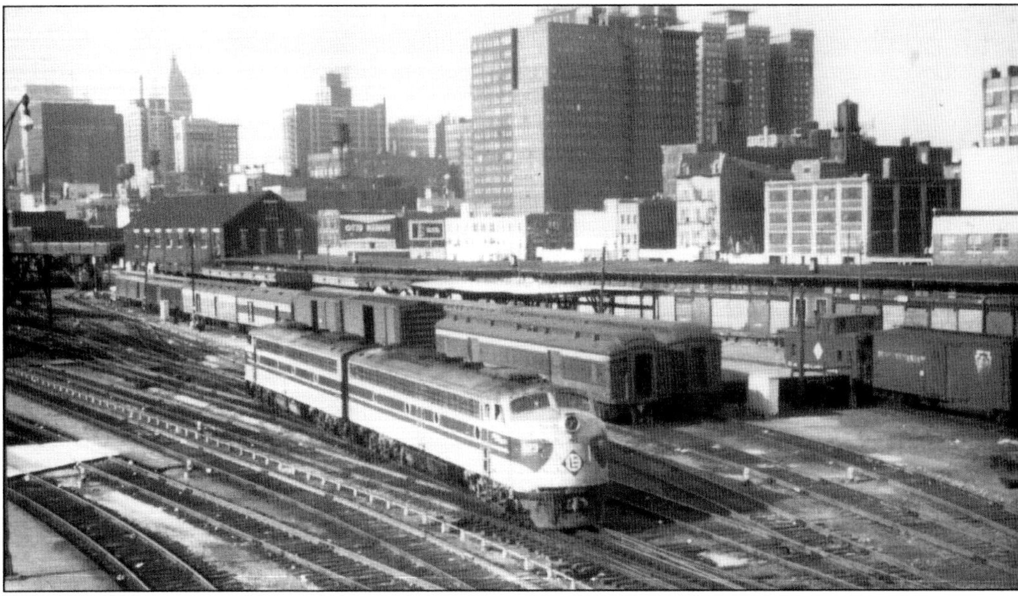

Erie-Lackawanna Railroad (EL) E8A No. 823 and its mate are shown above in May 1965 easing into Dearborn Station ready to couple onto EL train No. 2, the *Phoebe Snow.* The 823 was one of 14 E8A passenger diesel locomotives built for the Erie Railroad in the first three months of 1951. In the background to the right can be seen an Erie-Lackawanna steel caboose coupled to two Pennsylvania Railroad express cars. In the photograph below, E8A No. 823 and its mate are outbound for Hoboken, New Jersey, pulling the *Phoebe Snow,* which was equipped with mail and express cars, coaches, a diner, a sleeping car, and an observation lounge car. It was scheduled to depart from Chicago at 6:30 p.m. Central Standard Time and arrive at Hoboken 23 hours later at 6:30 p.m. Eastern Standard Time. This train was discontinued as of November 27, 1966.

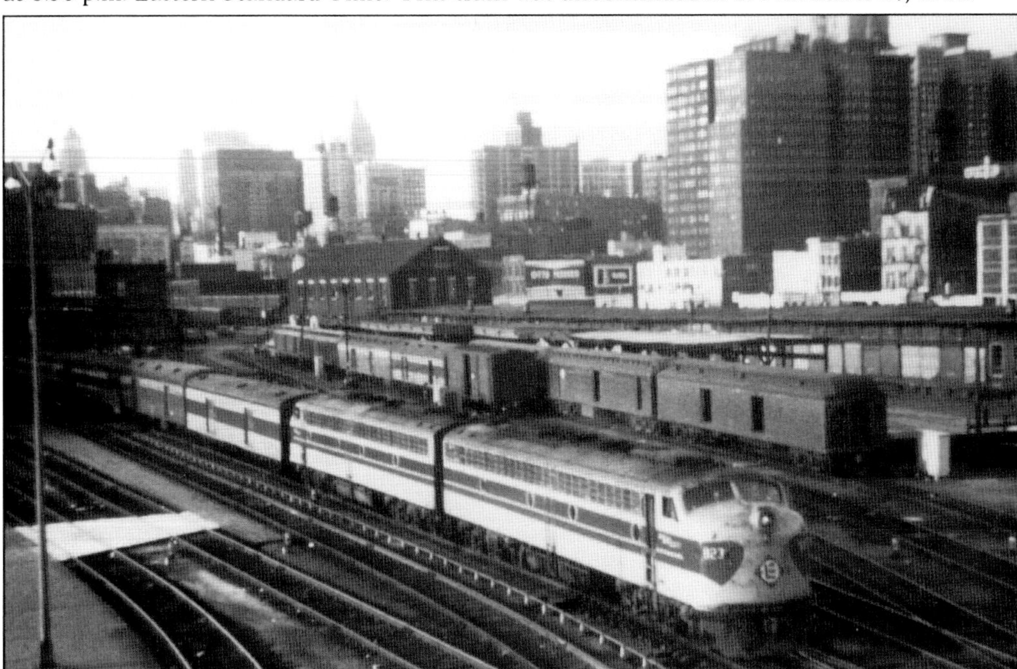

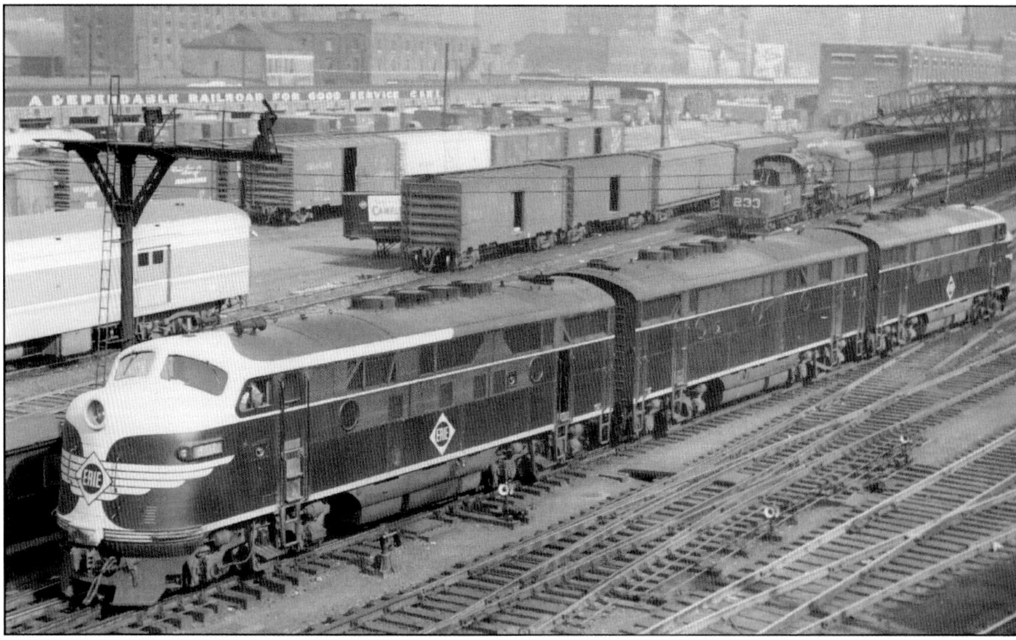

The Erie Railroad purchased its last new steam passenger locomotive in 1926, and it began ordering new diesel passenger locomotives like these immediately after World War II. The Electro-Motive Division of General Motors delivered this three-unit F3A-F3B-F3A set of locomotives to the Erie in November 1947. Each unit was powered by EMD's 16-cylinder 567B series prime mover, rated at 1,500 horsepower. (Courtesy of John Krause.)

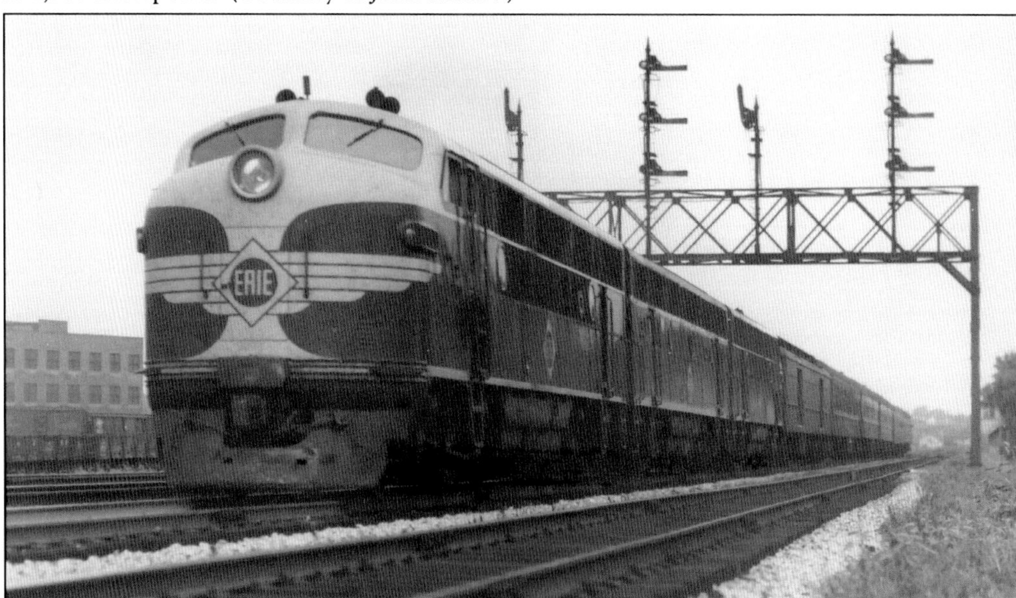

The Erie Railroad's diesel-powered train No. 6, the *Lake Cities*, shown here on the Chicago & Western Indiana Railroad's tracks at Eighty-First Street in 1949, departed every morning from Dearborn Station at 9:55 and arrived at Jersey City, New Jersey, the next morning at 7:50. This air-conditioned heavyweight train was equipped with individual reclining seat coaches, a diner-lounge car, and a 10-roomette, 6–double bedroom Pullman sleeping car. (Courtesy of Fred C. Stoes.)

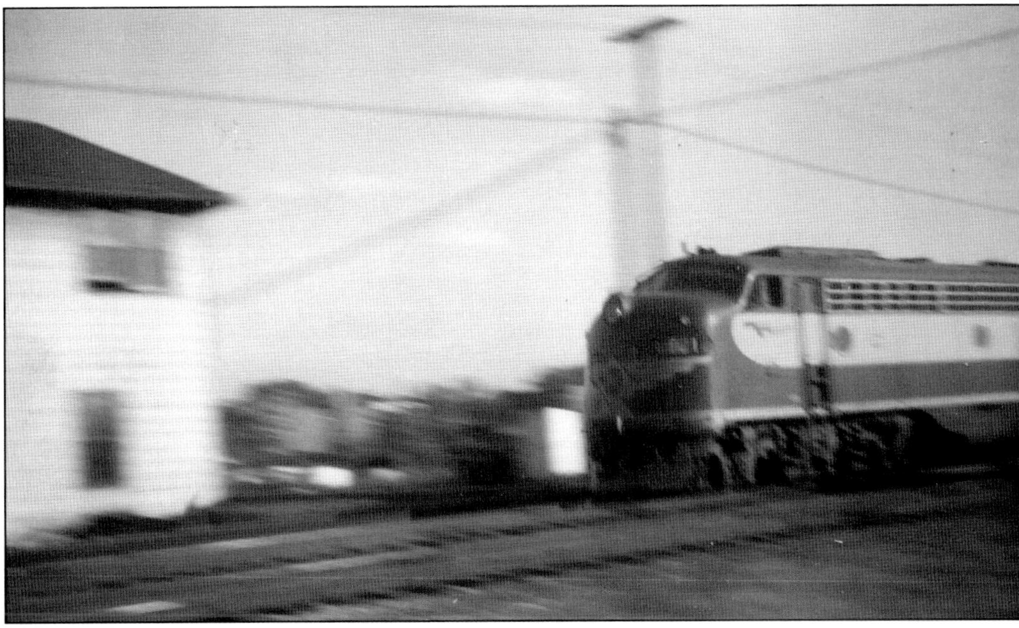

Another of young Bill Molony's photographs, taken in August 1956, shows the Erie's *Lake Cities Limited* inbound from Hoboken on C&WI tracks at the Ford interlocking tower, which was located between Fifty-Eighth and Fifty-Ninth Streets. The C&WI crossed the Pennsylvania Railroad's Englewood connecting line at this location.

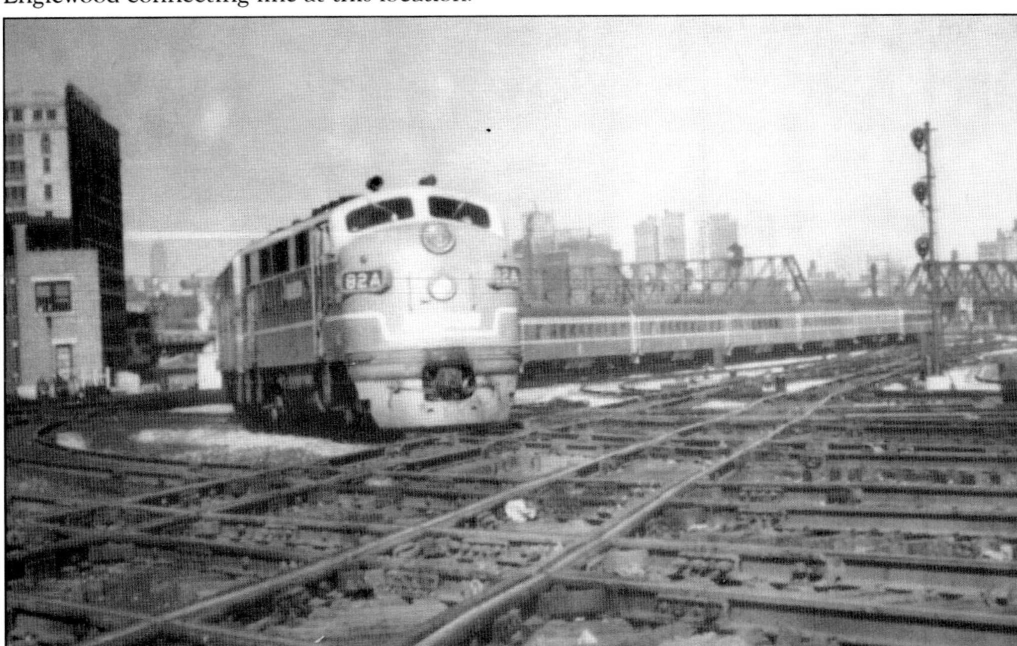

This particular train is No. 5, the *Thoroughbred*, the Monon Railroad's train that ran every afternoon from Dearborn Station in Chicago to Union Station in Louisville, Kentucky. It featured reclining seat coaches and an observation dining-parlor car. The Monon also purchased new F3A passenger diesel locomotives from EMD for its new streamlined passenger trains. (Courtesy of Norman G. Stockdale Jr.)

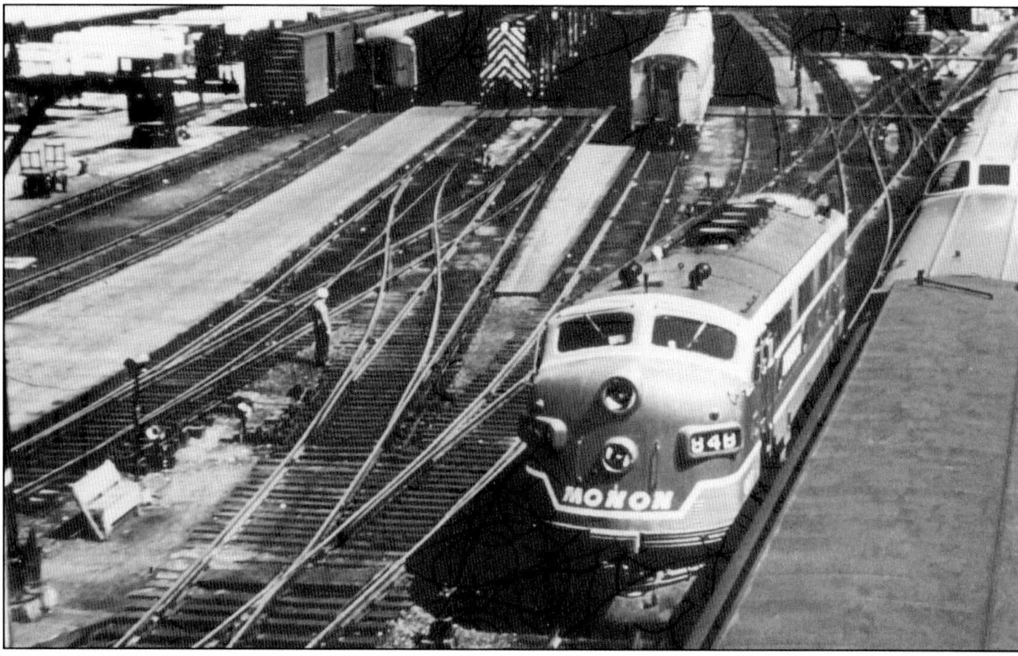

This Monon Railroad EMD F7A is backing into Dearborn Station in June 1961 and will be coupling on to its assigned passenger train. The train had been placed in the station earlier by a Chicago & Western Indiana Railroad RS-1 switch engine. The locomotive in the background is an Atchison, Topeka & Santa Fe Railway switch engine.

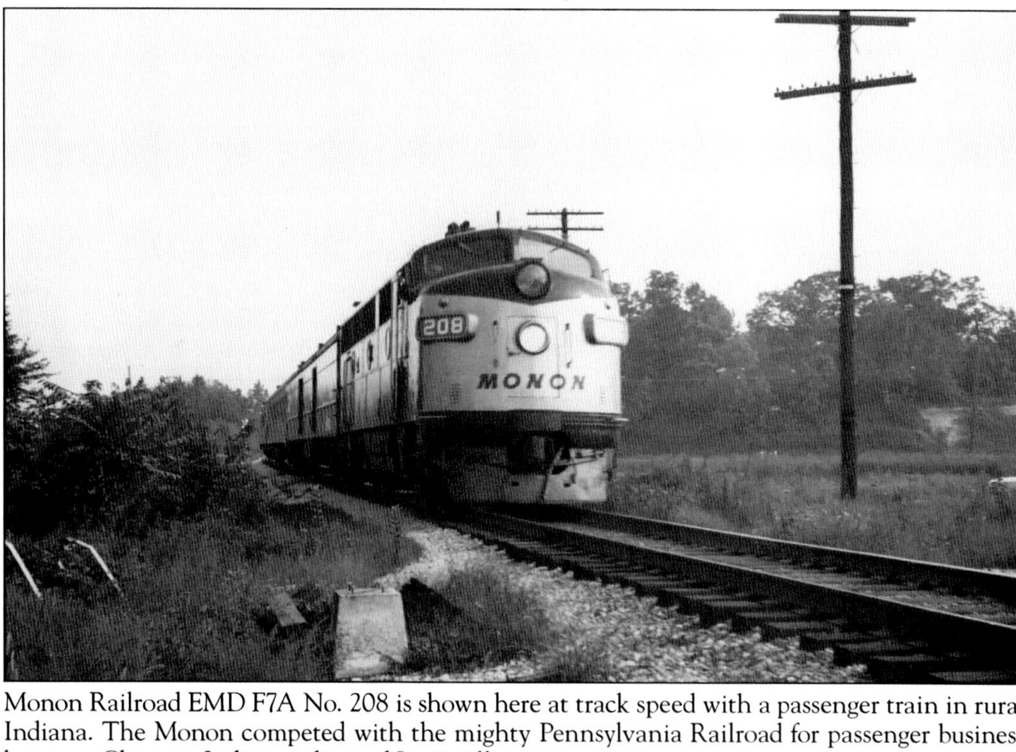

Monon Railroad EMD F7A No. 208 is shown here at track speed with a passenger train in rural Indiana. The Monon competed with the mighty Pennsylvania Railroad for passenger business between Chicago, Indianapolis, and Louisville.

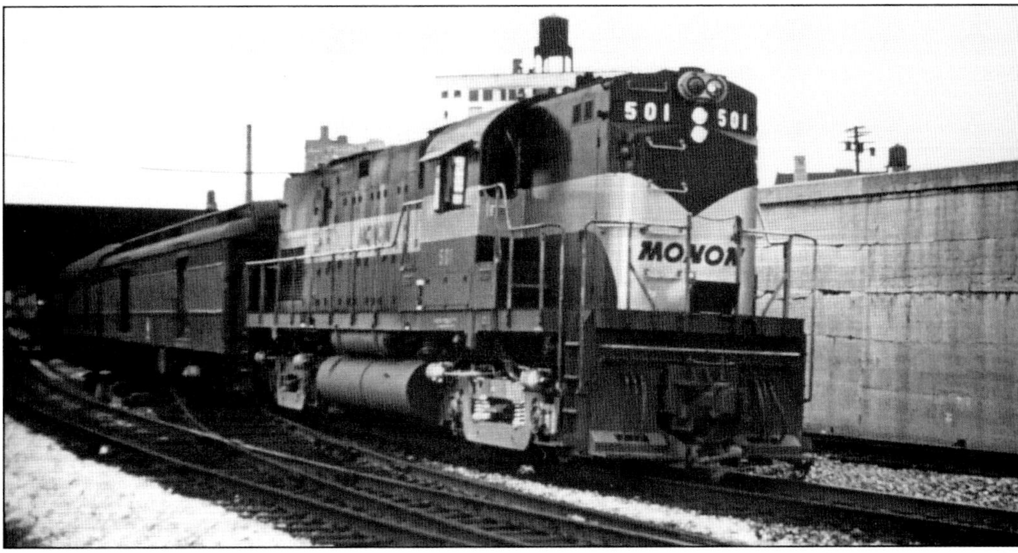

In 1966, the American Locomotive Company delivered two new passenger locomotives to the Monon. They were ALCO's Century 420 road switch engines and were equipped with 12-cylinder 251C prime movers, rated at 2,000 horsepower. Monon Railroad C-420 No. 501 is shown here in Chicago in June 1967. The high nose contained a steam generator that was used to provide heat to the passenger cars.

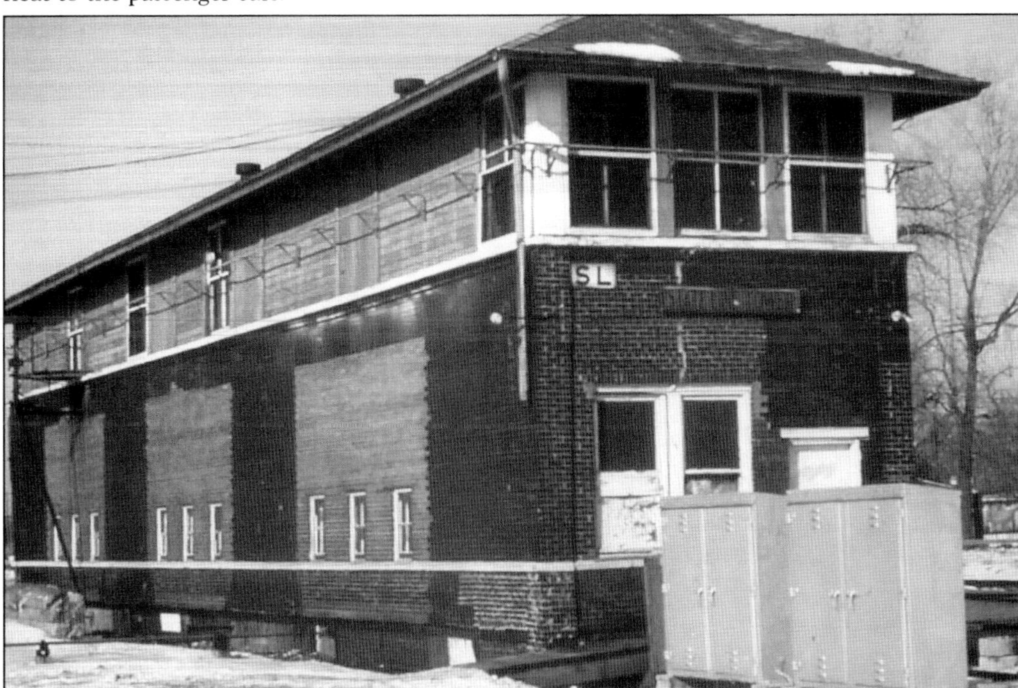

In 1956, the C&WI installed an illuminated board for each interlocking track circuit and each approach circuit at its State Line interlocking tower at the Indiana-Illinois border. The plant was still operated by C&WI personnel on a 24-hour/7-day-a-week schedule. In the late 1980s, however, the C&WI turned the operation over to the Indiana Harbor Belt Railroad Company. (Courtesy of Hammond Public Library.)

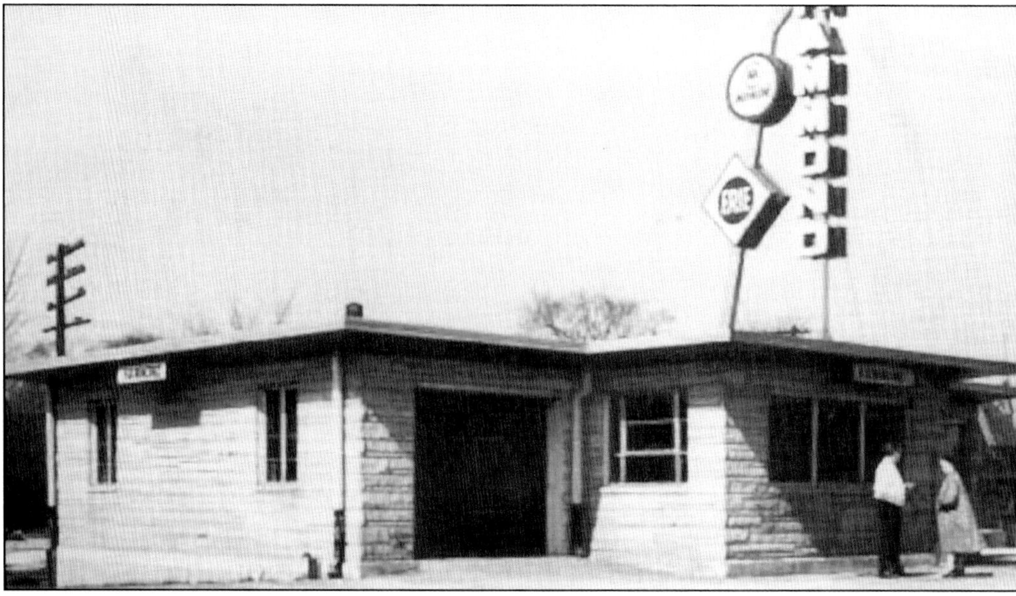

The Monon and Erie Railroads shared this post–World War II replacement station in South Hammond. From here, the Monon tracks headed south to Lowell, Indiana, while the Erie right-of-way headed southeast to Griffith. Each railroad had previously had its own station in downtown Hammond. Though smaller than the earlier stations, it was an improvement for passengers, especially with ample parking space for automobiles. (Courtesy of Hammond Public Library.)

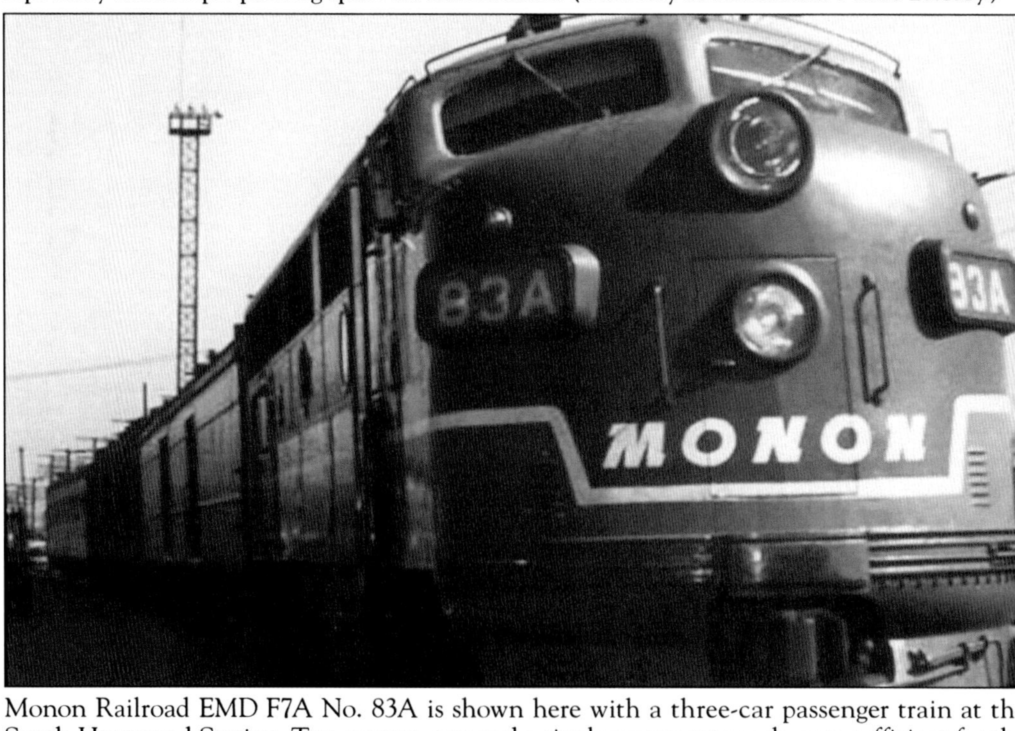

Monon Railroad EMD F7A No. 83A is shown here with a three-car passenger train at the South Hammond Station. Two express cars and a single passenger coach were sufficient for the company's business that day. The cart on the left is either waiting to unload an express car or has just deposited the day's freight into it. (Courtesy of Hammond Public Library.)

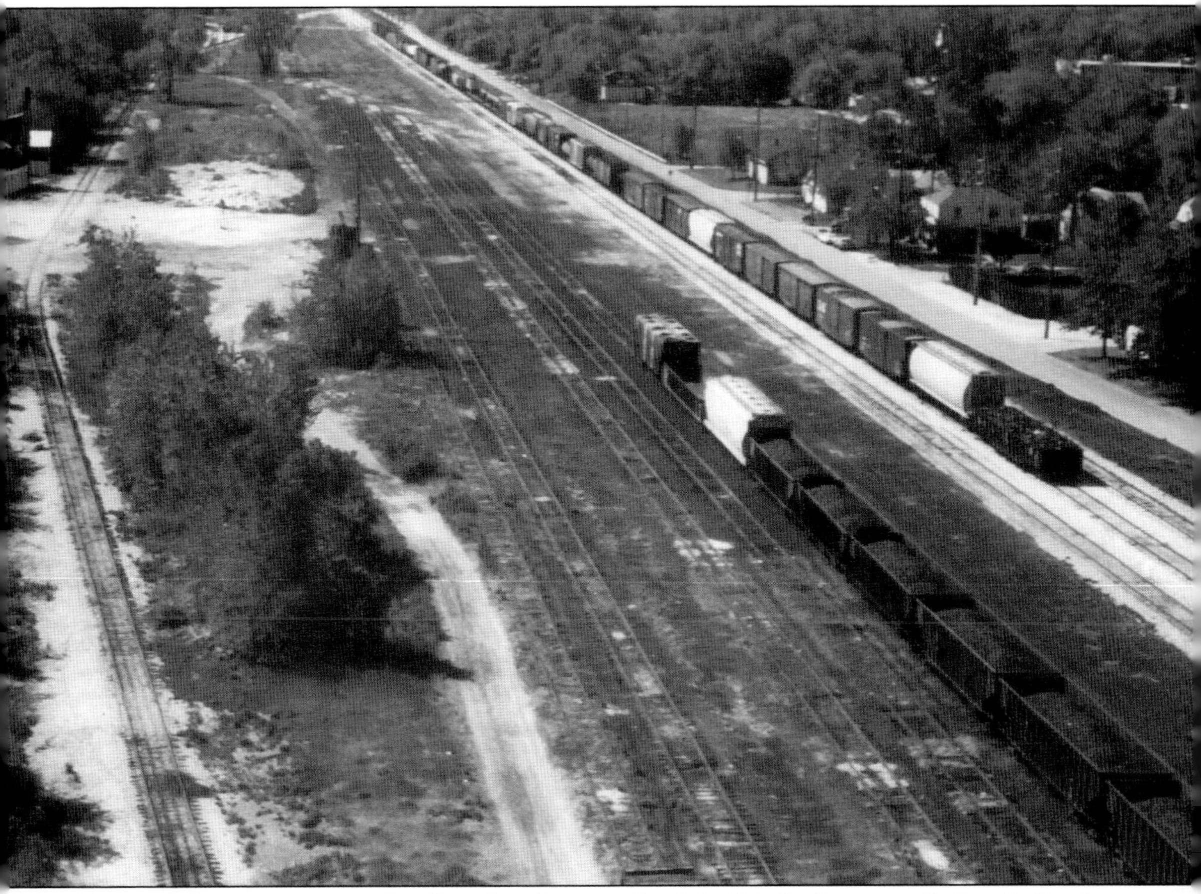

Not much business was in sight when this photograph of the Erie-Lackawanna Railroad's South Hammond Yard was taken from the Hammond water tower south of 173rd Street. In its heyday, the Erie yard had over 11 miles of track and an eight-locomotive roundhouse. Nearby had been a coal dump with bins that could hold up to 200 tons of coal. Head-end business in downtown Chicago was just a memory, and the mills on Chicago's southeast side had passed their post–World War II prime. Time was running out for the Erie-Lackawanna, as seen by the scarcity of freight cars in the yard. (Courtesy of Hammond Public Library.)

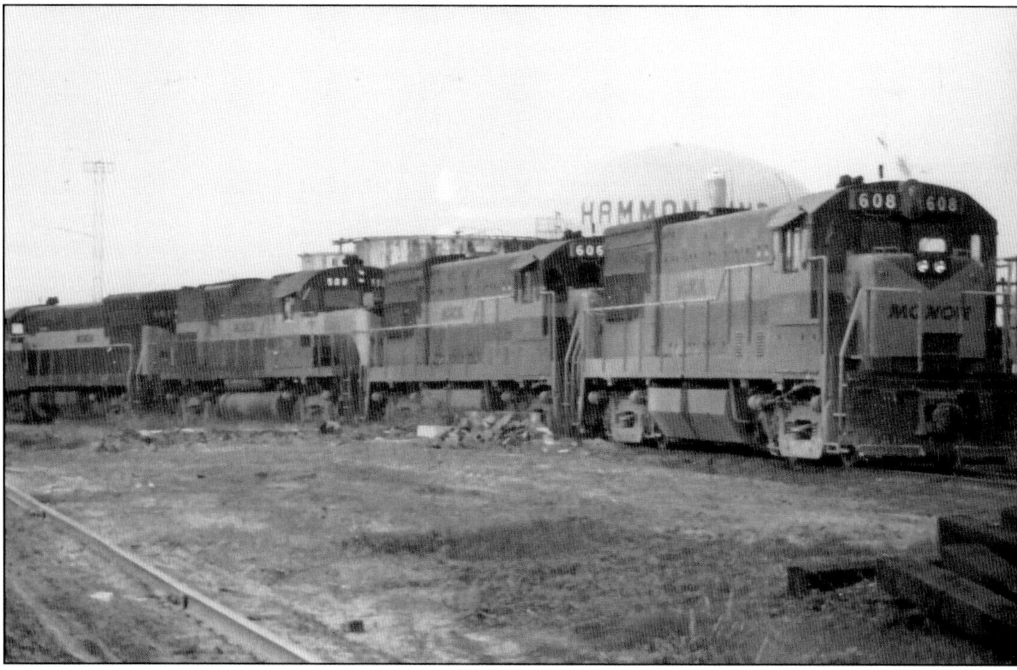

The Monon liked ALCO diesels for freight service, but when ALCO went out of business, the Monon began purchasing freight locomotives from General Electric. The second engine from the left in this photograph, taken in the South Hammond Yard, is an ALCO. The other three are General Electrics. (Courtesy of Hammond Public Library.)

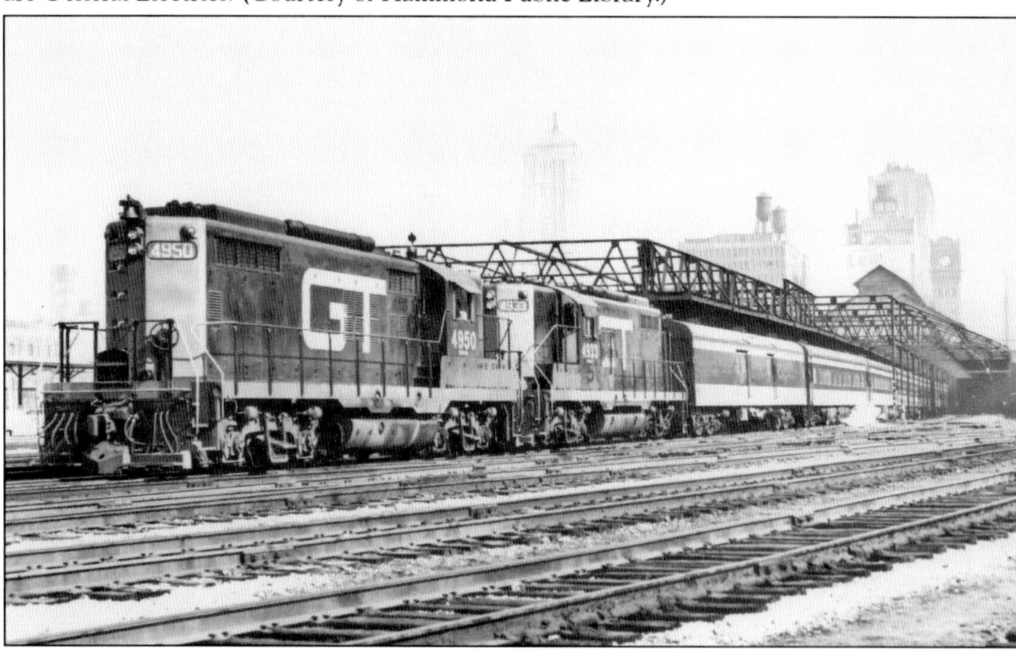

Two of the Grand Trunk Western's EMD road switch engines are ready to depart from Dearborn Station in Chicago with GTW train No. 20, the *Maple Leaf*, bound for Toronto. This train featured coaches, a dining car, and Pullman parlor cars. It was scheduled to depart from Chicago at 10:00 a.m. and arrive in Toronto at 10:05 p.m. the same day.

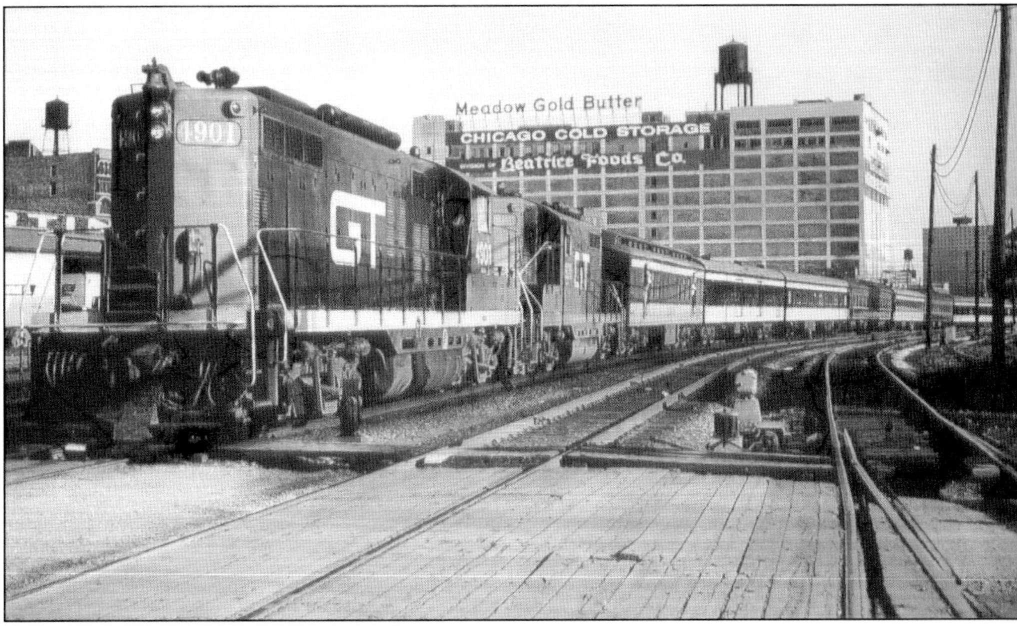

When the Grand Trunk Western Railroad decided to dieselize its passenger trains in the mid-1950s, it did so with GP9 road switch engines, built by the Electro-Motive Division of General Motors. Two of these units are shown arriving in Chicago with GTW train No. 15, the *International Limited*, from Montreal and Toronto. This train featured coaches, a dining car, and Pullman sleeping cars and parlor cars.

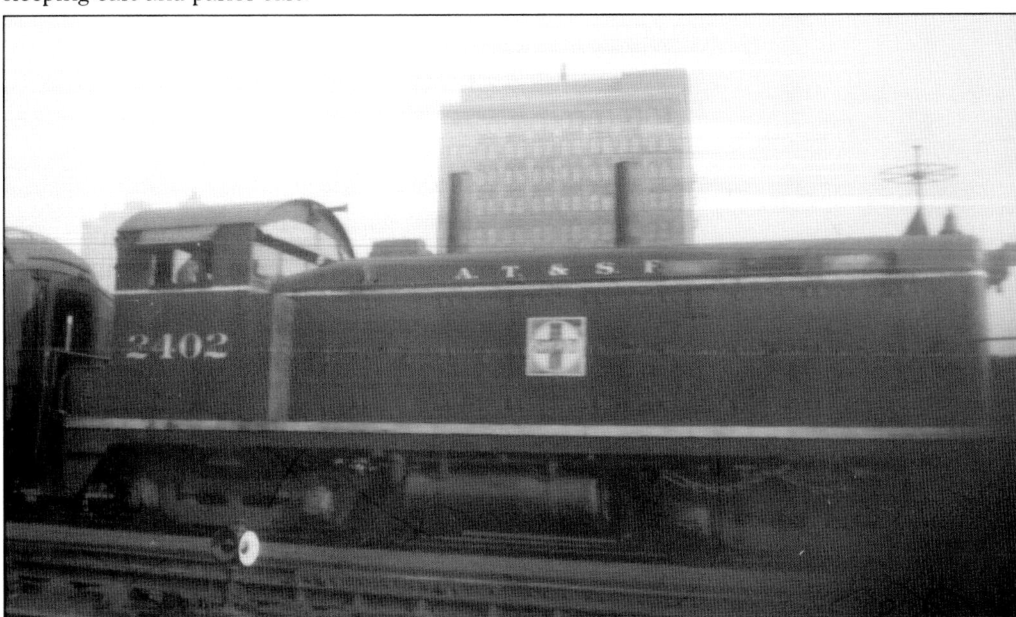

Atchison, Topeka & Santa Fe Railroad NW1 No. 2402 was built by the Electro-Motive Corporation at La Grange, Illinois, in September 1937 and was powered by a Winton Engine Company 12-cylinder 201-A series prime mover rated at 900 horsepower. It rode on AAR type A switcher trucks equipped with General Electric traction motors. In this photograph, it is switching a passenger car at Dearborn Station.

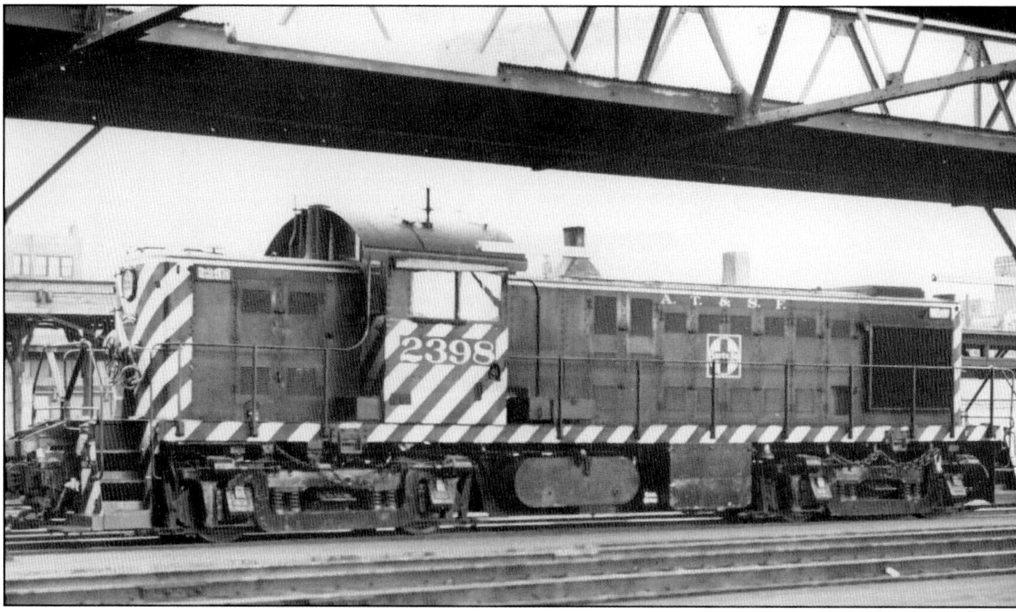

Santa Fe's No. 2398 is another one of five RS-1 road switchers built by the American Locomotive Company in 1950 at its Schenectady, New York, factory. It rode on AAR type B road trucks that were equipped with General Electric traction motors. In this photograph, it is working the Chicago & Western Indiana Railroad's Dearborn Station in September 1960. (Courtesy of the Dean Hale Collection.)

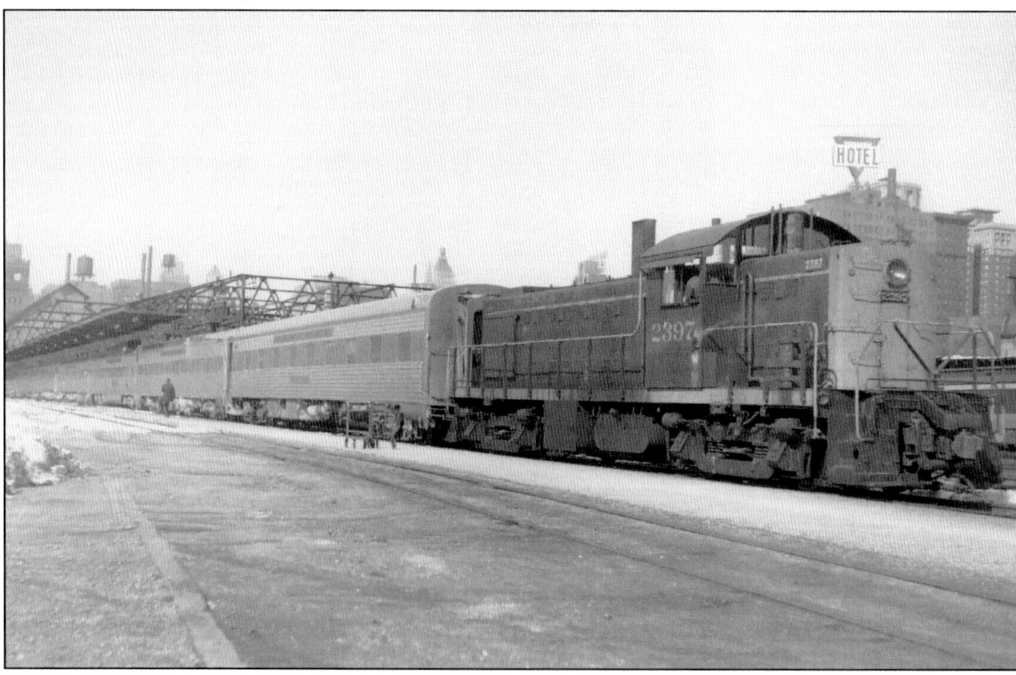

A Santa Fe passenger train is pictured being placed under the train shed at Dearborn Station in Chicago by switch engine No. 2397, a 1,000-horsepower RS-1 built for the Santa Fe by the American Locomotive Company in 1950. Once the switch engine pulled away, the road locomotives backed and coupled on to the train. (Courtesy of R.R. Enterprises.)

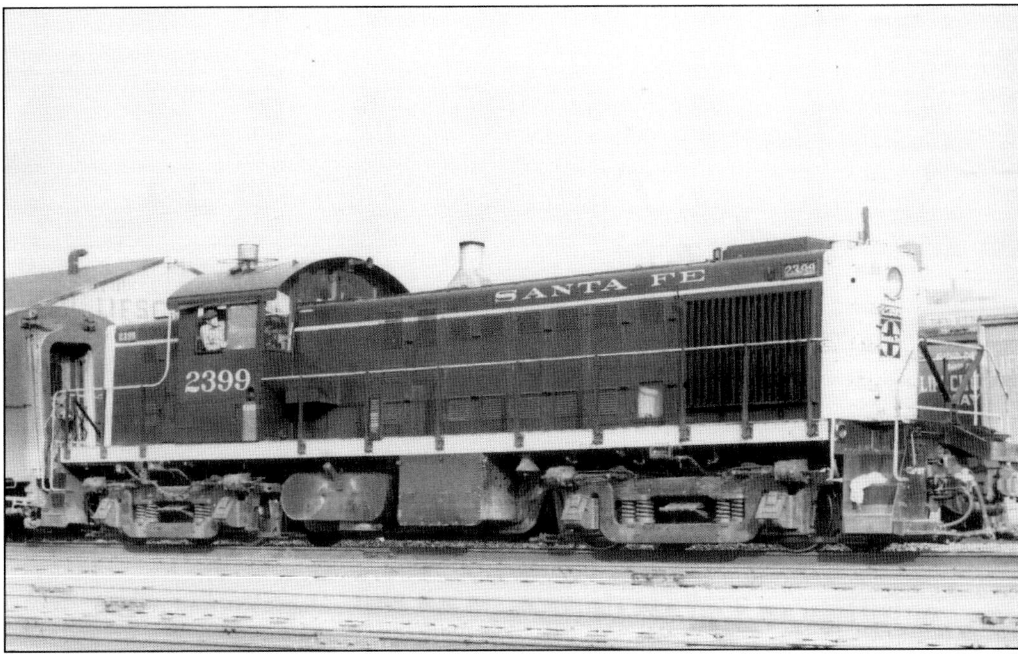

The Atchison, Topeka & Santa Fe Railroad did its own switching at Dearborn Station. One of the engines it used was RS-1 No. 2399, built in 1950 by the American Locomotive Company. The 2399 was powered by ALCO's six-cylinder 539-series prime move, rated at 1,000 horsepower. It is shown here in Chicago in November 1960 coupled to a passenger car.

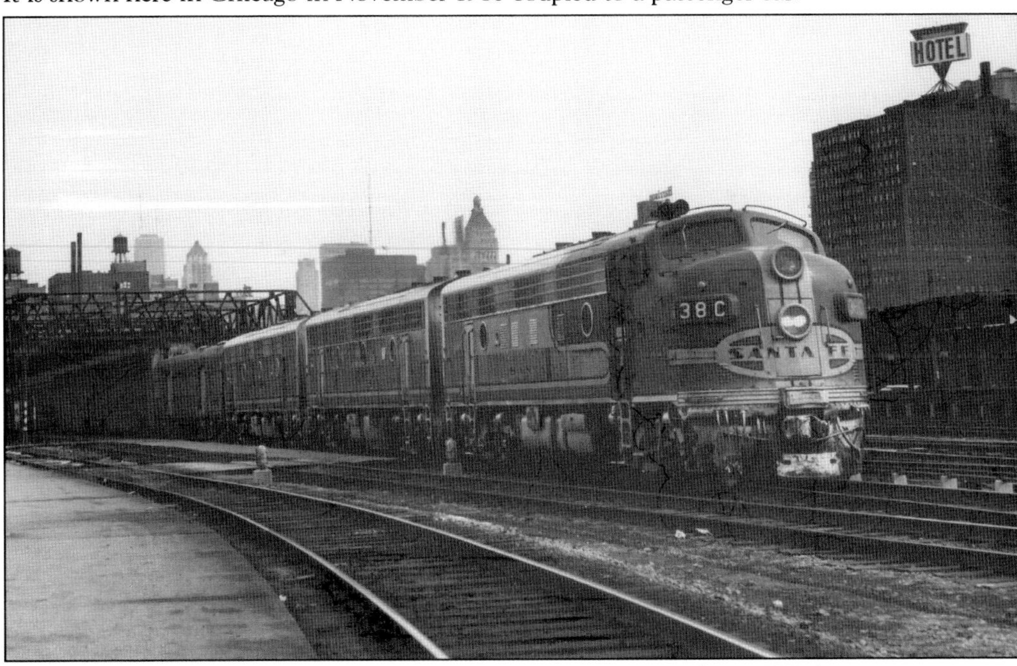

Atchison, Topeka & Santa Fe Railway EMD F7A No. 38C and two F7B booster units are at Dearborn Station in Chicago waiting to depart with AT&SF train No. 1, the *San Francisco Chief*. This all-reserved-seat train featured high-level coaches with reclining seats, a big dome lounge car, a dining car, Pullman sleeping cars, and a Pullman lounge car.

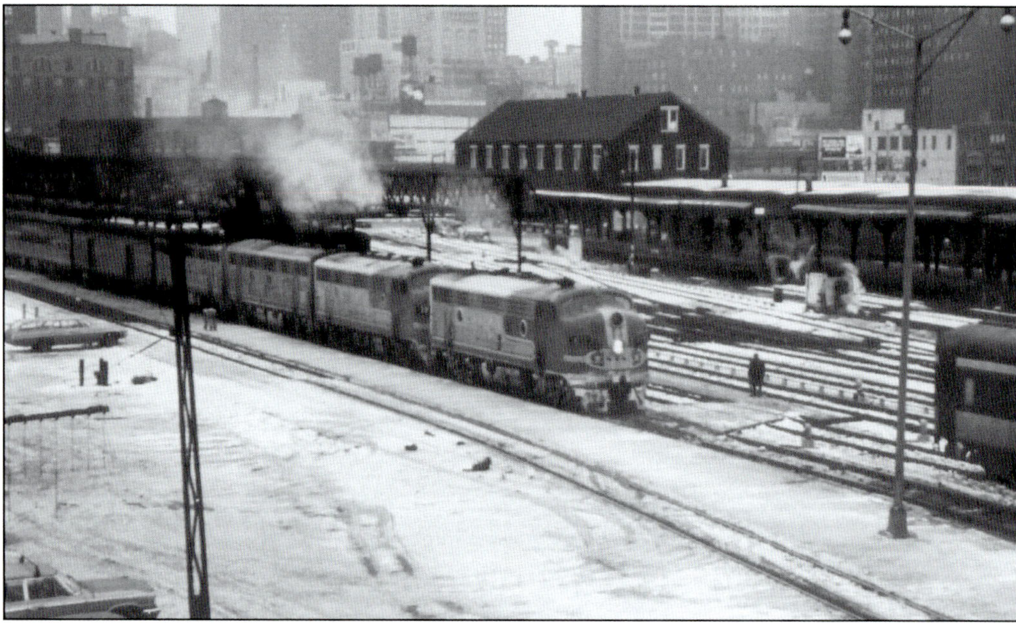

Two of the Santa Fe's F7As and two of its F7Bs are pictured at Dearborn Station in Chicago in January 1971, ready to depart with a westbound passenger train. By 1971, the Santa Fe was down to only four daily departures from and four daily arrivals at Chicago. (Courtesy of John Strombeck.)

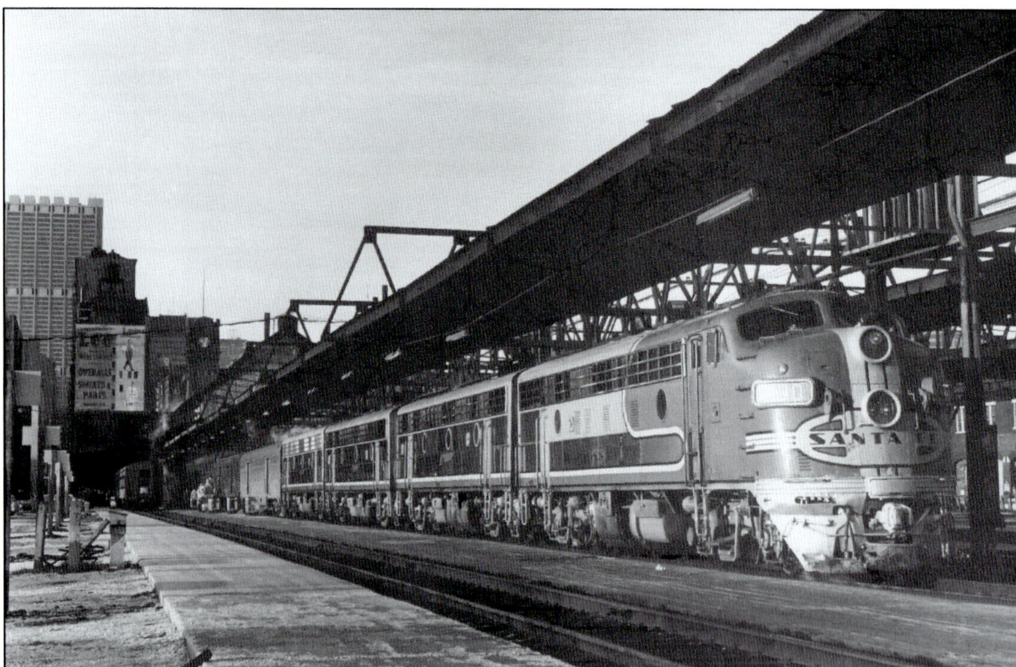

An EMD F7A and three EMD F7Bs are on the head end of the Santa Fe's train No. 17, the combined *Super Chief* extra-fare Pullman and the *El Capitan* extra-fare coach train, at Dearborn Station in April 1971, shortly before Amtrak took over this service. The Santa Fe was operating these two trains as a single consist but continued to maintain its high standard of deluxe passenger service to the very end. (Courtesy of Douglas Wornom.)

Six

The Final Run

After the fire of 1922, Dearborn Station was rebuilt in a somewhat less flamboyant style. Through the 1920s and 1930s, the golden era of train travel, rail business of all types increased, with enormous activity coming during World War II as soldiers passed through in the thousands and food and ordnance was shipped from one coast to the other. By 1946, however, that period was just a fond memory, as other transportation technologies nipped at rail business once again. Soon, people preferred airlines to rail lines for their cross-country trips. A day in a private automobile became preferable to taking the train "to grandma's." The post office and other express services found better efficiencies in moving their goods by truck and by air. Passenger service became more problematic as time went by, and one by one the Dearborn Station trunk lines abandoned them. As of August 16, 1964, the C&WI discontinued commuter service on the Dolton Line. For the next 20-some years, it was solely used to switch freight and passenger cars for its various owners until all of their passenger routes were discontinued. Amtrak assumed the remains of passenger service and consolidated all its routes out of Union Station on the west side of Chicago's Loop. This led to the closing of Dearborn in 1971. By 1985, the C&WI had become a railroad without trains or motive power, merely providing trackage and station service for its owners and tenants from Dearborn to Dolton Junction and to just over the state line into Hammond. The former site of the Dearborn Station train shed was redeveloped into a residential neighborhood called Dearborn Park. In 1994, even the C&WI itself was no longer in existence.

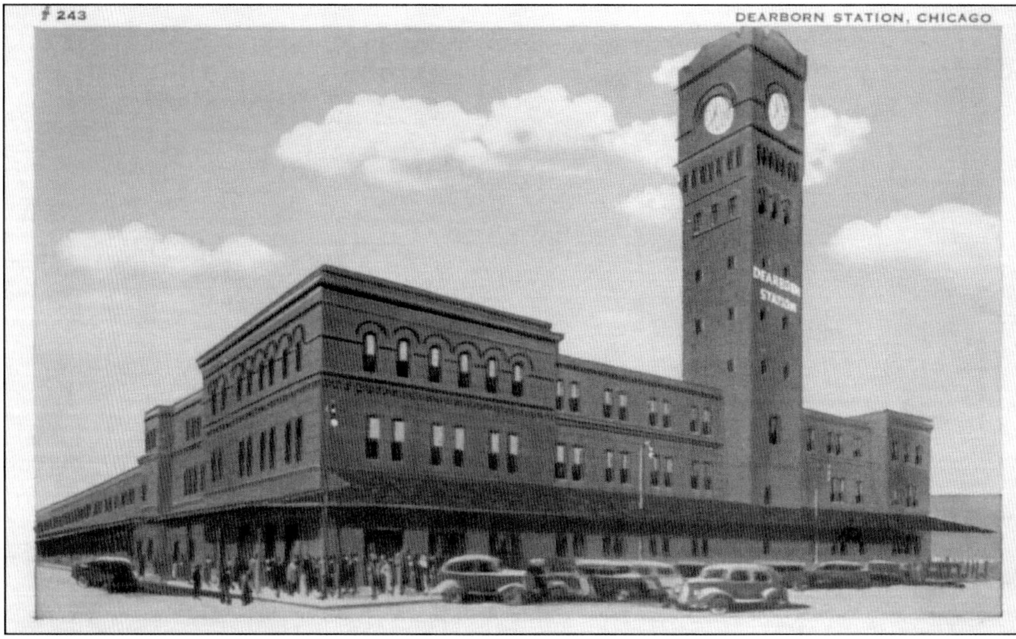

After the fire of 1922, Dearborn Station was rebuilt with some modifications. The central tower was truncated, and the third floor was remodeled with a flat roof, giving it more space for offices. This is the station as it looked in the early 1930s. (Courtesy of Max Rigot Selling Agency.)

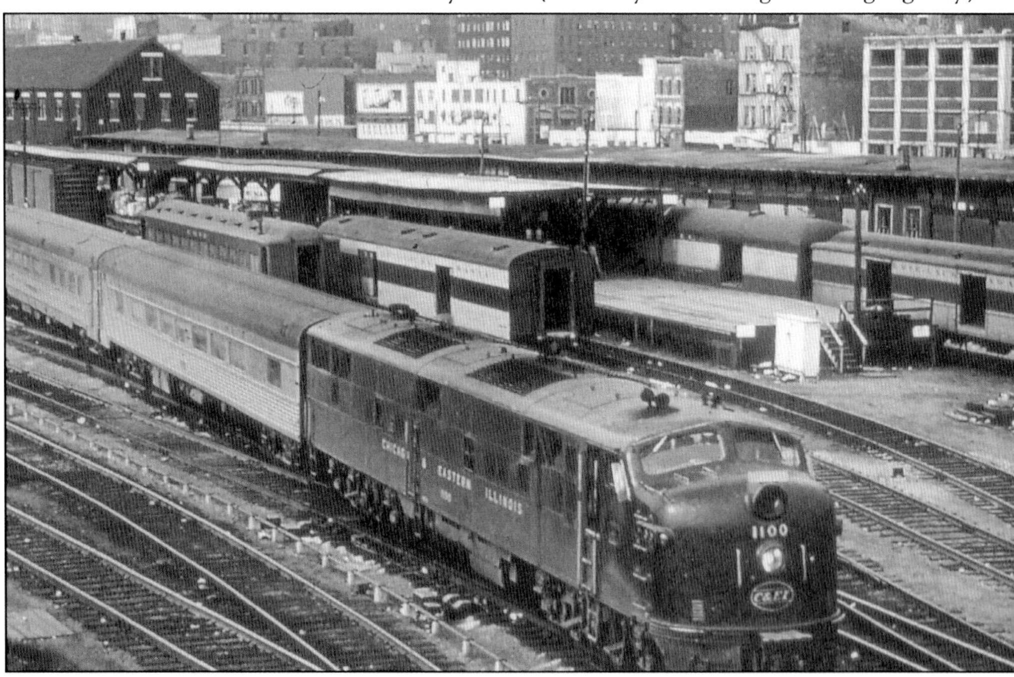

Chicago & Eastern Illinois Railroad E7A No. 1100 is shown here departing from Dearborn Station with C&EI train No. 3, the *Danville Flyer*. Up until the late 1960s, the C&WI and its owner railroads made a significant amount of their revenues carrying US Mail and Railway Express Agency packages. In the background can be seen the loading docks for mail and express that were on the east side of Dearborn Station.

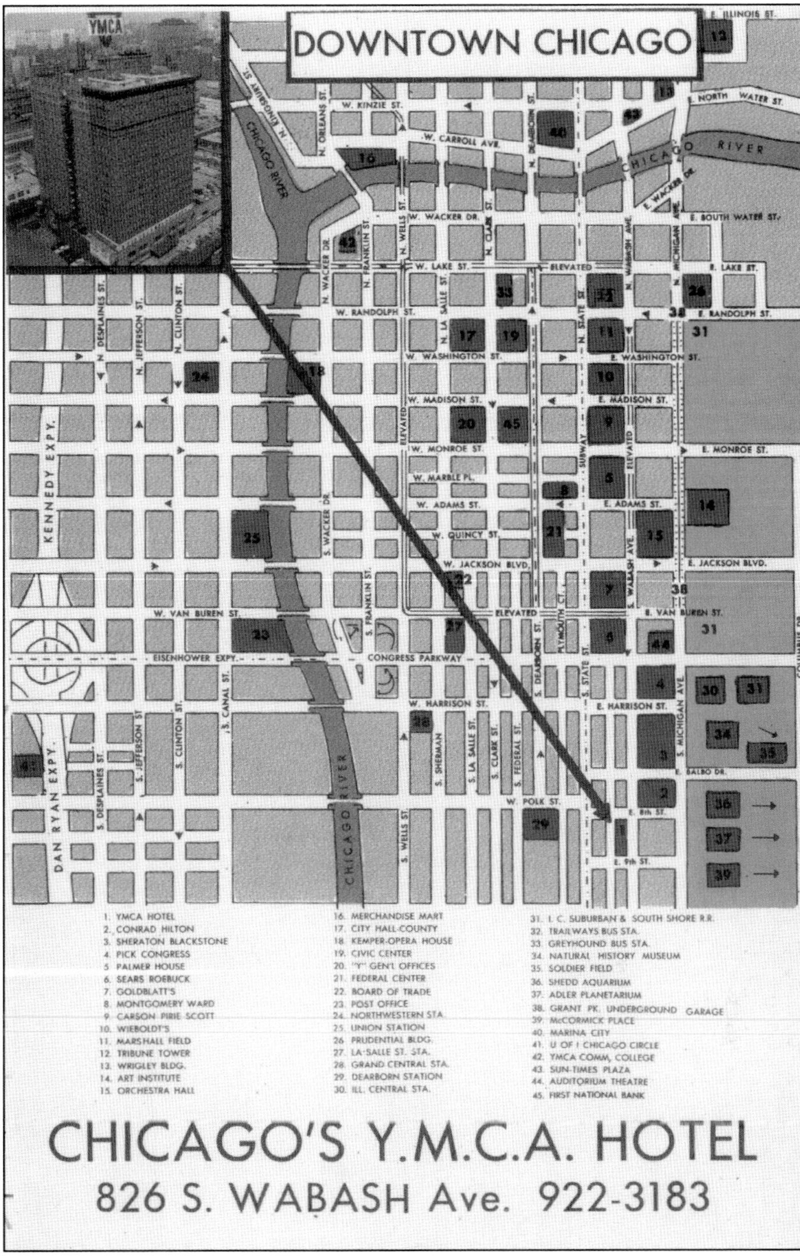

In the middle of the 20th century, Dearborn Station, at number 29 on the map, remained close to all the sights and hotels of downtown Chicago. Cross-country travelers found it easy to make connections with other railroad stations or to layover in the city. Day visitors from the south suburbs and beyond used the Wabash and C&EI via Dearborn for visits to museums and Loop shopping. The YMCA, at number 1, had developed into a family hotel. Printers Row (Dearborn Street north of the station), however, was seeing a change in its business atmosphere as printers and publishers began moving to the outskirts of the city, where land costs were cheaper and they were more easily accessed by trucks that hauled their printed products around the country. The appeal of air shipping was also beginning to be felt, and so they wanted to be closer to O'Hare and Midway Airports. (Courtesy of Cynthia Ogorek.)

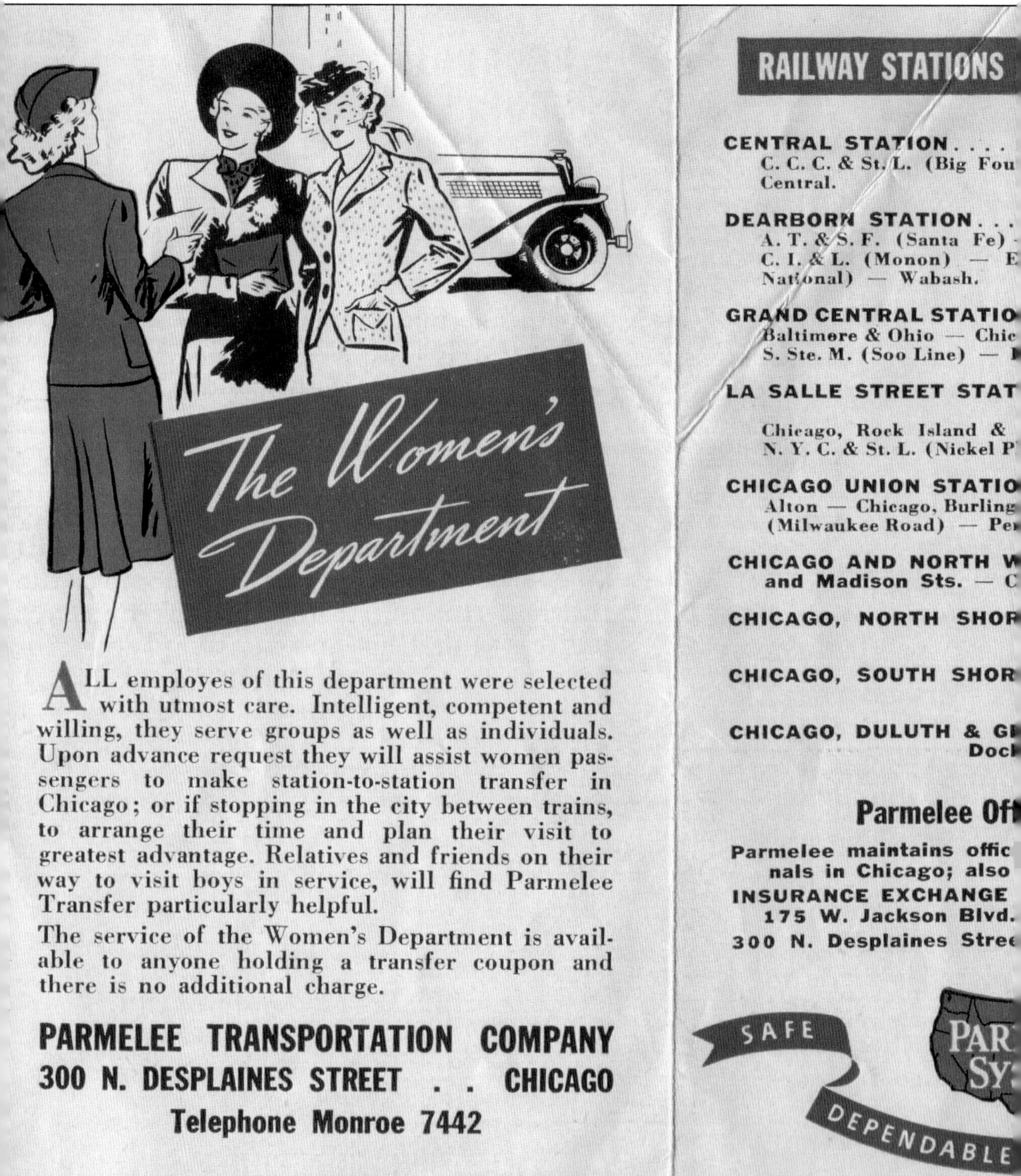

The Women's Department

ALL employes of this department were selected with utmost care. Intelligent, competent and willing, they serve groups as well as individuals. Upon advance request they will assist women passengers to make station-to-station transfer in Chicago; or if stopping in the city between trains, to arrange their time and plan their visit to greatest advantage. Relatives and friends on their way to visit boys in service, will find Parmelee Transfer particularly helpful.

The service of the Women's Department is available to anyone holding a transfer coupon and there is no additional charge.

PARMELEE TRANSPORTATION COMPANY
300 N. DESPLAINES STREET . . CHICAGO
Telephone Monroe 7442

RAILWAY STATIONS

CENTRAL STATION . . . .
C. C. C. & St. L. (Big Fou
Central.

DEARBORN STATION . . .
A. T. & S. F. (Santa Fe) -
C. I. & L. (Monon) — E
National) — Wabash.

GRAND CENTRAL STATIO
Baltimore & Ohio — Chic
S. Ste. M. (Soo Line) —

LA SALLE STREET STAT
Chicago, Rock Island &
N. Y. C. & St. L. (Nickel P

CHICAGO UNION STATIO
Alton — Chicago, Burling
(Milwaukee Road) — Pe

CHICAGO AND NORTH W
and Madison Sts. — C

CHICAGO, NORTH SHOR

CHICAGO, SOUTH SHOR

CHICAGO, DULUTH & G
Dock

Parmelee Of

Parmelee maintains offic
nals in Chicago; also
INSURANCE EXCHANGE
175 W. Jackson Blvd.
300 N. Desplaines Stre

Founded in 1853 and originally called the Parmelee Omnibus & Stage Company, the Parmelee Transportation Company offered assistance to strangers arriving in Chicago. For some 70 years, it was the "official transfer company for the railroads." A Parmelee transfer was free to all holders of through train tickets and enabled them to board a vehicle that moved them and their luggage from Dearborn Station to any of the other train stations and steamship terminals in the city.

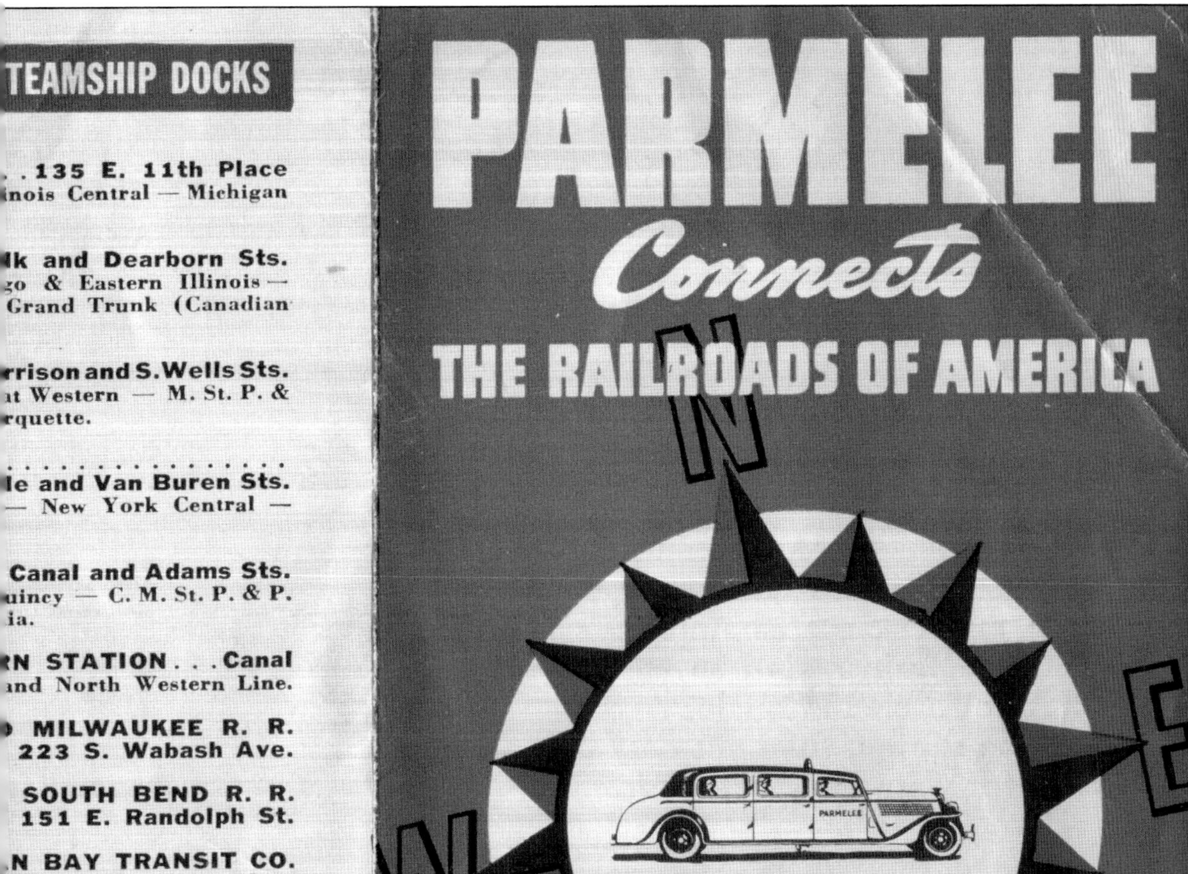

In the 19th century, the company used a fleet of horse-drawn wagons; in the second half of the 20th century, it became the Continental Air Transport Company, which indicates the change in travelers' arrangements. By the late 1960s, the company's coaches were picking up and dropping off airline passengers not at Dearborn Station but at the Palmer House and other hotels across the city.

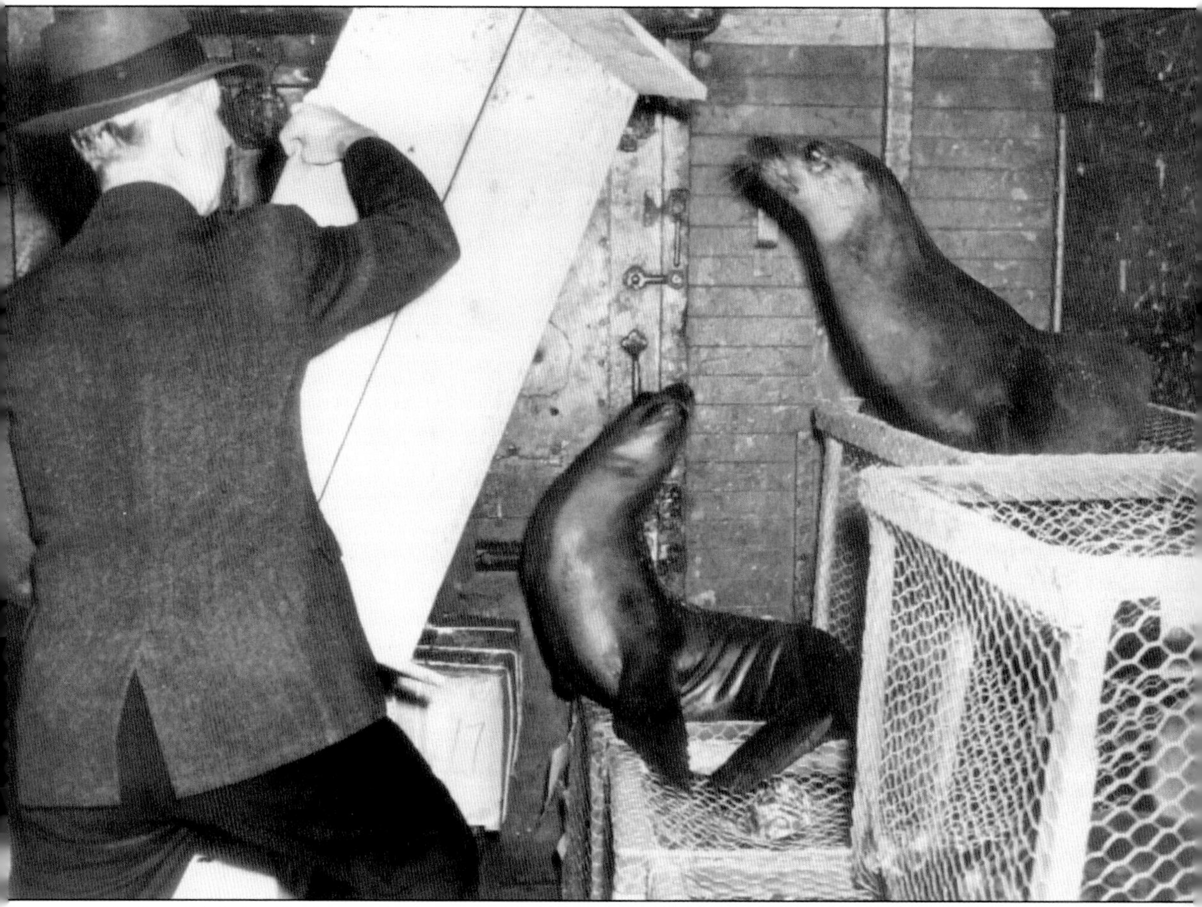

Richard Marlin Perkins, above, was the director of Chicago's Lincoln Park Zoo from 1944 until 1962. He was also well known as the host of *Zoo Parade*, a television program that originated from the Lincoln Park Zoo on NBC station WNBQ-TV. He is shown here welcoming to Chicago two sea lions who had escaped from their cages in the baggage room at Dearborn Station on May 14, 1947. Since the station's baggage men had been unable to handle the animals, Perkins was called to figure out a way to calm them and help them back into their temporary quarters. About 15 years earlier, "Public Enemy No. 1," Al Capone, was escorted by police into Dearborn Station, where he posed for photographs before taking his place in the last car of the *Dixie Flyer* on his way to the Atlanta Federal Penitentiary. Capone had often taken the C&EI to Miami, where he had a home. One of his relatives later remarked that he was a railroad buff and always set up a model electric train beneath his Christmas tree.

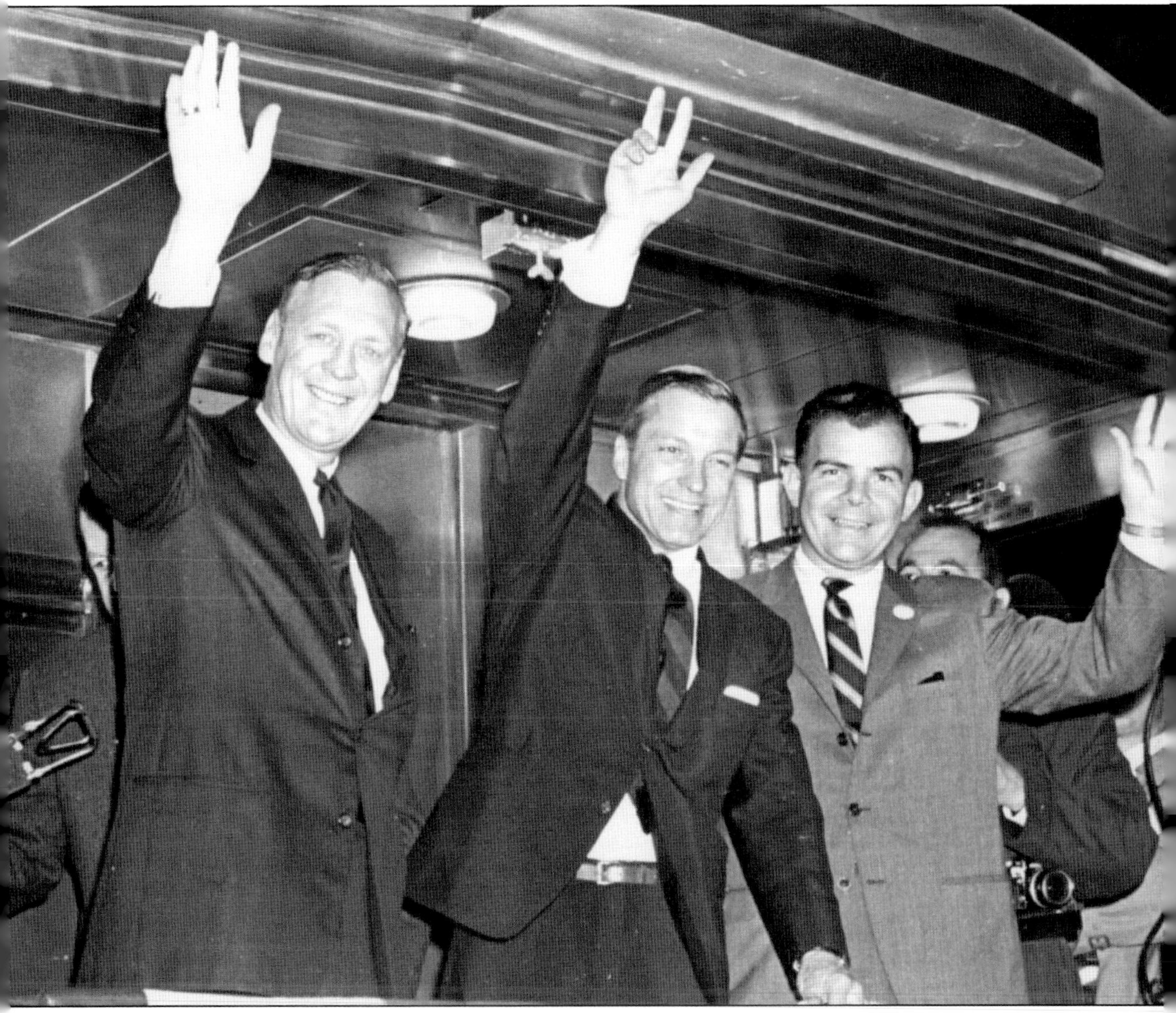

Well into the 1960s, politicians continued to make whistle-stop tours of their constituencies during campaign season. The 1966 Republican candidate for the US Senate, Charles H. Percy (center), is shown here standing on the rear platform of his campaign train at Dearborn Station in early November. On the left is Ray Page, the Republican candidate for Illinois superintendent of schools. On the right is Harris Rowe, Republican candidate for Illinois state treasurer. Percy won the senate race and was reelected in 1972 and 1978. Other celebrities arrived or departed on the Santa Fe's *Chief* or *Super Chief*, as noted in the Chicago papers—Henry Ford II, Conrad Hilton, Louis B. Mayer, and Cecil B. DeMille, to name a few. "Special Trains" were common on the C&EI. One in particular, *Operation POTUS*, carried Pres. Harry S. Truman, his staff, and his daughter, Margaret, on a whistle-stop tour through Illinois and Indiana. And, of course, baseball teams came and went through Dearborn before they took to the air during playing season.

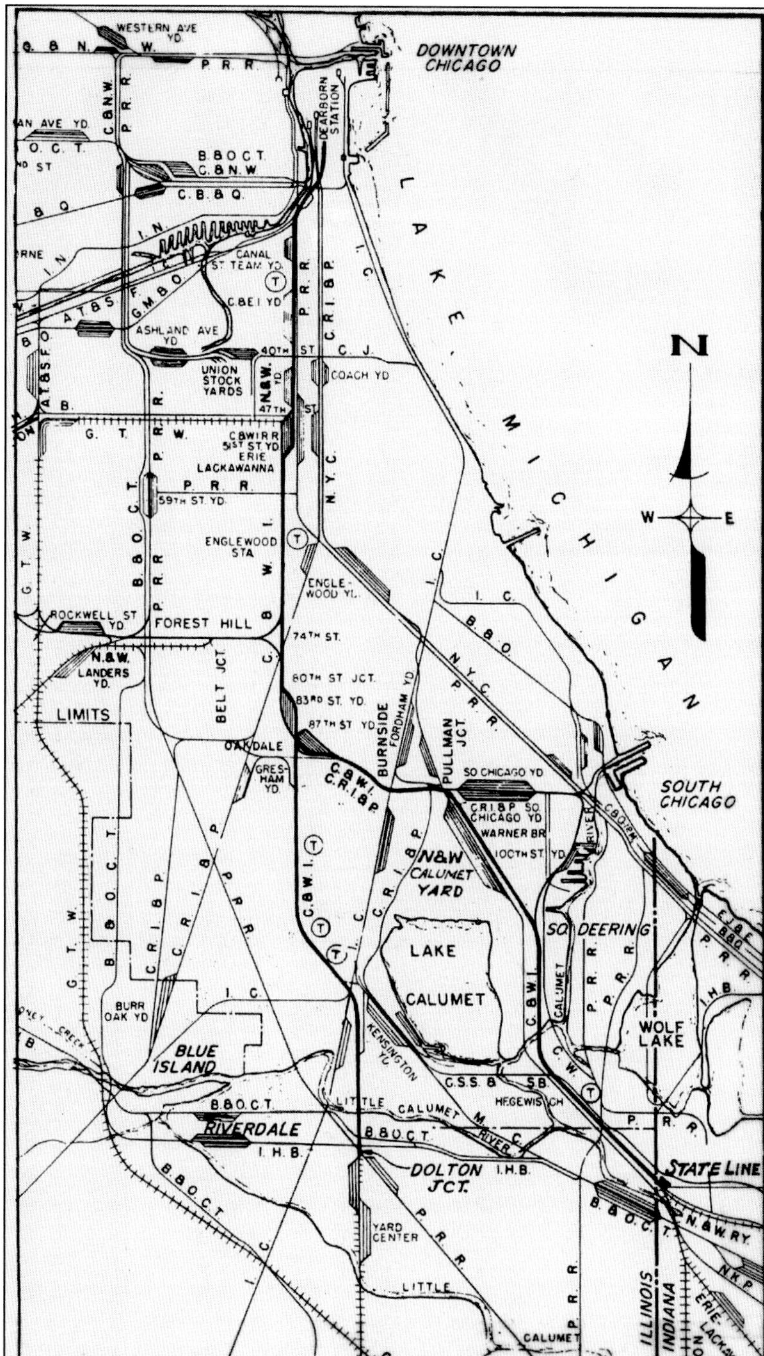

This 1966 map shows the aftermath of the C&WI's tenure through the South and Southeast Side of Chicago. By the time of its publication, the Norfolk & Western Railway (N&W) had absorbed the Wabash as well as the Nickel Plate Road, which had paralleled the C&WI right-of-way from Lake Calumet through Hegewisch to the Indiana border. The C&WI had already discontinued passenger service on its Dearborn-to-Dolton route. It continued to switch owner railroad cars at Dearborn until all of their passenger services were absorbed by Amtrak in 1971.

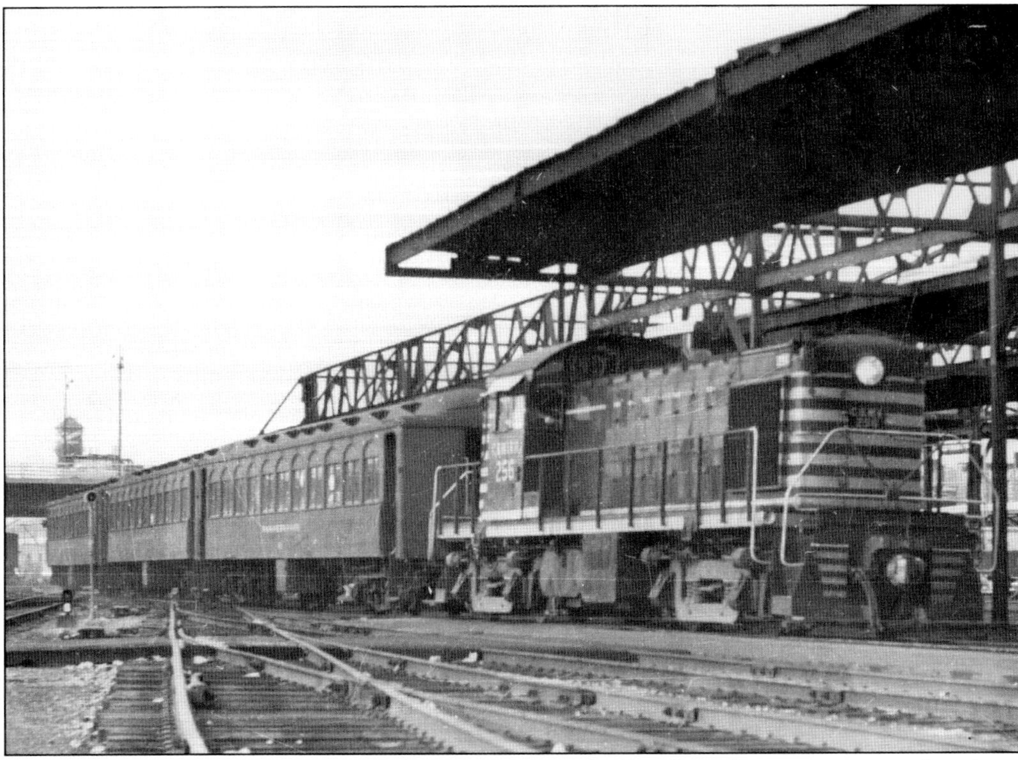

C&WI's ALCO RS-1 No. 256 is seen here arriving at the Dearborn Station annex with a three-car suburban train from Dolton around 1960. The demand for suburban commuter service on the C&WI declined over the years, but the cost of operating the service did not, and the C&WI discontinued the suburban service entirely in 1964.

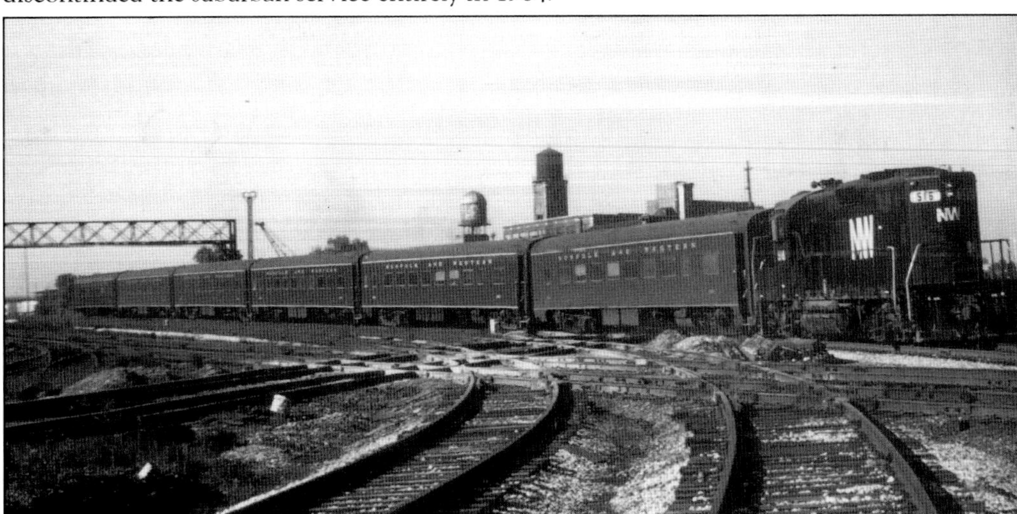

Norfolk & Western Railway's EMD GP9 No. 516 is seen here departing from downtown Chicago with a six-car commuter train on its way to Orland Park on May 27, 1974. Dearborn Station closed in 1971 with the coming of Amtrak, but the N&W's commuter train continued to use a platform next to the station. This train was equipped with streamlined coaches originally used for its long-distance trains between Norfolk and Cincinnati.

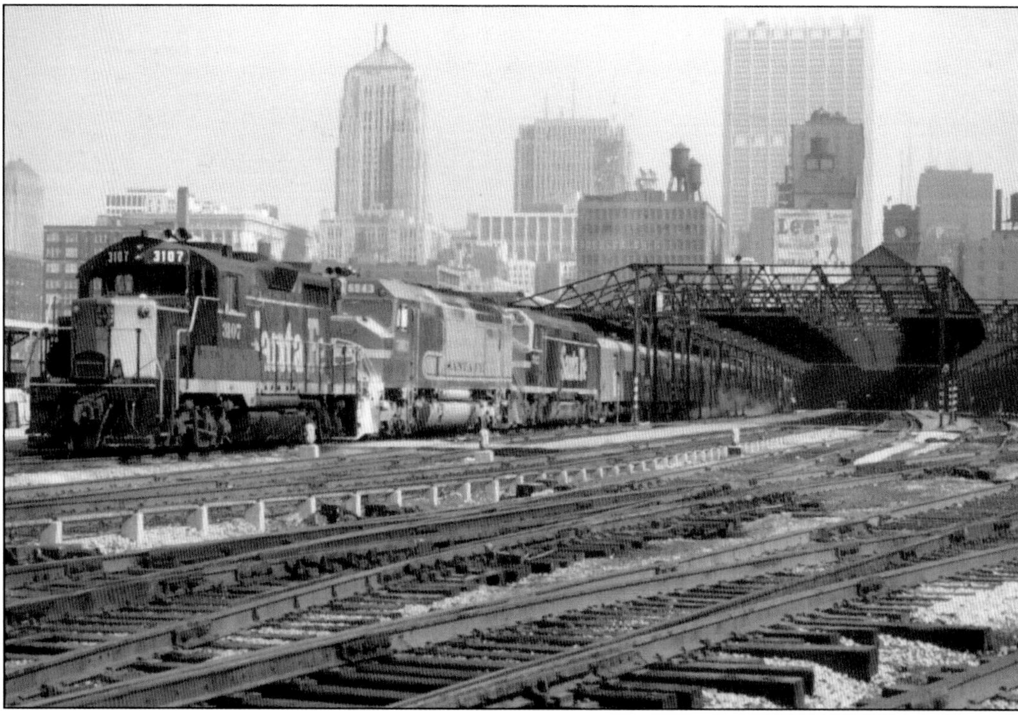

Santa Fe Railroad switch engine No. 3107 was still attached to this outbound passenger train at Dearborn Station when this photograph was taken in 1971. With the decline of intercity passenger train business at that time, most of Dearborn Station's capacity went unused. (Courtesy of Mark Lluanza.)

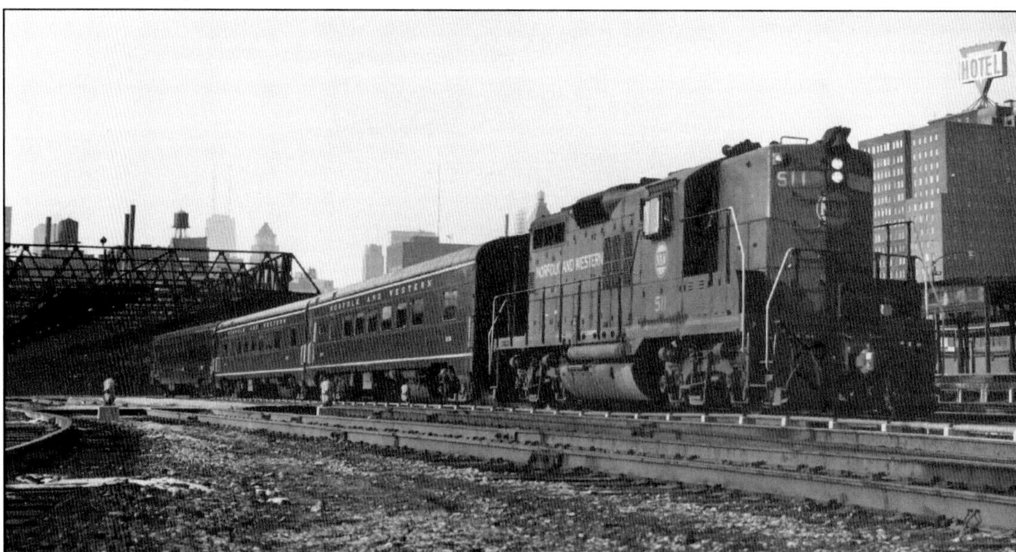

The Norfolk & Western Railroad acquired control of the Wabash Railroad in 1964 and continued to operate the ex-Wabash passenger trains. This is the N&W's *City of Decatur* passenger train departing from Dearborn Station in April 1971, just before Amtrak took over intercity passenger train service. This train was discontinued on April 30, 1971, and did not continue in operation under Amtrak. (Courtesy of Douglas Wornom.)

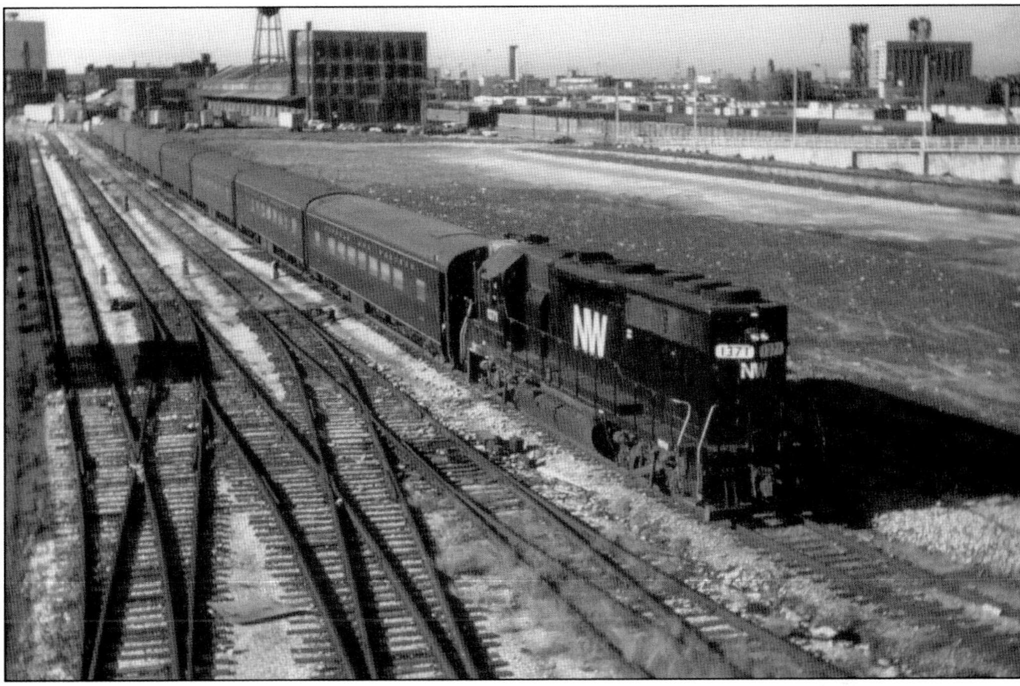

Norfolk & Western EMD GP9 No. 1371 is departing Chicago with the local commuter train to Orland Park. The N&W absorbed the Wabash Railroad in 1964 and continued to operate the weekday commuter service to the southwestern suburbs. (Courtesy of Mark Lluanza.)

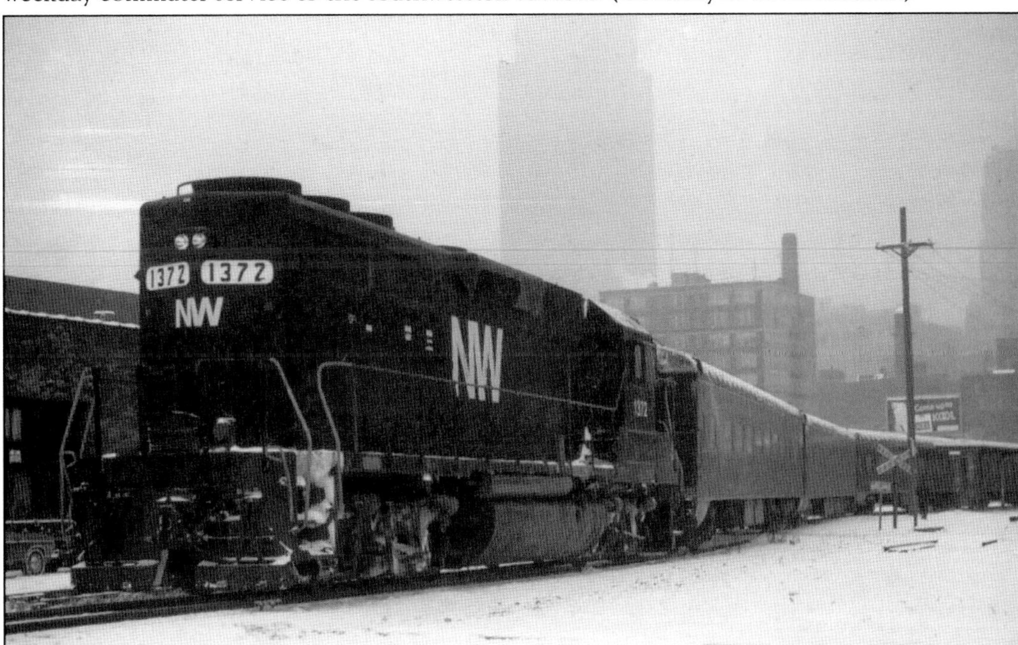

After Dearborn Station closed in 1971 with the coming of Amtrak, the Norfolk & Western used tracks and a platform on the west side of the station for its weekday commuter trains to and from Orland Park. N&W GP9 No. 1372 is shown here ready to depart on a snowy afternoon. (Courtesy of Mark Lluanza.)

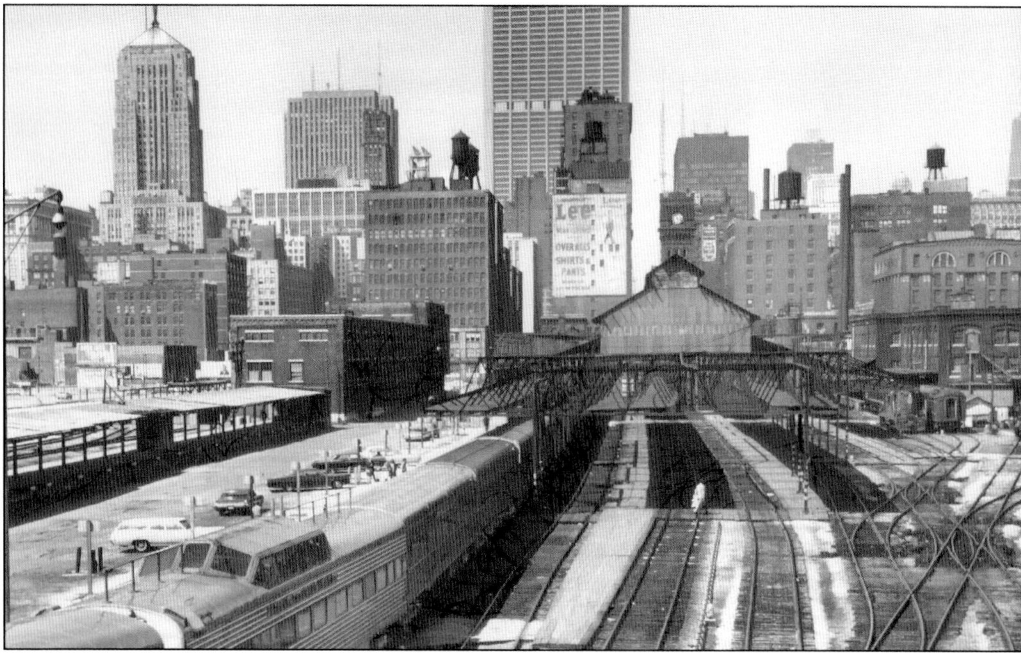

By 1971, passenger service out of Dearborn Station was on the decline. The passenger train on the left is the Santa Fe's. The last passenger arrival at Dearborn was the Santa Fe's *Grand Canyon* from Los Angeles. The last departure was the Grand Trunk's *International Ltd.*, bound for Port Huron on April 30, 1971. (Courtesy of Douglas Wornom.)

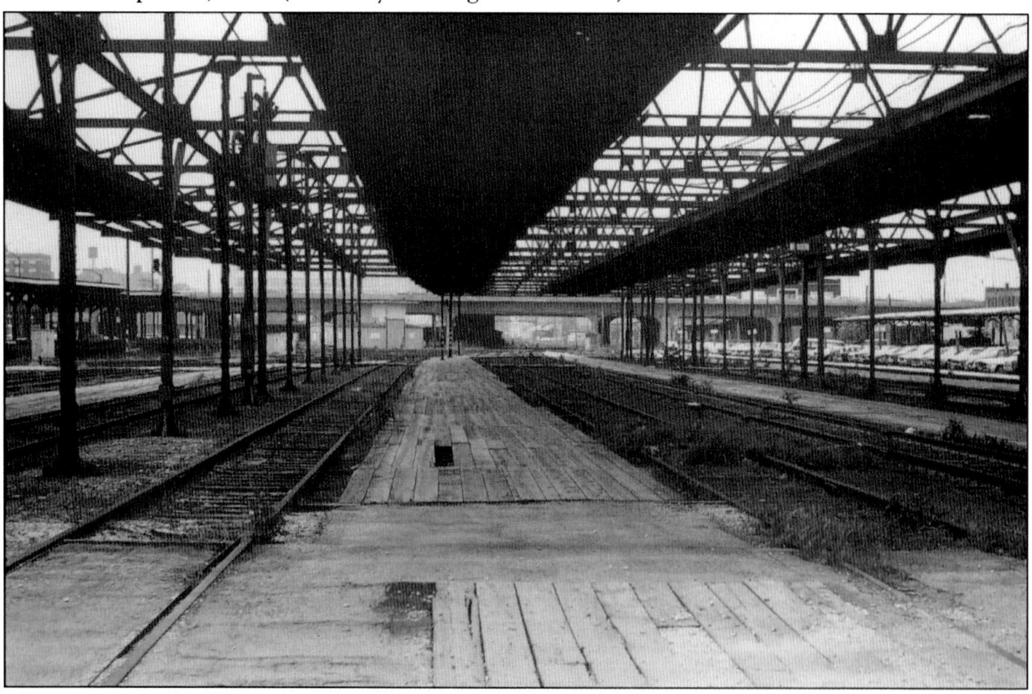

Photographer Mark Lluanza took this photograph of the Dearborn Station train shed in the 1970s, after the station had closed. Mark was standing at the north end of the station looking south toward Roosevelt Road. (Courtesy of Mark Lluanza.)

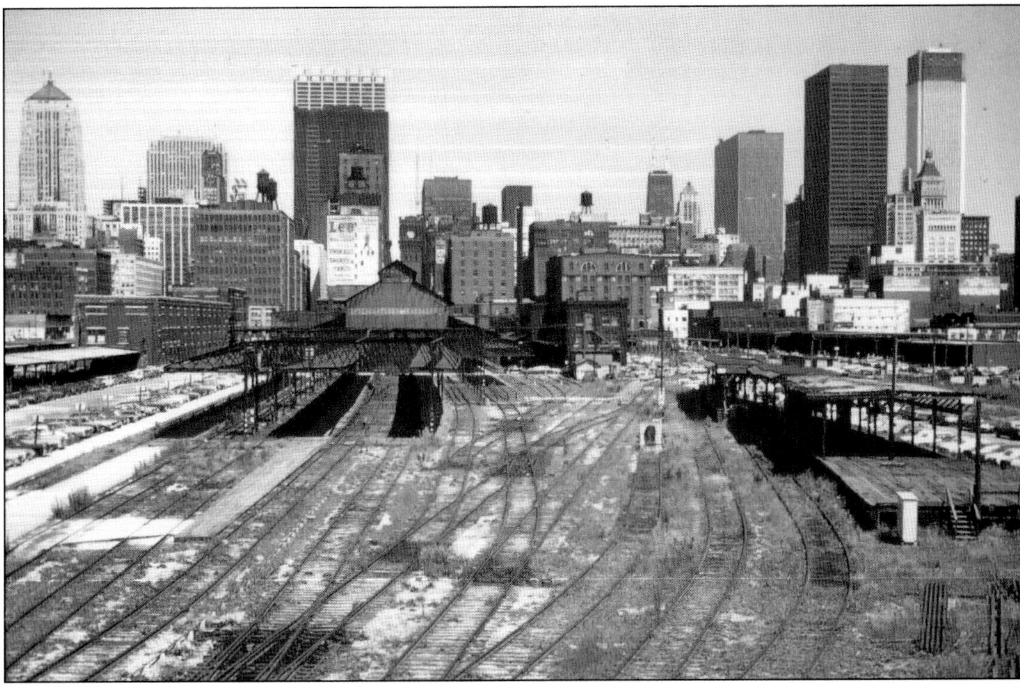

This is what Dearborn Station looked like in 1972, looking north from the Roosevelt Road–Twelfth Street overpass. With the coming of Amtrak in 1971, Dearborn Station was no longer needed to serve the remaining intercity passenger trains.

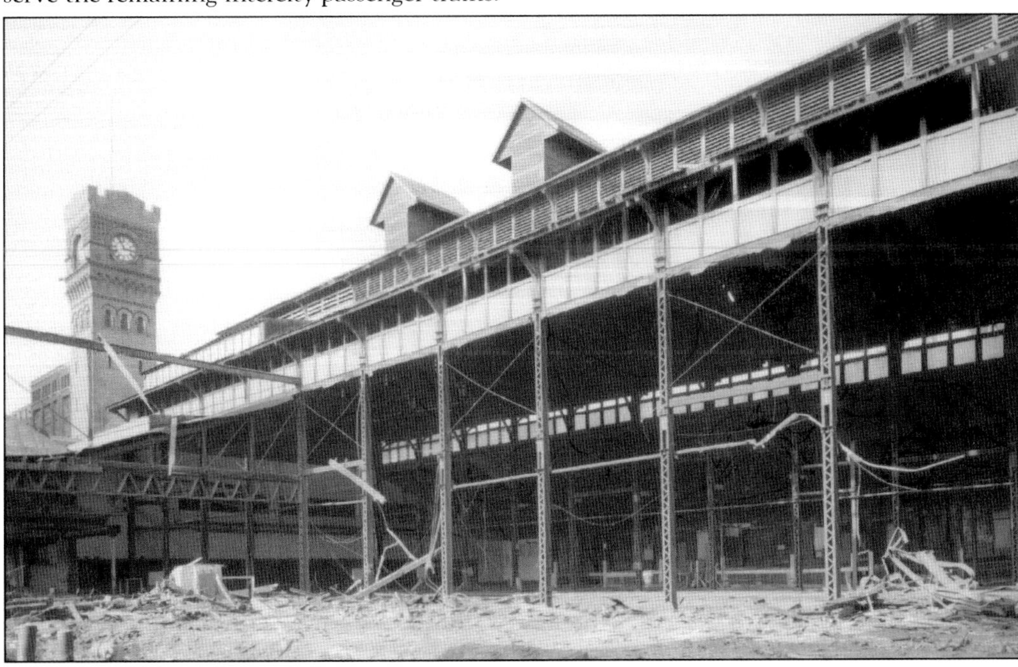

Intercity passenger train service to and from Dearborn Station was discontinued on May 1, 1971, when Amtrak consolidated all of the remaining service at Chicago Union Station on Canal Street. The grandiose Dearborn Station stood vacant and derelict for the next few years. The station tracks and the train sheds were removed in 1975.

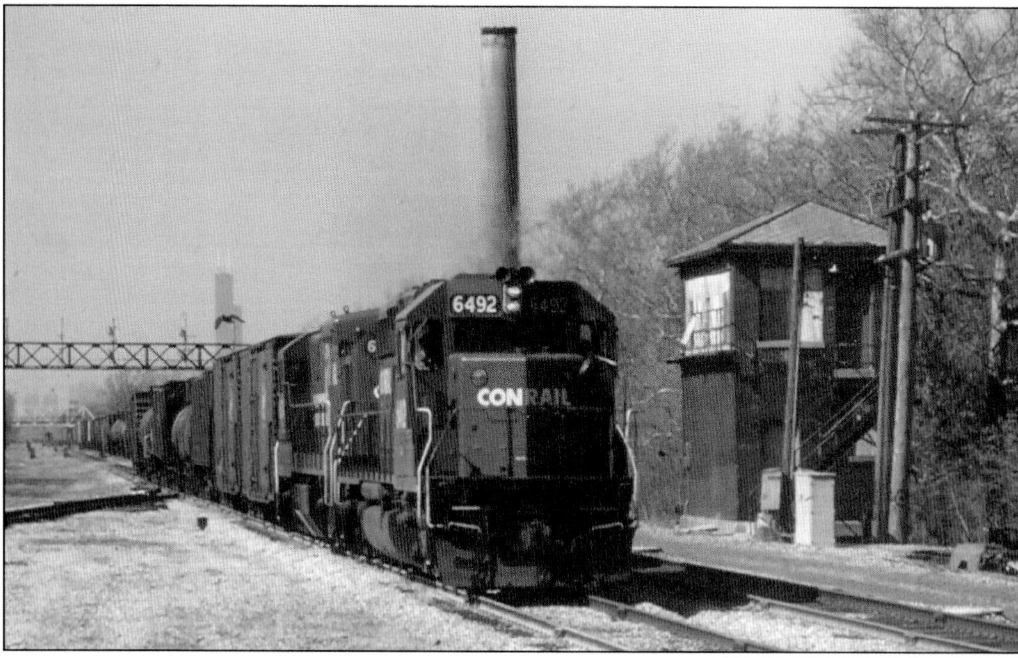

The Consolidated Rail Corporation, known simply as Conrail, was the federal government's answer to the collapse of freight rail service in the northeast in the early 1970s. It acquired pieces of the collapsed Penn Central and bankrupt Erie-Lackawanna Railroads in the Chicago area, along with several other railroad companies in the northeast. Conrail began operations on April 1, 1976.

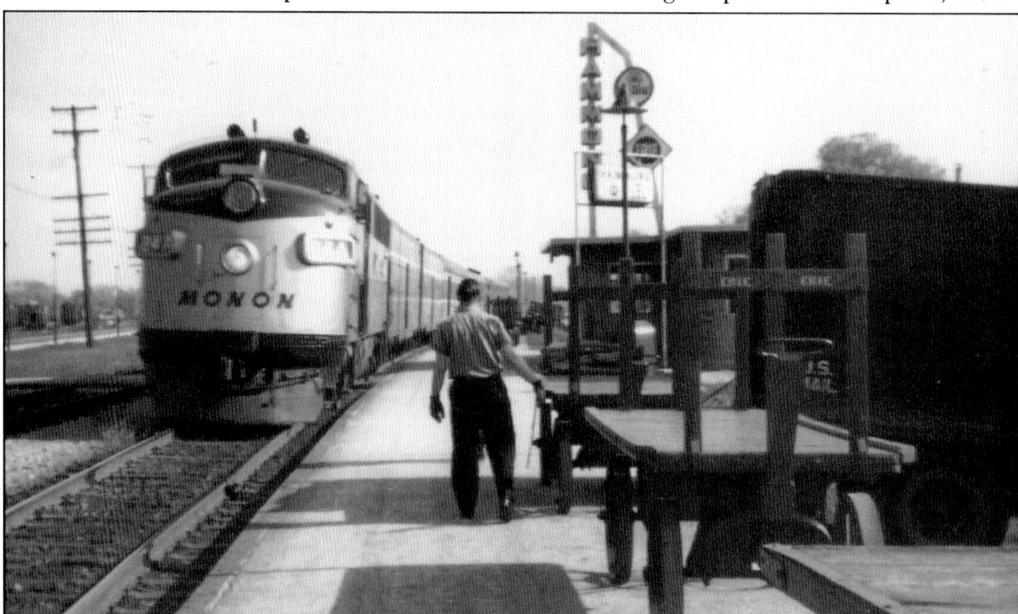

The station agent was standing by when this photograph was taken of a northbound Monon passenger train arriving on a sunny afternoon in Hammond. The Monon shared this post–World War II station with the Erie Railroad. It was located near 173rd Street in South Hammond. The last Monon passenger train to leave Dearborn Station was the *Thoroughbred*, bound for Louisville on September 30, 1967. (Courtesy of Hammond Public Library.)

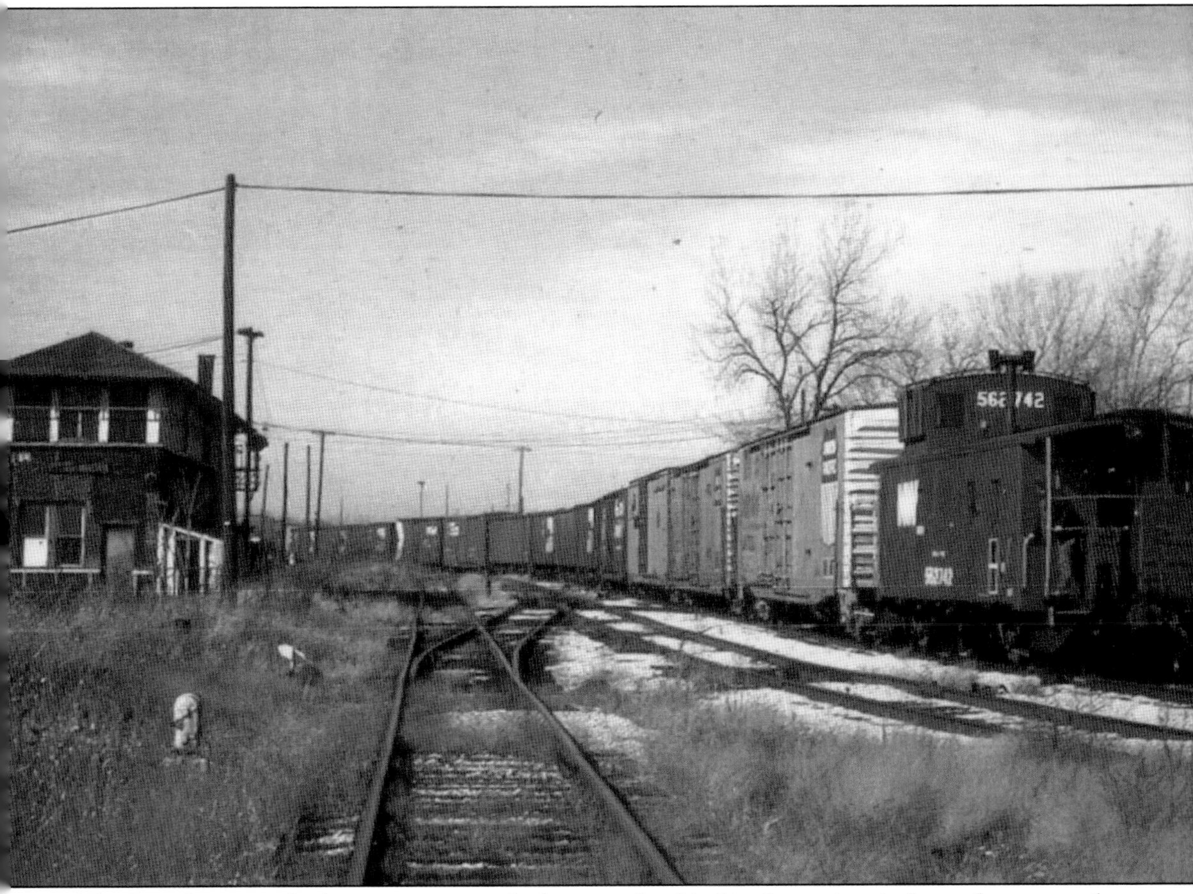

The State Line interlocking tower, once the biggest of its kind in the nation, is shown here toward the end of its existence. The only railroads still using it were the Indiana Harbor Belt Railroad (its owner), CSX Transportation, Inc., the Norfolk Southern Corporation, and the Northwest Indiana Commuter Transportation District, also known as the South Shore. The weeds and the forlorn appearance of the building itself indicated that it wasn't long before it would be gone. Throughout the 20th century, technological progress required the removal of tracks and the replacement of mechanical pipelines by electric signals and switches. By 1985, the C&WI tracks had been removed, and only the IHB, Baltimore & Ohio Chicago Terminal, CSS&SB, and New York, Chicago & St. Louis Railroads were using it. In August 2000, its owner, the IHB, moved the controlling works to a remote dispatching center in Calumet City, a mile or two beyond the freight in this photograph. That work was completed on August 14, 2000, and the tower was demolished on October 30. (Courtesy of Bob Lalich.)

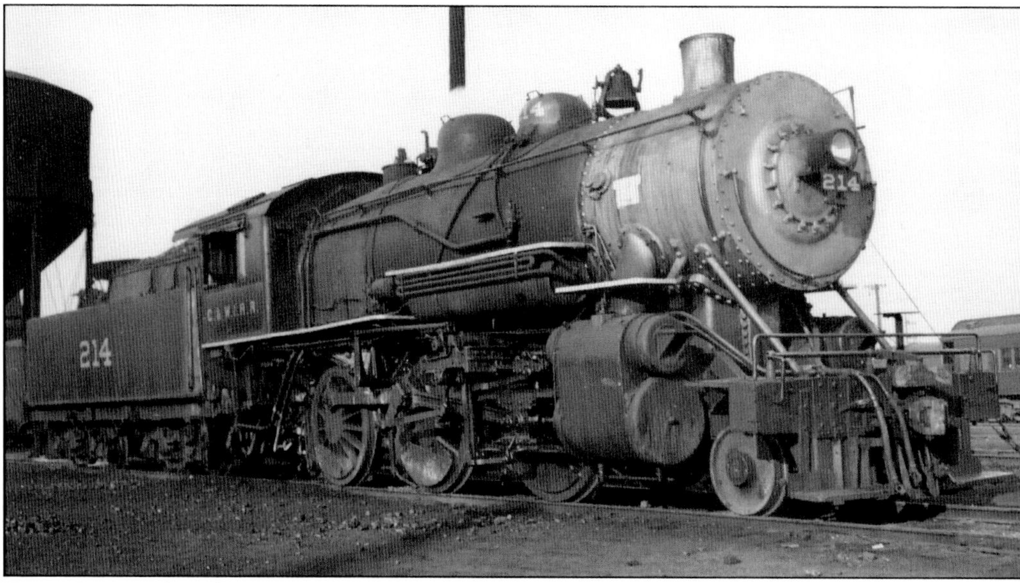

For 115 years, the Chicago & Western Indiana Railroad provided its owner railroads with access to Chicago, a terminal, freight yards, and freight houses. Switching cars was its most obvious service. Above is one of the C&WI's class J-2 2-6-0 Mogul-type locomotives, No. 214, awaiting servicing at the C&WI's Fifty-First Street coach yard. It came on line in 1914 and remained in service until the late 1940s, when ALCO diesel locomotives replaced steam. Below, three C&WI switchmen ride the front platform on ALCO RS-1 No. 252 as it eases into the Dearborn Station annex around 1960. To the right is Canadian National Railroad's sleeping car *Green Brook*. Built by Pullman Standard in 1954, it offered six open sections, six roomettes, and four double bedrooms. After Dearborn closed, the C&WI switched cars until 1985, then managed the Dolton and Main Lines until dissolution in 1994.

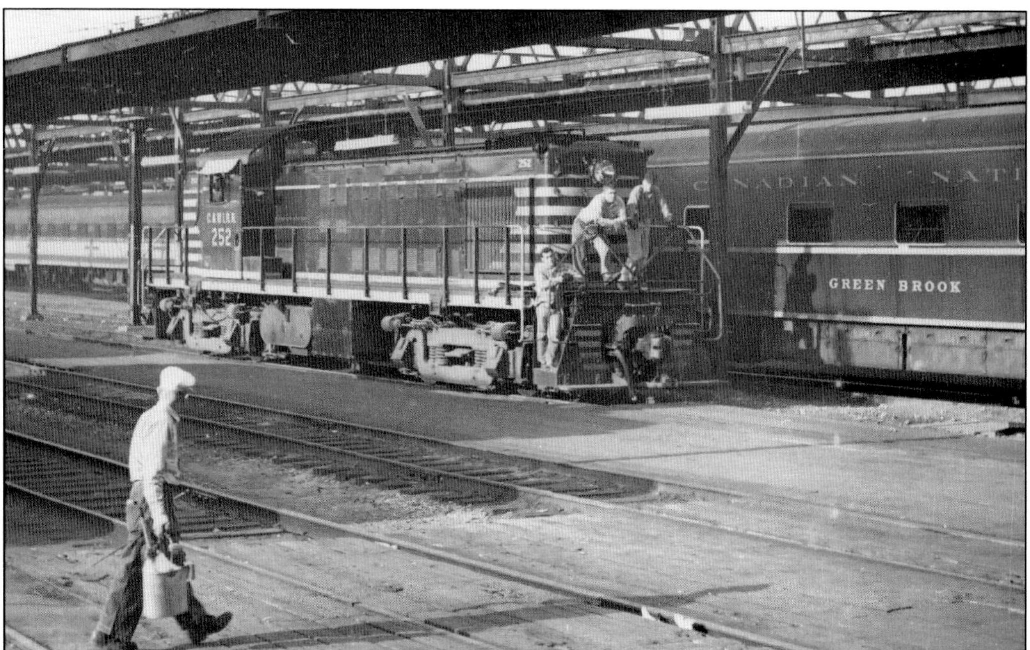

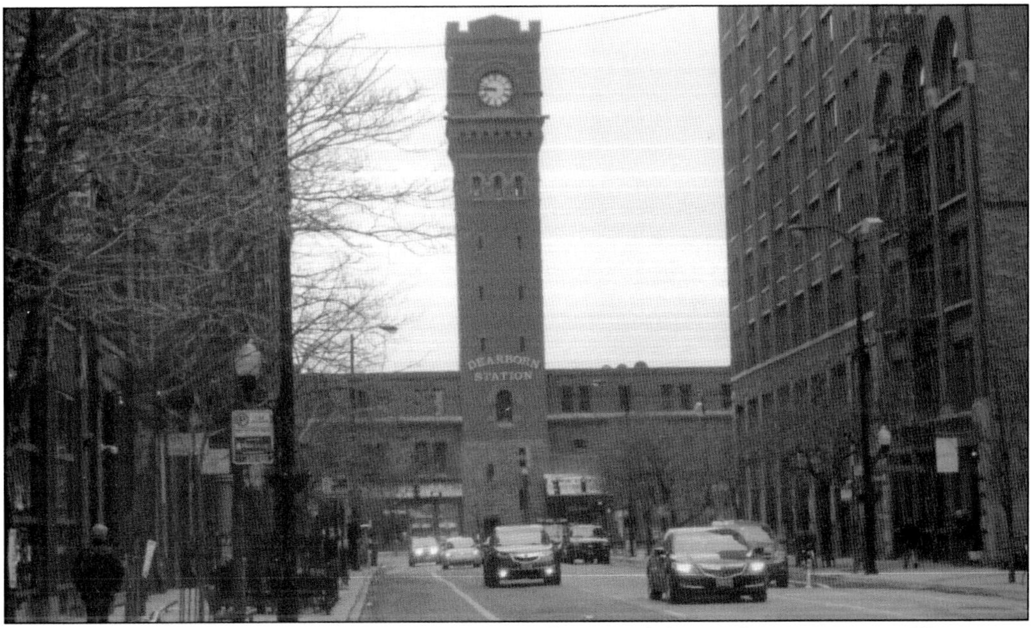

Dearborn Station, however, lived on and outlived most of the six big stations in Chicago in nearly original condition. After 1971, ownership of the building changed hands four times before it became the property of the City of Chicago. The building was given landmark status in 1982, and commercial redevelopment began in 1985, as it anchored a new residential neighborhood along Dearborn Street called Printers Row, commemorating the area's heyday. (Courtesy of Cynthia Ogorek.)

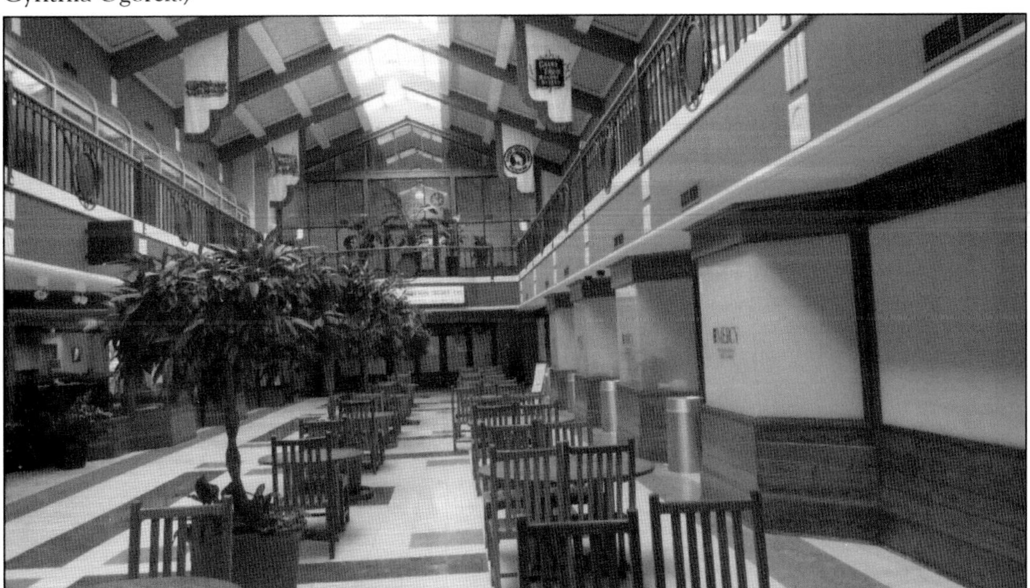

After World War II, renovations were made to the station that covered its old-style Victorian ornamentation with dropped ceilings, fluorescent lights, and other utilitarian finishes. A second-floor waiting room was opened with picture windows overlooking the track shed. Most of that remodeling has been removed, and many of the original architectural features are being enjoyed by the people who work in the building. (Courtesy of Cynthia Ogorek.)

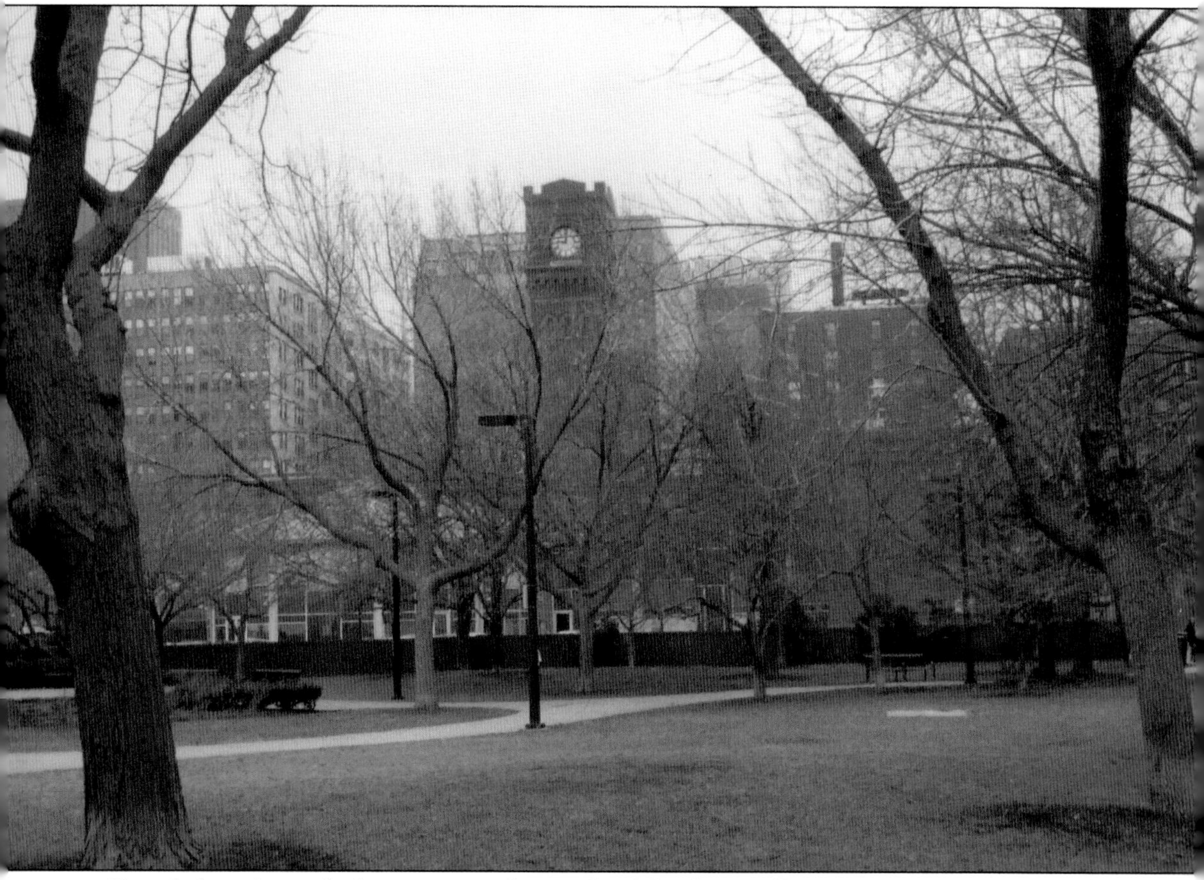

If one believed in such things, one might wonder if the ghosts of Brown, Kite, Torrence, Crawford, and Sawyer ever happen by the old Dearborn Station just to see how things are going. Would they be surprised at the lack of smoke and noise, no squealing metal or grunting switch engines or crowds of chattering people? All that is gone now. Newcomers to the city and tourists making their ways west or south no longer create a commotion in the main hall at Dearborn Station. Nobody buys a ticket or sends a telegram. Movie stars fly over Chicago instead of changing trains here. The railroaders might walk out back to where the track shed use to be, only to see a quiet park surrounded by apartment buildings and trees. Shaking their heads over the changes since their day, they might turn around and look up. Reassured, they would see that the clock tower is still there, and perhaps they would feel that at least Dearborn Station stands as a monument to their enterprise. (Courtesy of Cynthia Ogorek.)

Bibliography

The C&EI Flyer. Chicago & Eastern Illinois Railroad Historical Society. Numerous editions from January 1984 through Spring–Fall 1991.

Cook, Marlene. *Dolton Tattler, Fact, Fiction and Folklore, 1892–1992*. Dolton, IL: Marlene Cook, 1992.

"Dearborn Station Chicago, IL, A Time Machine Visit to 1930." *The Bulletin* 29, No. 1 (January-February 1995): 1–13. Railroad Station Historical Society, Inc.

Gero, Frank, publisher. [Hammond, Hegewisch, East Chicago] *Tri-Urban Directory, 1889–1890*. Reprint ed. Hammond, IN: Hammond Historical Society, n.d.

Gordon, Ron, and John Paulett. *Printers Row Chicago*. Chicago: Arcadia Publishing, 2003.

Hilton, George W. *Monon Route*. Berkeley: Howell-North Books, 1978.

Hungerford, Edward. *Men of Erie, A Story of Human Effort*. New York: Random House, 1946.

Lakeside Chicago City Directory 1892. chicagogenealogy.com.

McKinney, Kevin, and John Hilbron. "Chicago & Western Indiana, From Dearborn to Dolton (and Hammond): Remembering the Unremarked." *Passenger Train Journal* (August 1985): 26–29.

Moffat, Bruce. *Forty Feet Below, The Story of Chicago's Freight Tunnels*. Interurban Special 82. Glendale, CA: Interurban Press, 1982.

Rowlands, Marie K. *Down an Indiana Trail in 1849: The Story of Roseland*. Articles originally appearing in the *Calumet Index*, 1949. Book edition. Palos Heights, IL: The Dutch Heritage Center, Trinity Christian College, 1987.

Westing, Frederick, and Alvin F. Staufer, eds. *Erie Power, Steam and Diesel Locomotives of the Erie Railroad from 1840–1970*. Medina, OH: Alvin F. Staufer, 1970.

White, John H. Jr. *From the Wood-Car Era to the Coming of Steel: The American Railroad Freight Car*. Baltimore: The Johns Hopkins University Press, 1993.

Yenne, Bill, ed. *All Aboard! The Golden Age of American Rail Travel*. Greenwich, CT: Dorset Press Division of Marboro Books Corp., 1989.

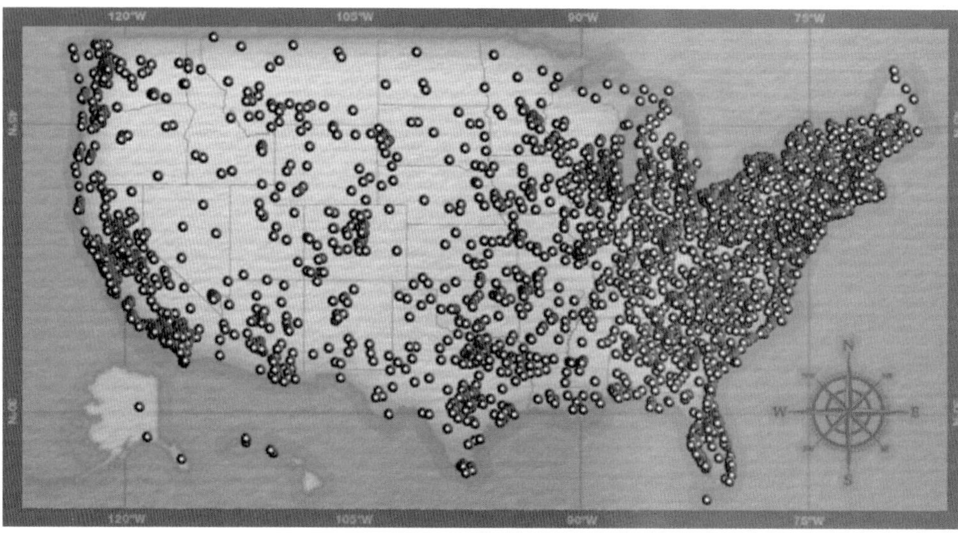